The F Programming Language

The F Programming Language

MICHAEL METCALF

*Computing and Networks Division
CERN, Geneva, Switzerland*

JOHN REID

*Computing and Information Systems Department
Rutherford Appleton Laboratory, Oxfordshire, UK*

OXFORD   NEW YORK   TOKYO
OXFORD UNIVERSITY PRESS
1996

Oxford University Press, Walton Street, Oxford OX2 6DP

Oxford NewYork
Athens Auckland Bangkok Bombay
Calcutta CapeTown DaresSalaam Delhi
Florence HongKong Istanbul Karachi
KualaLumpur Madras Madrid Melbourne
MexicoCity Nairobi Paris Singapore
Taipei Tokyo Toronto
and associated companies in
Berlin Ibadan

Oxford is a trade mark of Oxford University Press

Published in the United States by
Oxford University Press Inc., New York

A catalogue record for this book is available from the British Library

Library of Congress Cataloging in Publication Data
(Data applied for)

ISBN 0 19 850026 2

Typeset by the authors
Printed in Great Britain by
Bookcraft Ltd, Midsomer Norton, Avon

Preface

Fortran has always been the principal language used in the fields of scientific, numerical, and engineering programming, and a series of revisions to the standard defining successive versions of the language has progressively enhanced its power and kept it competitive with several generations of rivals.

Beginning in 1978, the technical committee responsible for the development of Fortran standards, X3J3, laboured to produce a new, much-needed modern version of the language, Fortran 90. Its purpose was to 'promote portability, reliability, maintainability, and efficient execution... on a variety of computing systems'. The standard was published in 1991, and a minor revision, known informally as Fortran 95, is due to be published in 1996.

Fortran, as a long-lived language with a tradition of backwards compatibility between successive standards, now carries a significant burden from its past. Fortran 90 is really two languages in one – an older language with an irregular syntax and dangerous features embedded in a modern language that has been carefully designed to be regular and safe to use. While this situation has certain advantages in those circumstances where long-lived programs have to be maintained, it creates an unnecessarily large language for teaching as a first programming language. It does nothing to combat Fortran's somewhat old-fashioned image.

This situation led a small group of people at Imagine1 Inc. to design a subset of Fortran 90, dubbed F, [1] that contains *only* the modern features and with a perfectly regular syntax. While this language is intended to be adequate for large programs, it is also ideally suited for teaching purposes. Any F program is a Fortran 90 program, so anyone skilled in F can acquire further Fortran 90 skills very easily, and any correct F program will work correctly using a Fortran 90 compiler.

As F compilers become available, so too must the accompanying documentation, and this book is intended as a complete description of the F language. It continues a series: the two editions of *Fortran 8x Explained* that described the two drafts of the standard (1987 and 1989), *Fortran 90 Explained* that described the Fortran 90 standard (1990), and *Fortran 90/95 Explained* that describes both the Fortran 90 and 95 standards.

In this book, an initial chapter sets out the background to the work on the standards, and the rationale of F. The following chapters describe F in a manner

---

[1] F is a trademark of Imagine1, Inc.

suitable both for grasping the implications of its features, and for writing programs. Some knowledge of programming concepts, although not necessarily of any version of Fortran, is assumed.

In order to make the book a complete reference work, it concludes with six appendices. They contain, successively, a list of F's intrinsic functions, a summary of F statements, a description of the differences between F and Fortran 90, an extended example illustrating the use of pointers and recursion, a glossary of F terms, and solutions to most of the exercises.

This book has been written in cooperation with Imagine1 Inc., to ensure that it accurately describes the F programming language as specified by Imagine1. They may be contacted at `info@imagine1.com`.

It is our hope that this book, by providing a complete description of F, will play a helpful role in its early years, as compilers are introduced and used, and will serve as a long-term reference to this compact and exciting language.

CERN, Switzerland	M.M.
Rutherford Appleton Laboratory, Oxfordshire	J.R.
March, 1996	

Acknowledgements

The Fortran 90 standard provides the foundations on which the F language is built. The development of the Fortran 90 standard was a long procedure involving several hundred people in many countries. The main burden fell on the principal members of X3J3, and especially on its then chairman, Jeanne Adams, the then Convenor of WG5, Jeanne Martin, and the present chairman of X3J3, Jerry Wagener. We extend our thanks to them and all our colleagues on X3J3 and elsewhere for their devotion to this important but thankless task, and for creating such a friendly working atmosphere.

This is the fifth Fortran 90 related book that we have jointly produced. One of us has also published an earlier Fortran book with Oxford University Press. We would like to express here our grateful thanks to the editor of all six of these volumes, Donald Degenhardt. He has been a constant encouragement to us both, and has been unwavering in his support for our endeavours. It has been a great pleasure to work under his guidance.

Finally, we would like to thank our supportive wives, Alison Reid and Beate Maeder-Metcalf, who have accepted so much of our time away from them even though we were at home.

Conventions used in this book

F displayed text is set in typewriter font:

```
integer :: i, j
```

and a line consisting of a colon indicates omitted lines:

```
subroutine sort
   :
end subroutine sort
```

Informal BNF terms are in italics:

```
if (scalar-logical-expr) then
```

Square brackets indicate optional items:

```
end do [name]
```

and an ellipsis represents an arbitrary number of repeated items:

```
[case selector
       block] ...
```

The italic letter *b* signifies a blank character.

Contents

1. Why F?

This book is concerned with the F programming language, setting out a reasonably concise description of the whole language. The form chosen for its presentation is that of a textbook intended for use in teaching or learning the language. Its description occupies Chapters 2 to 10, which are written in such a way that simple programs can already be coded after the first three of these chapters (on language elements, expressions and assignments, and control) have been read. Successively more complex programs can be written as the information in each subsequent chapter is absorbed. Chapter 5 describes the important concept of the module and the use of procedures, Chapter 6 completes the description of the powerful array features, Chapter 7 considers the details of specifying data objects including those of derived types, and Chapter 8 details the rich set of intrinsic procedures. Chapters 9 and 10 cover the whole of the input/output features in a manner such that the reader can also approach this more difficult area feature by feature, but always with a useful subset already covered. In a concluding section of each of Chapters 2 to 10, we summarize the differences between F and Fortran 77. Indeed, we intend this book to be readily accessible to existing Fortran 77 programmers.

This introductory chapter has the task of setting the scene for those that follow. The first section presents the Fortran language and its considerable evolution since it was first introduced over thirty years ago. The second continues with a justification for preparing a Fortran 90 standard, outlining how standards are developed, and summarizes its important new features; the third looks at the rationale for the F subset of the language. The fourth concludes by considering the requirements on programs and processors for conformance with the Fortran standard and hence the F language.

1.1 Fortran history

Programming in the early days of computing was tedious in the extreme. Programmers required a detailed knowledge of the instructions, registers, and other aspects of the central processing unit (CPU) of the computer for which they were writing code. The *source code* itself was written in a numerical notation, so-called *octal code*. In the course of time mnemonic codes were introduced, a form of coding known as *machine* or *assembly code*. These codes were translated into the instruction words by programs known as *assemblers*. In the 1950s it became increasingly apparent that this form of programming was highly inconvenient, although it did enable the CPU to be used in a very efficient way.

These difficulties spurred a team led by John Backus of IBM to develop one of the earliest high-level languages, Fortran. Their aim was to produce a language which would be simple to understand but almost as efficient in execution as assembly language. In this they succeeded beyond their wildest dreams. The language was indeed simple to learn, as it was possible to write mathematical formulae almost as they are usually written in mathematical texts. (In fact, the name Fortran is a contraction of Formula Translation.) This enabled working programs to be written faster than before, for only a small loss in efficiency, as a great deal of care was devoted to the construction of the compiler.

But Fortran was revolutionary as well as innovatory. Programmers were relieved of the tedious burden of using assembler language, and were able to concentrate more on the problem in hand. Perhaps more important, however, was the fact that computers became accessible to any scientist or engineer willing to devote a little effort to acquiring a working knowledge of Fortran; no longer was it necessary to be an expert on computers to be able to write application programs.

Fortran spread rapidly as it fulfilled a real need. Inevitably dialects of the language developed, which led to problems in exchanging programs between computers, and so, in 1966 the then American Standards Association (later the American National Standards Institute, ANSI) brought out the first ever standard for a programming language, now known as Fortran 66.

Fortran brought with it several other advances, apart from its ease of learning combined with a stress on efficient execution of code. It was, for instance, a language which remained close to, and exploited, the available hardware rather than being an abstract concept. It also brought with it the possibility for programmers to control storage allocation in a simple way, a feature which was very necessary in those early days of small memories, even if it is now regarded as being potentially dangerous.

The proliferation of dialects remained a problem after the publication of the 1966 standard. There was a widespread implementation in compilers of features which were essential for large-scale programs, but which were ignored by the standard. Different compilers implemented such facilities in different ways.

These difficulties were partially resolved by the publication of a new standard, in 1978, known as Fortran 77. It included several new features that were based on vendor extensions or pre-processors and it was, therefore, not simply a common subset of existing dialects. By the mid-1980s, the changeover to Fortran 77 was in full swing. It was a relatively simple matter to write new code under the new standard, and converting old standard-conforming code was usually easy as there is a large measure of compatibility between the two standards.

1.2   The drive for a new standard

After thirty years' existence, Fortran was far from being the only programming language available on most computers. In the course of time new languages had been developed, and where they were demonstrably more suitable for a particular type of application they had been adopted in preference to Fortran for that purpose. Fortran's superiority had always been in the area of numerical, scientific, engineering, and technical applications and, in order that it be brought properly up-to-date, the ANSI-accredited technical committee working as a development body for the ISO committee ISO/IEC JTC1/SC22/WG5 (which we abbreviate to WG5), once again prepared a new standard, formerly known as Fortran 8x and now as Fortran 90.

X3J3 itself is a body composed of representatives of computer hardware and software vendors, users, and academia. It is accredited to ANSI, the body that publishes final American standards, but reports directly to its parent committee, X3 (computer systems), which is responsible for actually adopting, or rejecting, the proposed draft standards presented to it. In these decisions, it tries to ensure that the proposals really do represent a consensus of those concerned. X3J3 acts as the development body for the corresponding international group, WG5, consisting of international experts responsible for recommending that a draft standard become an international standard. X3J3 maintains other close contacts with the international community by welcoming foreign members, including both the present authors.

What were the justifications for continuing to revise the definition of the Fortran language? As well as standardizing vendor extensions, there was a need to modernize it in response to the developments in language design which had been exploited in other languages, such as APL, Algol 68, Pascal, Ada, C and C++. Here, X3J3 could draw on the obvious benefits of concepts like data hiding. In the same vein was the need to begin to provide an alternative to dangerous storage association, to abolish the rigidity of the outmoded source form, and to improve further on the regularity of the language, as well as to increase the safety of programming in the language and to tighten the conformance requirements. To preserve the vast investment in Fortran 77 codes, the whole of Fortran 77 was retained as a subset. However, unlike the previous standard, which resulted almost entirely from an effort to standardize *existing practices*, the Fortran 90 standard is much more a *development* of the language, introducing features which are new to Fortran, but are based on experience in other languages.

The main features of Fortran 90 were, first and foremost, the array language and abstract data types. The former is built on whole array operations and assignments, array sections, intrinsic procedures for arrays, and dynamic storage. It was designed with optimization in mind. The latter is built on modules and module procedures, derived data types, operator overloading and generic interfaces, together with pointers. Also important are the new facilities for numerical computation including a set of numeric inquiry functions, the parametrization of the intrinsic types, new control constructs – `select case` and new forms of do, internal and recursive procedures and optional and keyword arguments, improved I/O facilities, and many new intrinsic procedures. Last but not least are the new free source form, an improved style of attribute-oriented specifications, the `implicit none` statement, and a mechanism for identifying redundant features for subsequent removal from the language. The requirement on compilers to be able to identify, for example, syntax extensions, and to report why a program has been rejected, are also significant. The resulting language is not only a far more powerful tool than its successor, but a safer and more reliable one too. Storage association, with its attendant dangers, is not abolished, but rendered unnecessary. Indeed, experience shows that compilers detect errors far more frequently than before, resulting in a faster development cycle. The array syntax and recursion also allow quite compact code to be written, a further aid to safe programming. Fortran 90 is fully described in *Fortran 90/95 Explained*, M. Metcalf and J. Reid, Oxford University Press, 1996.

1.3 The F language

Fortran is a long-lived language, and successive standards have been designed to maintain a large degree of backwards compatibility with each predecessor. The Fortran 90 standard was designed to provide the language with a quite regular syntax, but use of this syntax is to a large degree optional, as the older syntax, especially for older features, exists alongside the new. There is thus some degree of confusion, particularly for new users, as to what is allowed and what is not. For instance, if we wish to declare a variable to be of the real data type and to have the name `length`, we can write

```
real length
```

However, if we wish `length` to have the initial value 0.0, then we must use an extended syntax

```
real :: length = 0.0
```

with the `::` notation, separating the name of the type from the name of the variable. This `::` notation is, however, an allowed option even for the form without initialization – we could just as well have written

```
real :: length
```

In F there is no confusion – this form with `::` is the only one allowed in all circumstances.

A further drawback of Fortran 90 is that it contains many features that are, today, regarded as unsafe programming practice, another hangover from its past. Fortran 90 was designed to provide alternatives to such practices, but again their use is optional. For instance, we can call a variable, such as `length`, into being without any declaration whatsoever, just by using it, for instance in an assignment statement like

```
length = 3.3
```

However, when so doing, the rules of Fortran will cause, in this case, not a real variable to be created, but an integer one. The user might then be surprised to find that the value stored in length is not 3.3 but 3. In the F language, all variables must be declared in a type statement like those with the :: notation above.

These problems of learning (and teaching) and of safety led a small group of experts – Walt Brainerd, David Epstein, and Dick Hendrickson, in consultation with others including one of us (JR) – to specify a subset of Fortran 90 that would be both highly regular, and thus easy to learn, and quite safe, and thus reliable to use. It retains, nevertheless, Fortran's powerful features including the array language, pointers and derived data types. The formal syntax of the F language is such that any violation of its strict rules is detectable by an F compiler.

The result is a language that is compact in the style of Basic, C, or Pascal, yet far more powerful, especially for numerical applications. Furthermore, it is very regular, making it easier to learn than its parent language, and making it a significant competitor to these three older languages. It is our expectation that it will become a rival to all three of them, being far more modern with regard to its features, regularity, and safety. For advanced applications, it is just as suitable as Fortran 90 as a basis for the High Performance Fortran (HPF) extensions for using parallel computers to handle problems involving large sets of data that can be represented by regular grids.[1] In the future, F will be upgraded to follow developments in new Fortran standards, for instance to incorporate appropriate features from Fortran 95. Taking all this together, we can expect to see the huge body of experience in Fortran's design, implementation and use brought to a wider audience, in a new raiment.

1.4 Conformance

The Fortran standard and the rules of F are both almost exclusively concerned with the rules for programs rather than processors. A processor is required to accept a conforming program and to interpret it according to the standard, subject to limits that the processor may impose on the size and complexity of the program. The processor is allowed to accept further syntax and to interpret relationships that are not specified in the standard, provided they do not conflict with the standard. Of course, the programmer must avoid such syntax extensions if portability is desired.

The interpretation of some of the standard syntax is *processor dependent*, that is, may vary from processor to processor. For example, the set of characters allowed in character strings is processor dependent. Care must be taken whenever a processor-dependent feature is used in case it leads to the program not being portable to a desired processor.

---

[1] See *The High Performance Fortran Handbook*, C. Koebel et al., MIT Press, Cambridge, MA, 1994.

The syntax rules are expressed in a form of BNF with associated constraints, and the semantics are described by the text. This semi-formal style is not used in this book, so an example is perhaps helpful:

R609	*substring*	**is**	*parent-string(substring-range)*
R610	*parent-string*	**is**	*scalar-variable-name*
		or	*array-element*
		or	*scalar-structure-component*
R611	*substring-range*	**is**	[*scalar-int-expr*] : [*scalar-int-expr*]

Constraint: *parent-string* must be of type character.

 The first *scalar-int-expr* in *substring-range* is called the *starting point* and the second one is called the *ending point*. The length of a substring is the number of characters in the substring and is $\text{MAX}(\ell - f + 1, 0)$, where f and ℓ are the starting and ending points, respectively.

Here, the three production rules and the associated constraint for a character substring are defined, and the meaning of the length of such a substring explained. The full BNF description of F may be obtained via the World-Wide Web URL `http://www.imagine1.com/imagine1`.

The standard is written in such a way that a Fortran and hence F processor may, at compile-time, check that the program satisfies all the constraints that it imposes. Furthermore, it must be able to report the reason for rejecting a program. These capabilities are of great value in producing correct and portable code. Indeed, an F compiler applies even stricter conformance requirements.

2. Language elements

2.1 Introduction

Written prose in a natural language, such as an English text, is composed firstly of basic elements – the letters of the alphabet. These are combined into larger entities, words, which convey the basic concepts of objects, actions, and qualifications. The words of the language can be further combined into larger units, phrases and sentences, according to certain rules. One set of rules defines the grammar. This tells us whether a certain combination of words is correct in that it conforms to the *syntax* of the language, that is, those acknowledged forms which are regarded as correct renderings of the meanings we wish to express. Sentences can in turn be joined together into paragraphs, which conventionally contain the composite meaning of their constituent sentences, each paragraph expressing a larger unit of information. In a novel, sequences of paragraphs become chapters and the chapters together form a book, which usually is a self-contained work, largely independent of all other books.

2.2 The character set

Analogies to these concepts are found in a programming language. In F, the basic elements, or character set, are the 26 upper- and lower-case letters of the English alphabet, the 10 Arabic numerals, 0 to 9, the underscore, _, and the so-called special characters listed in Table 1. Within the F syntax, the case is significant[1]. The letters, numerals, and underscore are known as *alphanumeric* characters.

Except for the currency symbol, whose graphic may vary (for example, to be £ in the United Kingdom), the graphics are fixed, though their styles are not fixed. The special characters $, ?, ' and ; have no specific meaning within the F language.

In the course of this and the following chapters, we shall see how further analogies with natural language may be drawn. The unit of F information is the *lexical token*, which corresponds to a word or punctuation mark. Adjacent tokens are usually separated by spaces or the end of a line, but sensible exceptions are allowed just as for a punctuation mark in prose. Sequences of tokens form

---

[1]Unlike the Fortran 90 syntax where upper- and lower-case letters are equivalent and are distinguished only when they form part of character sequences.

Table 2.1. The special characters of the F language

Character	Name	Character	Name
=	Equals sign	:	Colon
+	Plus sign		Blank
−	Minus sign	!	Exclamation mark
*	Asterisk	"	Quotation mark
/	Slash	%	Percent
(	Left parenthesis	&	Ampersand
)	Right parenthesis	;	Semicolon
,	Comma	<	Less than
.	Decimal point	>	Greater than
$	Currency symbol	?	Question mark
'	Apostrophe		

statements, corresponding to sentences. Statements, like sentences, may be joined to form larger units like paragraphs. In F these are known as *program units*, and out of these may be built a *program*. A program forms a complete set of instructions to a computer to carry out a defined sequence of operations. The simplest program may consist of only a few statements, but programs of more than 100,000 statements are now quite common.

2.3　Tokens

Within the context of F, alphanumeric characters (the letters, the underscore, and the numerals) may be combined into sequences that have one or more meanings. For instance, the meaning of the sequence 999 is a constant in the mathematical sense. Similarly, the sequence date might represent, as one possible interpretation, a variable quantity to which we assign the calendar date.

The special characters are used to separate such sequences and also have various meanings. We shall see how the asterisk is used to specify the operation of multiplication, as in x*y, and has also a number of other interpretations.

Basic significant sequences of alphanumeric characters or of special characters are referred to as *tokens;* they are keywords, names, constants (other than complex literal constants), operators (listed in Table 3.4), and *separators*, which are

$$(\quad) \quad (/ \quad /) \quad , \quad = \quad => \quad : \quad :: \quad \%$$

For example, the expression x*y contains the three tokens x, *, and y.

Apart from within a token, blanks may be used freely to improve the layout. Thus, whereas the variable date may not be written as d a t e, the sequence x * y is syntactically equivalent to x*y. In this context, multiple blanks are syntactically equivalent to a single blank.

A name or a constant must be separated from an adjacent keyword, name, or constant by one or more blanks or by the end of a line. For instance, in

```
program main
use mod
do k=1,3
```

the blanks are required after program, use, and do. Likewise, adjacent keywords must normally be separated. However, the following pairs of keywords:

```
else if              end program
end do               end select
end file             end subroutine
end function         end type
end if               end where
end interface        in out
end module           select case
```

are not required to be separated. In each of these cases, the two tokens are interpreted together as a single token and they are not permitted to be separated by the end of a line.

All the language keywords are written in lower case, as in the examples of the previous paragraph.

2.4   Source form

The F source form is well adapted to use at a terminal. The statements of which a source program is composed are written on *lines*. Each line may contain up to 132 characters, and usually contains a single statement. Since leading spaces are not significant, it is possible to start all such statements in the first character position, or in any other position consistent with the user's chosen layout. A statement may thus be written as

```
x = (-y + root_of_discriminant)/(2.0*a)
```

In order to be able to mingle suitable comments with the code to which they refer, F allows any line to carry a trailing comment field, following an exclamation mark (!). An example is

```
x = y/a - b    ! Solve the linear equation
```

Any comment always extends to the end of the source line and may include processor-dependent characters (it is not restricted to the F character set, Section 2.2). Any line whose first non-blank character is an exclamation mark, or contains only blanks, or which is empty, is purely commentary, and is ignored by the compiler. Such comment lines may appear anywhere in a program unit, including ahead of the first statement (but not after the final program unit). A character constant is allowed to contain !, so the ! does not initiate a comment in this case; in all other cases it does.

Since it is possible that a long statement might not be accommodated in the 132 positions allowed in a single line, up to 39 additional continuation lines are allowed. The so-called *continuation mark* is the ampersand (&) character, and this is appended to each line that is followed by a continuation line. Thus, the first statement of this section (considerably spaced out) could be written as

```
x =                                                          &
    (-y + root_of_discriminant)                              &
/(2.0*a)
```

In this book, the ampersands will normally be aligned to improve readability. On a non-comment line, if & is the last non-blank character or the last non-blank character ahead of the comment symbol !, the statement continues from the character immediately preceding the &. Continuation is to the first character of the next non-comment line. Continuation within a token is not permitted, that is, each token must be contained within a single line.

Comments are allowed to contain any characters, including &, so they cannot be continued since a trailing & is taken as part of the comment. However, comment lines may be freely interspersed among continuation lines and do not count towards the limit of 39 lines.

No line is permitted to have & as its only non-blank character, or as its only non-blank character ahead of !. Such a line is really a comment and becomes a comment if & is removed.

2.5   Concept of type

In F, it is possible to define and manipulate various types of data. For instance, we may have available the value 10 in a program, and assign that value to an integer scalar variable denoted by i. Both 10 and i are of type integer; 10 is a fixed or *constant* value, whereas i is a *variable* which may be assigned other values. Integer expressions, such as $i+10$, are available too.

A *data type* consists of a set of data values, a means of denoting those values, and a set of operations that are allowed on them. For the integer data type, the values are $\ldots, -3, -2, -1, 0, 1, 2, 3, \ldots$ between some limits depending on the kind of integer and computer system being used. Such tokens as these are *literal constants*, and each data type has its own form for expressing them. Named scalar variables, such as i, may be established. During the execution of a program, the value of i may change to any valid value, or may become *undefined*, that is have no predictable value. The operations which may be performed on integers are those of usual arithmetic; we can write $1+10$ or $i-3$ and obtain the expected results.

Named constants may be established too; these have values that do not change during a given execution of the program.

Properties like those just mentioned are associated with all the data types of F, and will be described in detail in this and the following chapters. The language itself contains five data types whose existence may always be assumed. These are known as the *intrinsic data types*, whose literal constants form the subject of the next section. Except for character, of each intrinsic type there is a default kind and a processor-dependent number of other kinds. Each kind is associated with a non-negative integer value known as the *kind type parameter*. This is used as a means of identifying and distinguishing the various kinds available.

In addition, it is possible to define other data types based on collections of data of the intrinsic types, and these are known as *derived data types*. The ability to define data types of interest to the programmer – matrices, geometrical shapes, lists, interval numbers – is a powerful feature of the language, one which permits a high level of *data abstraction*, that is the ability to define and manipulate data objects without being concerned about their actual representation in a computer.

2.6   Literal constants of intrinsic type

The intrinsic data types are divided into two classes. The first class contains the three *numeric* types which are used mainly for numerical calculations – integer, real, and complex. The second class contains the two *non-numeric* types which are used for such applications as text-processing and control – character and logical. The numerical types are used in conjunction with the usual operators of arithmetic, such as + and -, which will be described in Chapter 3. Each includes a zero and the value of a signed zero is the same as that of an unsigned zero[2]. The non-numeric types are used with sets of operators specific to each type; for instance, character data may be concatenated. These too will be described in Chapter 3.

2.6.1   Integer literal constants

The first type of literal constant is the *integer literal constant*. The default kind is simply a signed or unsigned integer value, for example

```
1
0
-999
32767
+10
```

---

[2] Although the representation of data is processor dependent, for the numeric data types F defines model representations and means to inquire about the properties of those models. The details are deferred to Section 8.7.

The *range* of the default integers is not specified in the language, but on a computer with a word size of n bits, is often from -2^{n-1} to $+2^{n-1} - 1$. Thus on a 32-bit computer the range is often from -2147483648 to $+2147483647$.

To be sure that the range will be adequate on any computer requires the specification of the kind of integer by giving a value for the kind type parameter. This is done through a named integer constant. For example, if the range -999999 to 999999 is desired, k6 may be established as a constant with an appropriate value by the statement, fully explained later,

```
integer, parameter :: k6=selected_int_kind(6)
```

and used in constants thus:

```
-123456_k6
+1_k6
-2_k6
```

Here, selected_int_kind(6) is an intrinsic inquiry function call, and it returns a kind parameter value that yields the range -999999 to 999999 with the least margin (see Section 8.7.4).

On a given processor, it might be known that the kind value needed is 3. In this case, the declaration can be written

```
integer, parameter :: k6=3
```

but this form is less portable. If we move the code to another processor, this particular value may be unsupported, or might correspond to a different range.

Many implementations use kind values that indicate the number of bytes of storage occupied by a value, but greater flexibility is allowed. For example, a processor might have hardware only for 4-byte integers, and yet support kind values 1, 2, and 4 with this hardware (to ease portability from processors that have hardware for 1-, 2-, and 4-byte integers). However, F imposes no requirement on kind values or their order, except that the kind value is never negative.

The value of the kind type parameter for a given data type on a given processor can be obtained from the kind intrinsic function (Section 8.2):

```
kind(1)          for the default value
kind(2_k6)       for the example
```

and the decimal exponent range (number of decimal digits supported) of a given entity may be obtained from another function (Section 8.7.2), as in

```
range(2_k6)
```

which in this case would return a value of at least 6.

2.6.2 Real literal constants

The second type of literal constant is the *real literal constant*. The default kind is a floating-point form built of: a signed or unsigned integer part, a decimal point, a fractional part, and optionally a signed or unsigned exponent part. The exponent part is either absent or consists of the letter e followed by a signed or unsigned integer. An example is

```
-10.6e-11
```

meaning -10.6×10^{-11}, and other legal forms are

```
1.0e1
-0.1
1.9e-1
3.141592653
```

The default real literal constants are representations of a subset of the real numbers of mathematics, and the allowed range of the exponent and the number of significant digits represented varies from processor to processor. Many conform to the IEEE standard for floating-point arithmetic and have values of 10^{-37} to 10^{+37} for the range, and a precision of six decimal digits.

To be sure to obtain a desired range and significance requires the specification of a kind parameter value. For example,

```
integer, parameter :: long = selected_real_kind(9, 99)
```

ensures that the constants

```
1.7_long
12.3456789e30_long
```

have a precision of at least nine significant decimals, and an exponent range of at least 10^{-99} to 10^{+99}. The number of digits specified in the significand has no effect on the kind. In particular, it is permitted to write more digits than the processor can in fact use.

As for integers, many implementations use kind values that indicate the number of bytes of storage occupied by a value, but F requires only that the kind value is never negative. If the desired kind value is known it may be declared directly, as in the case

```
integer, parameter :: long = 8
```

but the resulting code is then less portable.

The processor must provide at least one representation with more precision than the default. For instance, on a machine with IEEE floating-point arithmetic, the range for double-width reals is 10^{-307} to 10^{+307} and the precision is 15 decimal digits.

The kind function is valid also for real values:

```
kind(1.0)           for the default value
kind(1.0_long)      for the example
```

In addition, there are two inquiry functions available which return the actual precision and range, respectively, of a given real entity (see Section 8.7.2). Thus, the value of

```
precision(1.7_long)
```

would be at least 9, and the value of

```
range(1.7_long)
```

would be at least 99.

2.6.3   Complex literal constants

F, as a language intended for scientific and engineering calculations, has the advantage of having as third literal constant type the *complex literal constant*. This is designated by a pair of real literal constants, separated by a comma and enclosed in parentheses. Examples are

```
(1.1, 3.2)
(1.9, 0.99e-2)
(1.0_long, 3.7_long)
```

where the first constant of each pair is the real part of the complex number, and the second constant is the imaginary part. Both parts must be of the same kind and with the same named constant, and this is the kind of the constant. If the kind value is specified for one, it must be specified for the other and with the same named constant. A default complex constant is one whose kind value is that of default real.

The kind, precision, and range functions are equally valid for complex entities.

Note that if an implementation uses the number of bytes needed to store a real as its kind value, the number of bytes needed to store a complex value of the corresponding kind is twice the kind value. For example, if the default real type has kind 4 and needs four bytes of storage, the default complex type has kind 4 but needs eight bytes of storage.

2.6.4   Character literal constants

The fourth type of literal constant is the *character literal constant*. It consists of a string of characters enclosed in a pair of quotation marks, for example

```
"Nuts & bolts"
```

The characters are not restricted to the F set (Section 2.2). Any graphic character supported by the processor is permitted, but not control characters such as 'new-line'. The quotation marks serve as *delimiters,* and are not part of the value of the constant. The value of the constant

```
"STRING"
```

is STRING.

A problem arises with the representation of a quotation mark in a character constant. A doubled quotation mark without any embedded intervening blanks is regarded as a single character of the constant. For example

```
"He said ""Hello"" to me"
```

has the value He said "Hello" to me.

The number of characters in a string is called its *length,* and may be zero. For instance, "" is a character constant of length zero.

We mention here the particular rule for the source form concerning character strings, namely that they must be written on one line. A long string must be broken up and expressed as a constant expression using the concatenation operator (Section 3.7). An example is

```
long_string =                                               &
    " Were I with her, the night would post too soon;"      &
// " But now are minutes added to the hours;"               &
// " To spite me now, each minute seems a moon;"            &
// " Yet not for me, shine sun to succour flowers!"         &
// "   Pack night, peep day; good day, of night now borrow:" &
// "   Short, night, to-night, and length thyself tomorrow."
```

On any computer, the characters have a property known as their *collating sequence.* One may ask the question whether one character occurs before or after another in the sequence. This question is posed in a natural form such as 'Does C precede M?', and we shall see later how this may be expressed in F terms. F requires the computer to use the collating sequence of the ASCII standard. This satisfies the following conditions:

- blank is less than 0;

- 0 is less than 1 is less than 2 ... is less than 8 is less than 9;

- 9 is less than A;

- A is less than B is less than C ... is less than Y is less than Z;

- Z is less than a;

- a is less than b is less than c ... is less than y is less than z;

In F, there are no kinds of character constants other than the default kind just described.

2.6.5 Logical literal constants

The fifth type of literal constant is the *logical literal constant.* The default kind has two constants, .true. and .false. . These logical constants are normally used only to initialize logical variables to their required values, as we shall see in Section 3.6.

The default kind has a kind parameter value which is processor dependent. The actual value is available as `kind(.true.)`. As for the other intrinsic types, the kind parameter may be specified by a named integer constant following an underscore, as in

```
.true._long
```

Non-default logical kinds are useful for storing logical arrays compactly; we defer further discussion until Section 6.14.

2.7   Names

An F program references many different entities by name. Such names must consist of between 1 and 31 alphanumeric characters (letters, underscores, and numerals) of which the first must be a letter and the last must not be an underscore. The case is significant, but for compatibility with Fortran 90, two names that differ only in the case of one or more letters cannot be used together. For example, where John is in use, `john` is not available. All the statement keywords, the names used for logical constants and operators, and all the names of the intrinsic procedures are reserved words that are not permitted for other purposes, even if some letters are capitalized. Some names of Fortran 90 and Fortran 95 are also reserved words. The complete set is listed in Appendix B.

We thus see that valid names are, for example,

```
a
a_thing
x1
Mass
q123
Time_of_flight
```

and invalid names are

`integer`	Statement keyword
`1a`	First character is not alphabetic
`integer_`	Final character is an underscore
`a thing`	Contains a blank
`$sign`	Contains a non-alphanumeric character
`any`	Name of an intrinsic procedure
`Any`	Name of an intrinsic procedure, apart from case

Within the constraints of the syntax, it is important for program clarity to choose names which have a clear significance – these are known as *mnemonic names.* Examples are day, month, and year, for variables to store the calendar date.

The use of names to refer to constants, already met in Section 2.6.1, will be fully described in Section 7.2.

2.8   Scalar variables of intrinsic type

We have seen in the section on literal constants that there exist five different intrinsic data types. Each of these types may have variables too. A variable must be declared to be of a particular type by specifying its name following :: in a *type declaration statement* such as

```
integer   :: i
real      :: a
complex   :: current
logical   :: pravda
character(len=1) :: letter
```

Here all the variables have default kind. Explicit requirements may also be specified for the first four through kind *type parameters*, as in the examples

```
integer(kind=k6)  :: i
real(kind=long)   :: a
```

The length of a character variable must always be specified.

2.9   Derived data types

When programming, it is often useful to be able to manipulate objects that are more sophisticated than those of the intrinsic types. Imagine, for instance, that we wished to specify objects representing persons. Each person in our application is distinguished by a name, an age, and an identification number. F allows us to define a corresponding data type in the following fashion:

```
type, public :: person
   character(len=10) :: name
   real :: age
   integer :: id
end type person
```

This is the *definition* of the type and it must be placed in a module (Section 5.5). A scalar object of such a type is called a *structure*. In order to create a structure of that type, we write an appropriate type declaration statement, such as

```
type(person) :: you
```

The scalar variable you is then a composite object of type person containing three separate components, one corresponding to the name, another to the age, and a third to the identification number. As will be described in Sections 3.8 and 3.9, a variable such as you may appear in expressions and assignments involving other variables or constants of the same or different types. In addition, each of the components of the variable may be referenced individually using the *component selector* character percent (%). The identification number of you would, for instance, be accessed as

```
you%id
```

and this quantity is an integer variable which could appear in an expression such as

```
you%id + 9
```

Similarly, if there were a second object of the same type:

```
type(person) :: me
```

the differences in ages could be established by writing

```
you%age - me%age
```

It will be shown in Section 3.8 how a meaning can be given to an expression such as

```
you - me
```

Just as the intrinsic data types have associated literal constants, so too may literal constants of derived type be specified. Their form is the name of the type followed by the constant values of the components, in order and enclosed in parentheses. Thus, the constant

```
person( "Smith", 23.5, 2541 )
```

may be written assuming the derived type defined at the beginning of this section, and could be *assigned* to a variable of the same type:

```
you = person( "Smith", 23.5, 2541 )
```

Any such *structure constructor* can appear only after the definition of the type.

A derived type may have a component that is of a previously defined derived type. This is illustrated in Figure 2.1. A variable of type triangle may be declared thus

```
type(triangle) :: t
```

and t has components t%a, t%b, and t%c all of type point, and t%a has components t%a%x and t%a%y of type real.

Figure 2.1

```
type, public :: point
   real :: x, y
end type point
type, public :: triangle
   type(point) :: a, b, c
end type triangle
```

2.10   Arrays of intrinsic type

Another compound object supported by F is the *array*. An array consists of a rectangular set of elements, all of the same type and type parameters. There are a number of ways in which arrays may be declared; for the moment we shall consider only the declaration of arrays of fixed sizes. To declare an array named a of 10 real elements, we add the dimension attribute to the type declaration statement thus:

```
real, dimension(10) :: a
```

The successive elements of the array are a(1), a(2), a(3), ..., a(10). The number of elements of an array is called its *size*. Each array element is a scalar.

Many problems require a more elaborate declaration than one in which the first element is designated 1, and it is possible in F to declare a lower as well as an upper *bound*:

```
real, dimension(-10:5) :: vector
```

This is a vector of 16 elements, vector(-10), vector(-9), ..., vector(5). We thus see that whereas we always need to specify the upper bound, the lower bound is optional, and by default has the value 1. The number of elements along a dimension of an array is known as the *extent* in that dimension. Thus, vector has an extent of 16.

An array may extend in more than one dimension, and F allows up to seven dimensions to be specified. For instance

```
real, dimension(5,4) :: b
```

declares an array with two dimensions, and

```
real, dimension(-10:5, -20:-1, 0:1, -1:0, 2, 2, 2) :: grid
```

declares seven dimensions, the first four with explicit lower bounds. It may be seen that the size of this second array is

$$16 \times 20 \times 2 \times 2 \times 2 \times 2 \times 2 = 10240,$$

and that arrays of many dimensions can thus place large demands on the memory of a computer. The number of dimensions of an array is known as its *rank*.

Thus, grid has a rank of seven. Scalars are regarded as having rank zero. The sequence of extents is known as the *shape*. For example, grid has the shape (16, 20, 2, 2, 2, 2, 2).

A derived type may contain an array component. For example, the following type

```
type, public :: triplet
    real                 :: u
    real, dimension(3)   :: du
    real, dimension(3,3) :: d2u
end type triplet
```

might be used to hold the value of a variable in three dimensions and the values of its first and second derivatives. If t is of type triplet, t%du and t%d2u are arrays of type real.

Some statements treat the elements of an array one-by-one in a special order which we call the *array element order*. It is obtained by counting most rapidly in the early dimensions. Thus, the elements of grid in array element order are

```
grid(-10, -20, 0, -1, 1, 1, 1)
grid( -9, -20, 0, -1, 1, 1, 1)
     :
grid(  5,  -1, 1,  0, 2, 2, 2).
```

This is illustrated for an array of two dimensions in Figure 2.2. Most implementations actually store arrays in contiguous storage in array element order, but we emphasize that the language does not require this.

Figure 2.2 The ordering of elements in the array b.

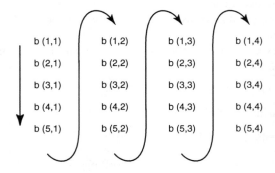

We reference an individual element of an array by specifying, as in the examples above, its *subscript* values. In the examples we used integer constants, but in general each subscript may be formed of a *scalar integer expression,* that is, any arithmetic expression whose value is scalar and of type integer. Each subscript must be within the corresponding ranges defined in the array declaration and the number of subscripts must equal the rank. Examples are

```
a(1)
a(i*j)          ! i and j are of type integer
a(nint(x+3.0))  ! x is of type real
t%d2u(i+1,j+2)  ! t is of derived type triplet
```

where nint is an intrinsic function to convert a real value to the nearest integer (see Section 8.3.1). In addition subarrays, called *sections*, may be referenced by specifying a range for one or more subscripts. The following are examples of array sections:

```
a(i:j)          ! Rank-one array of size j-i+1
b(k, 1:n)       ! Rank-one array of size n
c(1:i, 1:j, k)  ! Rank-two array with extents i and j
```

We describe array sections in more detail in Section 6.10. An array section is itself an array, but its individual elements must not be accessed through the section designator. Thus, b(k, 1:n)(1) cannot be written; it must be expressed as b(k, 1).

A further form of subscript is shown in

```
a(ipoint)       ! ipoint is an integer array
```

where ipoint is an array of indices, pointing to array elements. It may thus be seen that a(ipoint), which identifies as many elements of a as ipoint has elements, is an example of another *array-valued object*, and ipoint is referred to as a *vector subscript*. This will be met in greater detail in Section 6.10.

It is often convenient to be able to define an array constant. In F, a rank-one array may be constructed as a list of elements enclosed between the tokens (/ and /). A simple example is

```
(/ 1, 2, 3, 5, 10 /)
```

which is an array of rank one and size five. To obtain a series of values, the individual values may be defined by an expression that depends on an integer variable having values in a range, with an optional stride. Thus, the constructor

```
(/1, 2, 3, 4, 5/)
```

can be written as

```
(/ (i, i = 1,5) /)
```

and

```
(/2, 4, 6, 8/)
```

as

```
(/ (i, i = 2,8,2) /)
```

and

```
(/ 1.1, 1.2, 1.3, 1.4, 1.5 /)
```

as

```
(/ (i*0.1, i=11,15) /)
```

An array constant of rank greater than one may be constructed by using the function reshape (see Section 8.12.3) to reshape a rank-one array constant.

A full description of array constructors is reserved for Section 6.13.

2.11   Character substrings

It is possible to build arrays of characters, just as it is possible to build arrays of any other type:

```
character(len=1), dimension(80) :: line
```

declares an array, called line, of 80 elements, each one character in length. Each character may be addressed by the usual reference, line(i) for example. In this case, however, a more appropriate declaration might be

```
character(len=80) :: line
```

which declares a scalar data object of 80 characters. These may be referenced individually or in groups using a *substring* notation

```
line(i:j)    ! i and j are of type integer
```

which references all the characters from i to j in line. The colon is used to separate the two substring subscripts, which may be any scalar integer expressions. The colon is obligatory in substring references, so that referencing a single character requires line(i:i). There are default values for the substring subscripts. If the lower one is omitted, the value 1 is assumed; if the upper one is omitted, a value corresponding to the character length is assumed. Thus,

line(:i)	is equivalent to	line(1:i)
line(i:)	is equivalent to	line(i:80)
line(:)	is equivalent to	line or line(1:80)

If i is greater than j in line(i:j), the value is a zero-sized string.

We may now combine the length declaration with the array declaration to build arrays of character objects of specified length, as in

```
character(len=80), dimension(60) :: page
```

which might be used to define storage for the characters of a whole page, with 60 elements of an array, each of length 80. To reference the line j on a page we may write page(j), and to reference character i on that line we could combine the array subscript and character substring notations into

page(j)(i:i)

A substring of a structure component may also be formed:

you%name(1:2)

but a substring of a character constant is not permitted.

At this point we must note a limitation associated with character variables, namely that character variables must have a declared maximum length, making it impossible to manipulate character variables of variable length, unless they are defined appropriately as of a derived data type. Nevertheless, this data type is adequate for most character manipulation applications.

2.12   Objects and subobjects

We have seen that derived types may have components that are arrays, as in

```
type, public :: triplet
    real, dimension(3) :: vertex
end type triplet
```

and arrays may be of derived type as in the example

```
type(triplet), dimension(10) :: t
```

A single structure (for example, t(2)) is always regarded as a scalar, but it may have a component (for example, t(2)%vertex) that is an array. Derived types may have components of other derived types.

An object that is not part of a bigger object always has a name (up to 31 alphanumeric characters) and is called a *named object*. Its subobjects have *designators* (for example, t(1:7) and t(1)%vertex) that consist of the name of the object followed by one or more qualifiers. Each successive qualifier specifies a part of the object specified by the name or designator that precedes it.

The term 'array' is used for any object that is not scalar, including an array section or an array-valued component of a structure. The term 'variable' is used for any named object that is not specified to be a constant and for any part of such an object, including array elements, array sections, structure components, and substrings.

2.13   Pointers

In everyday language, nouns are often used in a way that makes their meaning precise only because of the context. 'The President said that...' will be understood precisely by the reader who knows that the context is the US government and that the President at that time was Bill Clinton.

Similarly, in a computer program it can be very useful to be able to use a name that can be made to refer to different objects during execution of the program. One example is the multiplication of a vector by a sequence of square matrices. We might write code that calculates

$$y_i = \sum_{j=1}^{n} a_{ij} x_j, \quad i = 1, 2, \ldots, n$$

from the vector x_j, $j = 1, 2, \ldots, n$. In order to use this to calculate

$$BCz$$

we might first make x refer to z and A refer to C, thereby using our code to calculate $y = Cz$, then make x refer to y and A refer to B so that our code calculates the result vector we finally want.

An object that can be made to refer to other objects in this way is called a *pointer*, and must be declared with the pointer attribute, for example

```
real, pointer              :: son
real, pointer, dimension(:)    :: x, y
real, pointer, dimension(:,:) :: a
```

In the case of an array, only the rank (number of dimensions) is declared, and the bounds (and hence shape) are taken from that of the object to which it points. Given such a declaration, the compiler arranges storage for a descriptor that is initially undefined but will later hold the address of the actual object (known as the *target*) and holds, if it is an array, its bounds and strides.

Besides pointing to existing variables, a pointer may be given fresh storage by an allocate statement such as

```
allocate (son, x(10), y(-10:10), a(n, n))
```

In the case of arrays, the lower and upper bounds are specified just as for the dimension attribute (Section 2.10) except that any scalar integer expression is permitted.

Components of derived types are permitted to have the pointer attribute. This enables a major application of pointers: the construction of linked lists. As a simple example, we might decide to hold a sparse vector as a chain of variables of the type shown in Figure 2.3, which allows us to access the entries one by one; if chain is a scalar of this type:

```
type(entry), pointer :: chain
```

holding a chain of length two, its entries are chain%i and chain%next%i. Additional entries may be created when necessary by an appropriate allocate statement. We defer the details to Section 3.12.

A subobject is not a pointer unless, as in the previous paragraph, it has a final component selector for the name of a pointer component.

Figure 2.3

```
type, public :: entry
   real :: value
   integer :: i
   type(entry), pointer :: next
end type entry
```

2.14 Summary

In this chapter we have introduced the elements of the F language. The character set has been listed, and the manner in which sequences of characters form literal constants and names explained. In this context we have encountered the five intrinsic data types defined in F, and seen how each data type has corresponding literal constants and named objects. We have seen how derived types may be constructed from the intrinsic types. We have introduced arrays and seen how their elements may be referenced by subscript expressions. The concepts of the array section, character substring, and pointer have been presented, and some important terms defined. Because of these possibilities, the terms 'array' and 'variable' are used with a more general meaning than in Fortran 77. In the following chapter we shall see how these elements may be combined into expressions and statements, F's equivalents of 'phrases' and 'sentences'.

With respect to Fortran 77, there are many changes in this area: dynamic arrays (which remedy a major deficiency of Fortran 77 and which will be discussed further in Section 6.5); the larger character set; a new source form; the significance of blanks; the parameterization of the intrinsic types; the ability to obtain a desired precision and range; quotation marks instead of apostrophes as character constant delimiters; longer names; derived data types; new array subscript notations; array constructors; and last, but not least, pointers. Together they represent a substantial improvement in the ease of use and power of the language.

2.15 Exercises

1. For each of the following assertions, state whether it is true or false, according to the F collating sequence:

```
B is less than M
8 is less than 2
blank is greater than A
blank is less than 6
```

2. Which of the lines of F in Figure 2.4 are correctly written according to the requirements of the F source form? Which ones contain commentary? Which lines are initial lines and which are continuation lines?

Figure 2.4

```
x = y
a = b+c ! add
word = "string"
song = "Life is just"&
    //" a bowl of cherries"
chide = "Waste not, &
    want not!"
c(3:4) = "up"
```

---

3. Classify the following literal constants according to the five intrinsic data types of F, when bit and short are integer constants with kind values that are valid for logical and integer constants, respectively. Which are not legal literal constants?

```
-43                "WORD"
4.39               1.9-4
0.0001e+20         "stuff & nonsense"
.1                 4.
4 9                (0.0,1.0)
(1.0e3,2.0)        "I can't"
"(4.3e9, 6.2)"     .true._bit
e5                 'shouldn' 't'
1_short            "O.K."
```

4. Which of the following names are legal F names?

```
name        name32
quotient    123
a182c3      no-go
stop!       burn_
size        long__name
```

5. What are the first, tenth, eleventh and last elements of the following arrays?

```
real, dimension(11)      :: a
real, dimension(0:11)    :: b
real, dimension(-11:0)   :: c
real, dimension(10,10)   :: d
real, dimension(5,9)     :: e
real, dimension(5,0:1,4) :: f
```

Write an array constructor of eleven integer elements.

6. Given the array declaration

```
character(len=10), dimension(0:5,3) :: c
```

which of the following subobject designators are legal?

```
c(2,3)           c(4:3)(2,1)
c(6,2)           c(5,3)(9:9)
c(0,3)           c(2,1)(4:8)
c(4,3)(:)        c(3,2)(0:9)
c(5)(2:3)        c(5:6)
c(5,3)(9)        c(,)
```

7. Write derived type definitions appropriate for:

  a) a vehicle registration;

  b) a circle;

  c) a book (title, author, and number of pages).

  Give an example of a derived type constant for each one.

8. Given the declaration for t in Section 2.12, which of the following objects and subobjects are arrays?

```
t                t(4)%vertex(1)
t(10)            t(5:6)
t(1)%vertex      t(5:5)
```

9. Write specifications for these entities:

  a) an integer variable inside the range -10^{20} to 10^{20};

  b) a real variable with a minimum of 12 decimal digits of precision and a range of 10^{-100} to 10^{100}.

3. Expressions and assignments

3.1 Introduction

We have seen in the previous chapter how we are able to build the 'words' of F – the constants, keywords, and names – from the basic elements of the character set. In this chapter we shall discover how these entities may be further combined into 'phrases' or *expressions*, and how these, in turn, may be combined into 'sentences', or *statements*.

In an expression, we describe a computation that is to be carried out by the computer. The result of the computation may then be assigned to a variable. A sequence of assignments is the way in which we specify, step-by-step, the series of individual computations to be carried out, in order to arrive at the desired result. There are separate sets of rules for expressions and assignments, depending on whether the operands in question are numeric, logical, character, or derived in type, and whether they are scalars or arrays. There are also separate rules for pointer assignments. We shall discuss each set of rules in turn, including a description of the relational expressions which produce a result of type logical and are needed in control statements (see next chapter). To simplify the initial discussion, we commence by considering expressions and assignments that are intrinsically defined and involve neither arrays nor entities of derived data types.

An expression in F is formed of operands and operators, combined in a way which follows the rules of F syntax. A simple expression involving a *dyadic* (or binary) operator has the form

operand *operator* operand

an example being

x+y

and a unary or *monadic* operator has the form

operator operand

an example being

-y

The operands may be constants, variables, or functions (see Chapter 5), and an expression may itself be used as an operand. In this way we can build up more complicated expressions such as

operand *operator* operand *operator* operand

where consecutive operands are separated by a single operator. Each operand must have a defined value and the result must be mathematically defined; for example, raising a negative real value to a real power is not permitted. Operators may be *intrinsic* (always available) or *defined* (see Section 3.8).

The rules of F state that the parts of expressions without parentheses are evaluated successively from left to right for operators of equal precedence, with the exception of ** (see Section 3.2). If it is necessary to evaluate part of an expression, or *subexpression,* before another, parentheses may be used to indicate which subexpression should be evaluated first. In

operand *operator* (operand *operator* operand)

the subexpression in parentheses will be evaluated, and the result used as an operand to the first operator.

If an expression or subexpression has no parentheses, the processor is permitted to evaluate an equivalent expression, that is an expression that always has the same value apart, possibly, from the effects of numerical round-off. For example, if a, b, and c are real variables, the expression

```
a/b/c
```

might be evaluated as

```
a/(b*c)
```

on a processor that can multiply much faster than it can divide. Usually, such changes are welcome to the programmer since the program runs faster, but when they are not (for instance because they would lead to more round-off) parentheses should be inserted because the processor is required to respect them.

If two operators immediately follow each other, as in

operand *operator operator* operand

the only possible interpretation is that the second operator is unary. Thus, there is a general rule that a binary operator must not follow immmediately after another operator.

3.2   Scalar numeric expressions

A *numeric expression* is an expression whose operands are one of the three numeric types – integer, real, and complex – and whose operators are

**	exponentiation
* /	multiplication, division
+ -	addition, subtraction

These operators are known as *numeric intrinsic* operators, and are listed here in their order of precedence. In the absence of parentheses, exponentiations will be carried out before multiplications and divisions, and these before additions and subtractions.

We note that the minus sign (-) and the plus sign (+) can be used as a unary operators, as in

    -tax

Because it is not permitted in ordinary mathematical notation, a unary minus or plus must not follow immediatedly after another operator. When this is needed, as for x^{-y}, parentheses must be placed around the operator and its operand:

    x**(-y)

The type and kind type parameter of the result of a unary operation are those of the operand.

The exception to the left-to-right rule noted in Section 3.1 concerns exponentiations. Whereas the expression

    -a+b+c

will be evaluated from left to right as

    ((-a)+b)+c

the expression

    a**b**c

will be evaluated as

    a**(b**c)

For integer data, the result of any division will be truncated towards zero, that is to the integer value whose magnitude is equal to or just less than the magnitude of the exact result. Thus, the result of

6/3	is 2
8/3	is 2
-8/3	is -2

This fact must always be borne in mind whenever integer divisions are written. Similarly, the result of

2**3	is 8

whereas the result of

$$2**(-3) \quad \text{is } 1/(2**3)$$

which is zero.

The rules of F allow a numeric expression to contain numeric operands of differing types or kind type parameters. This is known as a *mixed-mode expression*. Except when raising a real or complex value to an integer power, the object of the weaker (or simpler) of the two data types will be converted, or *coerced,* into the type of the stronger one. The result will also be that of the stronger type. If, for example, we write

$$a*i$$

when a is of type real and i is of type integer, then i will be converted to a real data type before the multiplication is performed, and the result of the computation will also be of type real. The rules are summarized for each possible combination for the operations +, -, * and / in Table 3.1, and for the operation ** in Table 3.2. The functions real, cmplx, and kind that they reference are defined in Section 8.3.1. In both Tables, I stands for integer, R stands for real, C stands for complex, and kinda and kindb have the kind values of *a* and *b*.

Table 3.1. Type of result of *a* .op. *b*, where .op. is +, -, * or /.

Type of *a*	Type of *b*	Value of *a* used	Value of *b* used	Type of result
I	I	*a*	*b*	I
I	R	real(*a*,kindb)	*b*	R
I	C	cmplx(*a*,0,kindb)	*b*	C
R	I	*a*	real(*b*,kinda)	R
R	R	*a*	*b*	R
R	C	cmplx(*a*,0,kindb)	*b*	C
C	I	*a*	cmplx(*b*,0,kinda)	C
C	R	*a*	cmplx(*b*,0,kinda)	C
C	C	*a*	*b*	C

If both operands are of type integer, the kind type parameter of the result is that of the operand with the greater decimal exponent range, or is processor dependent if the kinds differ but the decimal exponent ranges are the same. If both operands are of type real or complex, the kind type parameter of the result is that of the operand with the greater decimal precision, or is processor dependent if the kinds differ but the decimal precisions are the same. If one operand is of type integer and the other is of real or complex, the type parameter of the result is that of the real or complex operand.

Table 3.2. Type of result of $a**b$.

Type of a	Type of b	Value of a used	Value of b used	Type of result
I	I	a	b	I
I	R	real$(a,$kindb$)$	b	R
I	C	cmplx$(a,0,$kindb$)$	b	C
R	I	a	b	R
R	R	a	b	R
R	C	cmplx$(a,0,$kindb$)$	b	C
C	I	a	b	C
C	R	a	cmplx$(b,0,$kinda$)$	C
C	C	a	b	C

In the case of raising a complex value to a complex power, the principal value[1] is taken.

3.3 Defined and undefined variables

In the course of the explanations in this and the following chapters, we shall often refer to a variable becoming *defined* or *undefined*. In the previous chapter, we showed how a scalar variable may be called into existence by a statement like

```
real :: speed
```

In this simple case, the variable speed has, at the beginning of the execution of the program, no defined value. It is undefined. No attempt must be made to reference its value since it has none. A common way in which it might become defined is for it to be assigned a value:

```
speed = 2.997
```

After the execution of such an *assignment statement* it has a value, and that value may be referenced, for instance in an expression:

```
speed*0.5
```

For a compound object, it is necessary for all its subobjects to be individually defined before the object as a whole is regarded as defined. Thus, an array is said to be defined only when each of its elements is defined, an object of a derived data type is defined only when each of its components is defined, and a character variable is defined only when each of its characters is defined.

A variable that is defined does not necessarily retain its state of definition throughout the execution of a program. As we shall see in Chapter 5, a variable

---

[1] The principal value of a^b is $\exp(b(\log|a| + i \arg a))$, with $-\pi < \arg a \leq \pi$.

that is local to a single subprogram usually becomes undefined when control is returned from that subprogram. In certain circumstances it is even possible that a single array element becomes undefined: this causes the array considered as a whole to become undefined; a similar rule holds for entities of derived data type and for character variables.

In the case of a pointer, the pointer association status may be *undefined* (its initial state), *associated* with a target, or *disassociated*, which means that it is not associated with a target but has a definite status that may be tested by the function `associated` (Section 8.2). Even though a pointer is associated with a target, the target itself may be defined or undefined.

3.4   Scalar numeric assignment

The general form of a scalar numeric assignment is

   variable = *expr*

where *variable* is a scalar numeric variable and *expr* is a scalar numeric expression. If *expr* is not of the same type or kind as *variable*, it will be converted to that type and kind before the assignment is carried out, according to the set of rules given in Table 3.3, where kindv has the kind value of *variable* (the function int is defined in Section 8.3.1).

Table 3.3. Numeric conversion for assignment statement *variable* = *expr*

Type of *variable*	Value assigned
integer	int(*expr*, kindv)
real	real(*expr*, kindv)
complex	cmplx(*expr*, kindv)

We note that if the type of *variable* is integer but *expr* is not, then the assignment will result in a loss of precision unless *expr* happens to have an integral value. Similarly, assigning a real expression to a real variable of a kind with less precision will also cause a loss of precision to occur, and the assignment of a complex quantity to a non-complex variable involves the loss of the imaginary part. Thus, the values in i and a following the assignments

```
i = 7.3                    ! i of type default integer
a = (4.01935, 2.12372)     ! a of type default real
```

are 7 and 4.01935, respectively.

3.5   Scalar relational operators

It is possible in F to test whether the value of one numeric expression bears a certain relation to that of another, and similarly for character expressions. The relational operators are

<	less than
<=	less than or equal
==	equal
/=	not equal
>	greater than
>=	greater than or equal

If either or both of the expressions are complex, only the operators == and /= are available.

The result of such a comparison is one of the default logical values .true. or .false., and we shall see in the next chapter how such tests are of great importance in controlling the flow of a program. Examples of relational expressions (for i and j of type integer, a and b of type real, and char1 of type default character) are

i < 0	integer relational expression
a < b	real relational expression
a+b > i-j	mixed-mode relational expression
char1 == "Z"	character relational expression

In the third expression above, we note that the two components are of different numeric types. In this case, and whenever either or both of the two components consist of numeric expressions, the rules state that the components are to be evaluated separately, and converted to the type and kind of their sum before the comparison is made. Thus, a relational expression such as

a+b <= i-j

will be evaluated by converting the result of (i-j) to type real.

For character comparisons, the letters are compared from the left until a difference is found or the strings are found to be identical. If the lengths differ, the shorter one is regarded as being padded with blanks on the right. Two zero-sized strings are considered to be identical.

No other form of mixed mode relational operator is intrinsically available, though such an operator may be defined (Section 3.8). The numeric operators take precedence over the relational operators.

3.6 Scalar logical expressions and assignments

Logical constants, variables, and functions may appear as operands in logical expressions. The logical operators, in decreasing order of precedence, are:

unary operator:

> `.not.`   logical negation

binary operators:

> `.and.`   logical intersection
>
> `.or.`   logical union
>
> `.eqv.` and `.neqv.`   logical equivalence and non-equivalence

If we assume a logical declaration of the form

> `logical :: i,j,k,l`

then the following are valid logical expressions:

> `.not.j`
> `j .and. k`
> `i .or. l .and. .not.j`
> `( .not.k .and. j .neqv. .not.l) .or. i`

In the first expression we note the use of `.not.` as a unary operator. In the third expression, the rules of precedence imply that the subexpression `l.and..not.j` will be evaluated first, and the result combined with `i`. In the last expression, the two subexpressions `.not.k.and.j` and `.not.l` will be evaluated and compared for non-equivalence. The result of the comparison, `.true.` or `.false.`, will be combined with `i`.

The kind type parameter of the result is that of the operand for `.not.`, and for the others is that of the operands if they have the same kind or processor dependent otherwise.

We note that the `.or.` operator is an inclusive operator; the `.neqv.` operator provides an exclusive logical or (`a.and..not.b .or. .not.a.and.b`).

The result of any logical expression is the value true or false, and this value may then be assigned to a logical variable such as element 3 of the logical array `flag` in the example

> `flag(3) = ( .not. k .eqv. l) .or. j`

The kind type parameter values of the variable and expression need not be identical.

A logical variable may be set to a predetermined value by an assignment statement:

> `flag(1) = .true.`
> `flag(2) = .false.`

In the foregoing examples, all the operands and results were of type logical – no other data type is allowed to participate in an intrinsic logical operation or assignment.

The results of several relational expressions may be combined into a logical expression, and assigned, as in

```
real :: a, b, x, y
logical :: cond
:
cond = a>b .or. x<0.0 .and. y>1.0
```

where we note the precedence of the relational operators over the logical operators. If the value of such a logical expression can be determined without evaluating a subexpression, a processor is permitted not to evaluate the subexpression. An example is

```
i<=10 .and. ary(i)==0
```

when i has the value 11. However, the programmer must not rely on such behaviour. For example, when ary has size 10, an out-of-bounds subscript might be referenced if the processor chooses to evaluate the right-hand subexpression before the left-hand one. We return to this topic in Section 5.9.1.

3.7   Scalar character expressions and assignments

The only intrinsic operator for character expressions is the concatenation operator //, which has the effect of combining two character operands into a single character result. For example, the result of concatenating the two character constants AB and CD, written as

```
"AB"//"CD"
```

is the character string ABCD. The operands may be character variables, constants, or functions. For instance, if word1 and word2 are both of length 4, and contain the character strings LOOP and HOLE respectively, the result of

```
word1(4:4)//word2(2:4)
```

is the string POLE.

The length of the result of a concatenation is the sum of the lengths of the operands. Thus, the length of the result of

```
word1//word2//"S"
```

is 9, which is the length of the string LOOPHOLES.

The result of a character expression may be assigned to a character variable. Assuming the declarations

```
character(len=4) :: char1, char2
character(len=8) :: char8
```

we may write

```
char1 = "any "
char2 = "book"
char8 = char1//char2
```

In this case, char8 will now contain the string any book. We note in these examples that the lengths of the left- and right-hand sides of the three assignments are in each case equal. If, however, the length of the result of the right-hand side is shorter than the length of the left-hand side, then the result is placed in the left-most part of the left-hand side and the rest is filled with blank characters. Thus, in

```
character(len=5) :: fill
fill(1:4) = "AB"
```

fill(1:4) will have the value AB*bb* (where *b* stands for a blank character). The value of fill(5:5) remains undefined, that is, it contains no specific value and should not be used in an expression. As a consequence, fill is also undefined. On the other hand, when the left-hand side is shorter than the result of the right-hand side, the right-hand end of the result is truncated. The result of

```
character(len=5) :: trunc8
trunc8 = "TRUNCATE"
```

is to place in trunc8 the character string TRUNC. If a left-hand side is of zero length, no assignment takes place.

The left-hand and right-hand sides of an assignment may overlap. In such a case, it is always the old values that are used in the right-hand side expression. For example, the assignment

```
char8(3:5) = char8(1:3)
```

is valid and if char8 began with the value ABCDEFGH, it would be left with the value ABABCFGH.

Other means of manipulating characters and strings of characters, via intrinsic functions, are described in Sections 8.5 and 8.6.

3.8   Structure constructors and scalar defined operators

No operators for derived types are automatically available, but a structure may be constructed from expressions for its components, just as a constant structure may be constructed from constants (Section 2.9). The general form of a *structure constructor* is

> *type-name* (*expr-list*)

where the *expr-list* specifies the values of the components. For example, given the type

```
type, public :: string
   integer :: length
   character(len=10) :: value
end type string
```

and the variables

```
character(len=4) :: char1, char2
```

the following is a value of type string

```
string(8, char1//char2)
```

Each expression in *expr-list* corresponds to a component of the structure; if it is not a pointer component, the value is assigned to the component under the rules of intrinsic assignment; if it is a pointer component, the expression must be a valid target for it,[2] as in a pointer assignment statement (Section 3.12).

When a programmer defines a derived type and wishes operators to be available, he or she must define the operators, too. For a binary operator this is done by writing a module (Section 5.5) containing a function, with two intent in arguments, that specifies how the result depends on the result depends on the operands, and an interface block that associates the function with the operator token (functions and interface blocks will be explained fully in Chapter 5). For example, given the type

```
type, public :: interval
    real :: lower, upper
end type interval
```

that represents intervals of numbers between a lower and an upper bound, we may define addition by the procedure

```
function add_interval(a,b) result(c)
    type(interval), intent(in) :: a, b
    type(interval)             :: c
    c%lower = a%lower + b%lower ! Production code would
    c%upper = a%upper + b%upper ! allow for roundoff.
end function add_interval
```

and the interface block (Section 5.16)

```
interface operator(+)
    module procedure add_interval
end interface
```

This function would be invoked in an expression such as

```
x = y + z
```

to perform this programmer-defined add operation for scalar variables x, y, and z of type interval. A unary operator is defined by an interface block and a function with one intent in argument.

The operator token may be any of the tokens used for the intrinsic operators or may be a name (Section 2.7) consisting entirely of letters and enclosed in decimal points. An example is

---

[2] In particular, it must not be a constant.

```
.add.
```

In this case, the header line of the interface block would be written as

```
interface operator(.add.)
```

and the expression as

```
x = y.add.z
```

If an intrinsic token is used, the number of arguments must be the same as for the intrinsic operation, the priority of the operation is as for the intrinsic operation, and a unary minus or plus must not follow immediately after another operator. Otherwise, it is of highest priority for defined unary operators and lowest priority for defined binary operators. The complete set of priorities is given in Table 3.4. Where another priority is required within an expression, parentheses must be used.

Table 3.4. Relative precedence of operators (in decreasing order)

Type of operation when intrinsic	Operator
-	monadic (unary) defined operator
Numeric	`**`
Numeric	`* or /`
Numeric	monadic + or –
Numeric	dyadic + or –
Character	`//`
Relational	`== /= < <= > >=`
Logical	`.not.`
Logical	`.and.`
Logical	`.or.`
Logical	`.eqv. or .neqv.`
-	dyadic (binary) defined operator

Retaining the intrinsic priorities is helpful both to the readability of expressions and to the efficiency with which a compiler can interpret them. For example, if + is used for set union and * for set intersection, we can interpret the expression

```
i*j + k
```

for sets i, j, and k without difficulty.

Note that a defined unary operator not using an intrinsic token may follow immediately after another operator as in

```
y .add. .inverse. x
```

Operators may be defined for any types of operands, except where there is an intrinsic operation for the operator and types. For example, we might wish to be able to add an interval number to an ordinary real, which can be done by adding the procedure

```
function add_interval_real(a,b) result(c)
    type(interval), intent(in) :: a
    real, intent(in)           :: b
    type(interval)             :: c
    c%lower = a%lower + b ! Production code would
    c%upper = a%upper + b ! allow for roundoff.
end function add_interval_real
```

to the module and changing the interface block to

```
interface operator(+)
    module procedure add_interval, add_interval_real
end interface
```

The result of a defined operation may have any type. The type of the result, as well as its value, must be specified by the function.

Note that an operation that is defined intrinsically cannot be redefined; thus in

```
real :: a, b, c
:
c = a + b
```

the meaning of the operation is always unambiguous.

3.9 Scalar defined assignments

Assignment of an expression of derived type to a variable of the same type is automatically available. For example, if a is of the type interval defined at the start of Section 3.8, we may write

```
a = interval(0.0, 1.0)
```

(structure constructors were met in Section 3.8, too). This assignment may be redefined or another assignment may be defined by a subroutine with two arguments, the first having intent out or intent inout and corresponding to the variable and the second having intent in and corresponding to the expression (subroutines will also be dealt with fully in Chapter 5). For example, assignment of reals to intervals and vice versa might be defined by a module containing the subroutines

```
subroutine real_from_interval(a,b)
    real, intent(out)          :: a
    type(interval), intent(in) :: b
    a = (b%lower + b%upper)/2
end subroutine real_from_interval
```

and

```
subroutine interval_from_real(a,b)
   type(interval), intent(out) :: a
   real, intent(in)            :: b
   a%lower = b
   a%upper = b
end subroutine interval_from_real
```

and the interface block

```
interface assignment(=)
   module procedure real_from_interval, interval_from_real
end interface
```

Given this we may write

```
type(interval) :: a
a = 0.0
```

A defined assignment may not redefine the meaning of an intrinsic assignment for intrinsic types, that is an assignment between two objects of numeric type, logical type, or character type, but may redefine the meaning of an intrinsic assignment for two objects of the same derived type. For instance, for an assignment between two variables of the type string (Section 3.8) that copies only the relevant part of the character component, we might write

```
subroutine assign_string (left, right)
   type(string), intent(out) :: left
   type(string), intent(in)  :: right
   left%length = right%length
   left%value(1:left%length) = right%value(1:right%length)
end subroutine assign_string
```

3.10   Array expressions

So far in this chapter, we have assumed that all the entities in an expression are scalar. However, any of the unary intrinsic operations may also be applied to an array to produce another array of the same shape (identical rank and extents, see Section 2.10) and having each element value equal to that of the operation applied to the corresponding element of the operand. Similarly, binary intrinsic operations may be applied to a pair of arrays of the same shape to produce an array of that shape, with each element value equal to that of the operation applied to corresponding elements of the operands. One of the operands to a binary operation may be a scalar, in which case the result is as if the scalar had been broadcast to an array of the same shape as the array operand. Given the array declarations

```
real, dimension(10,20) :: a,b
real, dimension(5)     :: v
```

the following are examples of array expressions:

```
a/b         ! Array of shape (10,20), with elements a(i,j)/b(i,j)
v+1.0       ! Array of shape (5), with elements v(i)+1.0
5/v+a(1:5,5) ! Array of shape (5), with elements 5/v(i)+a(i,5)
a==b        ! Logical array of shape (10,20), with elements
            ! .true. if a(i,j)==b(i,j), and .false. otherwise
```

Two arrays of the same shape are said to be *conformable* and a scalar is conformable with any array.

Note that the correspondence is by position in the extent and not by subscript value. For example,

```
a(2:9,5:10) + b(1:8,15:20)
```

has element values

```
a(i+1,j+4) + b(i,j+14), i=1,2,...,8, j=1,2,...,6.
```

This may be represented pictorially as in Figure 3.1.

Figure 3.1 The sum of two array sections.

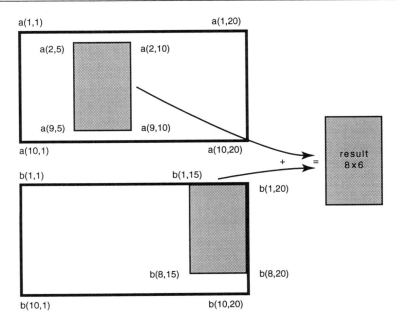

The order in which the scalar operations in any array expression are executed is not specified, thus enabling a compiler to arrange efficient execution on a vector or parallel computer.

Any scalar intrinsic operator may be applied in this way to arrays and array-scalar pairs. For derived operators, the programmer must define operators directly for array operands, for each rank or pair of ranks involved. For example, the type

```
type, public :: matrix
   real :: element
end type matrix
```

might be defined to have scalar operations that are identical to the operations for reals, but for arrays of ranks one and two the operator * defined to mean matrix multiplication. The type matrix would therefore be suitable for matrix arithmetic, whereas reals are not suitable because multiplication for real arrays is done element by element. This is further discussed in Section 6.7.

3.11   Array assignment

By intrinsic assignment, an array expression may be assigned to an array variable of the same shape, which is interpreted as if each element of the expression were assigned to the corresponding element of the variable. For example, with the declarations of the beginning of the last section, the assignment

```
a = a + 1.0
```

replaces $a(i,j)$ by $a(i,j)+1.0$ for $i = 1, 2, \ldots, 10$ and $j = 1, 2, \ldots, 20$. Note that, as for expressions, the element correspondence is by position within the extent rather than by subscript value. This is illustrated by the example

```
a(1,11:15) = v       ! a(1,j+10) is assigned from
                     ! v(j), j=1,2,...,5
```

A scalar expression may be assigned to an array, in which case the scalar value is broadcast to all the array elements.

If the expression includes a reference to the array variable or to a part of it, the expression is interpreted as being fully evaluated before the assignment commences. For example, the statement

```
v(2:5) = v(1:4)
```

results in each element $v(i)$ for $i = 2, 3, 4, 5$ having the value that $v(i-1)$ had prior to the commencement of the assignment. This rule exactly parallels the rule for substrings that was explained in Section 3.7. The order in which the array elements are assigned is not specified, in order to allow optimizations.

Sets of numeric and mathematical intrinsic functions, whose results may be used as operands in scalar or array expressions and in assignments, are described in Sections 8.3 and 8.4.

For a defined assignment (Section 3.9), a separate subroutine must be provided for each combination of ranks for which it is required. Intrinsic assignment is overridden only for those combinations of ranks for which a corresponding defined assignment is accessible.

3.12 Pointers in expressions and assignments

A pointer may appear as a variable in the expressions and assignments that we have considered so far in this chapter, provided it has a valid association with a target. The target is accessed implicitly (that is, without any need for an explicit dereferencing symbol). In particular, if two pointers appear on opposite sides of an assignment statement, data are copied from one target to the other target.

Sometimes the need arises for another sort of assignment. We may want the left-hand pointer to point to another target, rather than that its current target acquire fresh data. This is called *pointer assignment* and takes place in a pointer assignment statement:

   pointer => *target*

where *pointer* is the name of a pointer or the designator of a structure component that is a pointer, and *target* is usually a variable but may also be an expression that has the pointer attribute. For example, the statements

```
x => z
a => c
```

are needed for the first matrix multiplication of Section 2.13, in order to make x refer to z and a to refer to c. Pointer assignment also takes place for a pointer component of a structure when the structure appears on the left-hand side of an ordinary assignment. For example, suppose we have used the type entry of Section 2.13 to construct a chain of entries and wish to add a fresh entry at the front. If first points to the first entry and the pointer variable current is currently allocated, the statements

```
current = entry(new_value, new_index, first)
first => current
```

link a new entry into the top of the chain, with currrent%next pointing to the old first entry, and redefine first to point at the new first entry. In the case where the chain began with length 2 and consisted of

```
first :        (1.0, 10, associated)
first%next :  (2.0, 15, null)
```

following the execution of these statements it would have length 3 and might consist of

```
first :              (4.0, 16, associated)
first%next :         (1.0, 10, associated)
first%next%next :   (2.0, 15, null)
```

If the *target* in a pointer assignment statement is a variable that is not itself a pointer or a subobject of a pointer, it must have the `target` attribute. For example, the statement

```
real, dimension(10), target :: y
```

declares y to have the `target` attribute. Any subobject of an object with the `target` attribute also has the `target` attribute. The `target` attribute is required for the purpose of code optimization by the compiler. It is very helpful to the compiler to know that a variable that is not a pointer or a target may not be accessed by a pointer.

The target in a pointer assignment statement may be a subobject of a pointer. For example, given the declaration

```
character(len=80), dimension(:), pointer :: page
```

and an appropriate association, the following are all permitted targets:

```
page, page(10), page(2:4), page(2)(3:15)
```

If the *target* in a pointer assignment statement is itself a pointer, then a straightforward copy of the pointer takes place. If it is undefined or disassociated, this state is copied; otherwise the targets become identical.

The type, type parameters, and rank of the *pointer* and *target* in a pointer assignment statement must each be the same. If the *pointer* is an array, it takes its shape and bounds from the *target*. The bounds are as would be returned by the functions lbound and ubound (Section 8.11.2) for the target, which means that an array section or array expression is always taken to have the value 1 for a lower bound and the extent for the corresponding upper bound.

F is unusual in not requiring a special character for a reference to a pointer object, but requiring one for distinguishing pointer assignment from ordinary assignment. The reason for this choice was the expectation that most engineering and scientific programs will refer to target data far more often than they change targets.

3.13 Summary

In this chapter, we have seen how scalar and array expressions of numeric, logical, character, and derived types may be formed, and how the corresponding assignments of the results may be made. The relational expressions and the use of pointers have also been presented. We now have the information required to write short sections of code forming a sequence of statements to be performed one after the other. In the following chapter we shall see how more complicated sequences, involving branching and iteration, may be built up.

Features described in this chapter that are not in Fortran 77 are the use of the representations <, <=, ... for the relational operators; the ability of the two sides of a character assignment to overlap; structure constructors; defined operators and assignment; array expressions and assignment; and the use of pointers in expressions and assignment.

3.14   Exercises

1. If all the variables are numeric scalars, which of the following are valid numeric expressions?

```
a+b                 -c
a+-c                d+(-f)
(a+c)**(p+q)        (a+c)(p+q)
-(x+y)**i           4.((a-d)-(a+4.0*x)+1)
```

2. In the following expressions, add the parentheses which correspond to F's rules of precedence (assuming a, c-f are real scalars, i-n are logical scalars, and b is a logical array), for example

```
a+d**2/c      becomes      a+((d**2)/c)

c+4.0*f
4.0*g-a+d/2.0
a**e**c**d
a*e-c**d/a+e
i .and. j .or. k
.not. l .or.   .not. i .and. m .neqv. n
b(3).and.b(1).or.b(6).or..not.b(2)
```

3. What are the results of the following expressions?

```
3+4/2           6/4/2
3.0*4**2        3.0**3/2
-1.0**2         (-1.0)**3
```

4. A scalar character variable r has length 8. What are the contents of r after each of the following assignments?

```
r = "ABCDEFGH"
r = "ABCD"//"01234"
r(:7) = "ABCDEFGH"
r(:6) = "ABCD"
```

5. Which of the following logical expressions are valid if b is a logical array?

```
.not.b(1).and.b(2)      .or.b(1)
b(1).or..not.b(4)       b(2)(.and.b(3).or.b(4))
```

6. If all the variables are real scalars, which of the following relational expressions are valid?

```
d <= c              p < t > 0
x-1 /= y            x+y < 3 .or. > 4.
d<c.and.3.0         q==r .and. s>t
```

7. Write expressions to compute:

    a) the perimeter of a square of side 1;

    b) the area of a triangle of base b and height h;

    c) the volume of a sphere of radius r, given that pi has the value π.

8. An item costs n cents. Write a declaration statement for suitable variables and assignment statements which compute the change to be given from a $1 bill for any value of n from 1 to 99, using coins of denomination 1, 5, 10, and 25 cents.

9. Given the type declaration for interval in Section 3.8, the definitions of + given at the end of Section 3.8, the definitions of assignment given in Section 3.9, and the declarations

```
type(interval) :: a,b,c,d
real :: r
```

which of the following statements are valid?

```
a = b + c
c = b + 1.0
d = b + 1
r = b + c
a = r + 2
```

10. Given the type declarations

```
real, dimension(5,6) :: a, b
real, dimension(5)   :: c
```

which of the following statements are valid?

```
a = b                c = a(:,2) + b(5,:5)
a = c+1.0            c = a(2,:) + b(:,5)
a(:,3) = c           b(2:,3) = c + b(:5,3)
```

4. Control constructs

4.1 Introduction

We have learnt in the previous chapter how assignment statements may be written, and how these may be ordered one after the other to form a sequence of code which is executed step-by-step. In most computations, however, this simple sequence of statements is by itself inadequate for the formulation of the problem. For instance, we may wish to follow one of two possible paths through a section of code, depending on whether a calculated value is positive or negative. We may wish to sum 1000 elements of an array, and to do this by writing 1000 additions and assignments is clearly tedious; the ability to iterate over a single addition is required instead.

For such purposes, we have available in F various facilities to enable the logical flow through the program statements to be controlled. The facilities contained in F correspond to those now widely regarded as being the most appropriate for a modern programming language. Their general form is that of a *block* construct, which begins with an initial keyword statement, may have intermediate keyword statements, and ends with a matching terminal statement. Each sequence of statements between keywords is called a *block*. A block may be empty, though such cases are rare.

Executable constructs may be *nested*, that is a block may contain another executable construct. In such a case, the block must contain the whole of the inner construct. Execution of a block always begins with its first executable statement.

4.2 The if construct

The if construct allows either the execution of a sequence of statements (a block) to depend on a condition, or the execution of alternative sequences of statements (blocks) to depend on alternative conditions. The simplest of its three forms is

```
if (scalar-logical-expr) then
    block
end if
```

where *scalar-logical-expr* is any scalar logical expression and *block* is any sequence of executable statements (but not an incomplete construct). The *block* is executed if *scalar-logical-expr* evaluates to the value true, and is not executed if it evaluates to the value false.

We notice that the if construct is a compound statement, the beginning being marked by the if...then, and the end by the end if. An example is

```
if (x < y) then
    temp = x
    x = y
    y = temp
end if
```

in which we notice also that the block inside the if construct is indented with respect to its beginning and end. This is not obligatory, but makes the logic easier to understand, especially in nested if constructs as we shall see at the end of this section.

In the second form of the if construct, an alternative block of statements is executable, for the case where the condition is false. The general form is

```
if (scalar-logical-expr) then
    block1
else
    block2
end if
```

in which the first block of statements (*block1*) is executed if the condition is true and the second block (*block2*), following the else statement, is executed if the condition is false. An example is

```
if (x < y) then
    x = -x
else
    y = -y
end if
```

in which the sign of x is changed if x is less than y, and the sign of y is changed if x is greater than or equal to y.

The third and most general type of if construct uses the else if statement to make a succession of tests, each of which has its associated block of statements. The tests are made one after the other until one is fulfilled, and the associated statements of the relevant if or else if block are executed. Control then passes to the end of the if construct. If no test is fulfilled, no block is executed, unless there is a final 'catch-all' else clause. The general form is shown in Figure 4.1. Here, and later in the book, we use the notation [ ] to indicate an optional item and [ ]... to indicate an item that may occur any number of times (including zero). There can be any number (including zero) of else if statements, and zero or one else statements.

It is permitted to nest if constructs within one another to an arbitrary depth, as shown to two levels in Figure 4.2, in which we see again the necessity to

Figure 4.1

```
if (scalar-logical-expr) then
    block
[else if (scalar-logical-expr) then
    block]...
[else
    block]
end if
```

indent the code in order to be able to understand the logic easily. For even deeper nesting, appending matching comments to each if, else if, else, and end if statement is to be recommended. The constructs must be properly nested, that is each construct must be wholly contained in a block of the next outer construct.

Figure 4.2

```
if (i < 0) then
    if (j < 0) then
        x = 0.0
        y = 0.0
    else
        z = 0.0
    end if
else if (k < 0) then
    z = 1.0
else
    x = 1.0
    y = 1.0
end if
```

4.3   The case construct

F provides another means of selecting one of several options, rather similar to that of the if construct. The principal differences between the two constructs are that, for the case construct, only *one* expression is evaluated for testing, and the evaluated expression may belong to no more than one of a series of pre-defined sets of values. The form of the case construct is shown by:

```
select case (expr)
    [case selector
        block]...
end select
```

The expression *expr* must be scalar and of type character or integer, and the specified values in each *selector* must be of this type. In the character case, the lengths are permitted to differ. In the integer case, the kinds may differ. The simplest form of *selector* is a scalar initialization expression[1] in parentheses, such as in the statement

```
case(1)
```

A range may be specified by a lower and an upper scalar initialization expression separated by a colon:

```
case (low:high)
```

Either *low* or *high*, but not both, may be absent; this is equivalent to specifying that the case is selected whenever *expr* evaluates to a value that is less than or equal to *high*, or greater than or equal to *low*, respectively. An example is shown in Figure 4.3. Though we recommend that the values be in order, as in this example, this is not required.

Figure 4.3

```
select case (number)      ! number is of type integer
case (:-1)                ! all values below 0
   n_sign = -1
case (0)                  ! only 0
   n_sign = 0
case (1:)                 ! all values above 0
   n_sign = 1
end select
```

The general form of *selector* is a list of non-overlapping values and ranges, all of the same type as *expr*, enclosed in parentheses, such as

```
case (1, 2, 7, 10:17, 23)
```

Overlapping values are not permitted within one *selector*, nor between different ones in the same construct.

The form

```
case default
```

is available as the final case selector and is equivalent to a list of all the possible values of *expr* that are not included in the other selectors of the construct. An example is shown in Figure 4.4.

---

[1]An initialization expression is a restricted form of constant expression (the restrictions being chosen for ease of implementation). The details are tedious and are deferred to Section 7.2. In this section, all examples are the simplest form of initialization expression: the literal constant.

Figure 4.4

```
select case (ch)          ! ch of type character
case ("c", "d", "r":)
    ch_type = .true.
case ("i":"n")
    int_type = .true.
case default
    real_type = .true.
end select
```

Since the values of the selectors are not permitted to overlap, at most one selector may be satisfied; if none is satisfied, control passes to the next executable statement following the end select statement.

Like the if construct, case constructs may be nested inside one another.

4.4 The do construct

Many problems in mathematics require, for their representation in a programming language, the ability to *iterate*. If we wish to sum the elements of an array a of length 10, we could write

```
sum_a = a(1)
sum_a = sum_a+a(2)
:
sum_a = sum_a+a(10)
```

which is clearly laborious. F provides a facility known as the do construct which allows us to reduce these ten lines of code to

```
sum_a = 0.0
do  i = 1,10
    sum_a = sum_a+a(i)
end do
```

In this fragment of code we first set sum_a to zero, and then require that the statement between the do statement and the end do statement shall be executed ten times. For each iteration there is an associated value of an index, kept in i, which assumes the value 1 for the first iteration through the loop, 2 for the second, and so on up to 10. The variable i must be a locally declared integer variable. It must not be explicitly modified within the do construct.

The do statement has more general forms. If we wished to sum the fourth to ninth elements we would write

```
do  i = 4, 9
```

thereby specifying the required first and last values of i. If, alternatively, we wished to sum all the odd elements, we would write

    do i = 1, 9, 2

where the third of the three loop *parameters,* namely the 2, specifies that i is to be incremented in steps of 2, rather than by the default value of 1, which is assumed if no third parameter is given. In fact, we can go further still, as the parameters need not be constants at all, but integer expressions, as in

    do i = j+4, m, -k(j)**2

in which the first value of i is j+4, and subsequent values are decremented by k(j)**2 until the value of m is reached. Thus, do constructs may run 'backwards' as well as 'forwards'. If any of the three parameters is a variable or is an expression that involves a variable, the value of the variable may be modified within the loop without affecting the number of iterations, as the *initial* values of the parameters are used for the control of the loop.

The general form of this type of bounded do construct control clause is

[*name*:]   do *variable* = *expr1, expr2* [*,expr3*]
                block
            end do [*name*]

where *variable* is a named scalar integer variable, *expr1, expr2,* and *expr3* (*expr3* is optional but must be nonzero when present) are any valid scalar integer expressions, and *name* is the optional construct name. The do index must be a local variable declared in the scoping unit and is not permitted to be a dummy argument, function result, or pointer. The do and end do statements must either both bear the same *name*, or both be unnamed.

The number of iterations of a do construct is given by the formula

    max((*expr2-expr1+expr3*)/*expr3*, 0)

where max is a function which we shall meet in Section 8.3.2 and which returns either the value of the expression or zero, whichever is the larger. There is a consequence following from this definition, namely that if a construct begins with the statement

    do i = 1, n

then its body will not be executed at all if the value of n on entering the loop is zero or less. This is an example of the *zero-trip loop,* and results from the application of the max function.

A very simple form of the do statement is the unbounded

    [*name*:] do

which specifies an endless loop. In practice, a means to exit from an endless loop is required, and this is provided in the form of the exit statement:

```
exit [name]
```

where *name* is optional and is used to specify from which construct the exit should be taken in the case of nested constructs. Execution of an exit statement causes control to be transferred to the next executable statement after the end do statement to which it refers. If no name is specified, it terminates execution of the innermost do construct in which it is enclosed. As an example of this form of the do, suppose we have used the type entry of Section 2.13 to construct a chain of entries in a sparse vector, and we wish to find the entry with index 10, known to be present. If first points to the first entry, the code in Figure 4.5 is suitable.

Figure 4.5

```
type(entry), pointer :: first, current
:
current => first
do
    if (current%i == 10) then
        exit
    end if
    current => current%next
end do
```

The exit statement is also useful in a bounded loop when all iterations are not always needed.

A related statement is the cycle statement

```
cycle [name]
```

which transfers control to the end do statement of the corresponding construct. Thus, if further iterations are still to be carried out, the next one is initiated.

The value of a do construct index (if present) is incremented at the end of every construct iteration for use in the subsequent iteration. As the value of this index is available outside the construct after its execution, we have three possible situations, each illustrated by the following construct:

```
do  i = 1, n
    :
    if (i==j) then
        exit
    end if
    :
end do
l = i
```

The situations are:

i) If, at execution time, n has the value zero or less, i is set to 1 but the loop is not executed, and control passes to the statement following the end do statement.

ii) If, on the other hand, n has a value which is greater than or equal to j, an exit will be taken at the if statement, and l will acquire the last value of i, which is of course j.

iii) If, as a third possibility, the value of n is greater than zero but less than j, the loop will be executed n times, with the successive values of i being 1, 2, ... *etc.* up to n. When reaching the end of the loop for the *nth* time, i will be incremented a final time, acquiring the value n+1, which will then be assigned to l.

We see how important it is to make careful use of loop indices outside the do block, especially when there is the possibility of the number of iterations taking on the boundary value of the maximum for the construct.

The do block, just mentioned, is the sequence of statements between the do statement and the end do statement.

It is illegal for the block of a do construct (or an if, case, or where construct, see Section 6.8), to be only partially contained in a block of another construct. The construct must be completely contained in the block. The following two sequences are thus legal:

```
if (scalar-logical-expr) then
    do i = 1, n
       :
    end do
else
    :
end if
```

and

```
do i = 1, n
    if (scalar-logical-expr) then
       :
    end if
end do
```

but this third sequence is not:

```
if (scalar-logical-expr) then
    do  i = 1, 10
       :
    end if   ! illegal position of if construct termination
    :
end do
```

Any number of do constructs may be nested provided that the range of each nested construct is completely contained within the range of another. We may thus write a matrix multiplication as shown in Figure 4.6.

Figure 4.6

```
do   i = 1, n
   do  j = 1, m
      a(i,j) = 0.0
      do  l = 1, k
         a(i,j) = a(i,j)+b(i,l)*c(l,j)
      end do
   end do
end do
```

Another example is the summation loop in Figure 4.7.

Figure 4.7

```
do   i = 1, n
   sum_b = 0.0
   do  j = 1,i
      sum_b = sum_b+b(j,i)
   end do
   a(i) = sum_b
end do
```

Finally, it should be noted that many short do-constructs can be expressed alternatively, and better, in the form of array expressions and assignments. However, this is not always possible, and a particular danger to watch for is where one iteration of the construct depends upon a previous one. Thus, the construct

```
do i = 2, n
   a(i) = a(i-1) + b(i)
end do
```

cannot be replaced by the statement

```
a(2:n) = a(1:n-1) + b(2:n)          ! Beware
```

4.5 Summary

In this chapter we have introduced the three main features by which the control in F code may be programmed – the if statement and construct, the case construct and the do construct. The effective use of these features is the key to sound code.

We have touched upon the concept of a *program unit* as being like the chapter of a book. Just as a book may have just one chapter, so a complete program may consist of just one program unit, which is known as a *main program*. In its simplest form it consists of a series of statements of the kinds we have been dealing with so far, starting with a program statement and terminating with an end program statement, which acts as a signal to the computer to stop processing the current program.

In order to test whether a program unit of this type works correctly, we need to be able to output, to a terminal or printer, the values of the computed quantities. This topic will be fully explained in Chapter 9, and for the moment we need to know only that this can be achieved by a statement of the form

```
print * , " var1 = ", var1 , " var2 = ", var2
```

which will output a line such as

```
var1 = 1.0   var2 = 2.0
```

Similarly, input data can be read by statements like

```
read *, val1, val2
```

This is sufficient to allow us to write simple programs like that in Figure 4.8, which outputs the converted values of a temperature scale between specified limits. Valid inputs are shown at the end of the example.

The case construct is not present in to Fortran 77 and the do construct takes a different form, not relying on labels.

4.6   Exercises

1. Write a program which

   a) defines an array to have 100 elements;

   b) assigns to the elements the values 1, 2, 3, . . . , 100;

   c) reads two integer values in the range 1 to 100;

   d) reverses the order of the elements of the array in the range specified by the two values.

2. The first two terms of the Fibonacci series are both 1, and all subsequent terms are defined as the sum of the preceding two terms. Write a program which reads an integer value limit and which computes and prints the coefficients of the first limit terms of the series.

Figure 4.8

```
program temp_convert
!   Print a conversion table of the Farenheit and Celsius
!   temperature scales between specified limits.
!
    real :: celsius, farenheit
    integer :: low_temp, high_temp, temperature
    character(len=1) :: temp_scale
!
read_loop:   do
!
!   Read scale and limits
        read *, temp_scale, low_temp, high_temp
!
!   Check for valid data
        if (temp_scale /= "C" .and. temp_scale /= "F") then
            exit read_loop
        end if
!
!   Loop over the limits
        do  temperature = low_temp, high_temp
!
!   Choose conversion formula
            select case (temp_scale)
            case ("C")
                celsius = temperature
                farenheit = 9.0/5.0*celsius + 32.0
            case ("F")
                farenheit = temperature
                celsius = 5.0/9.0*(farenheit-32.0)
            end select
!
!   Print table
            print *, celsius, " degrees C correspond to",  &
                     farenheit, " degrees F"
        end do
    end do read_loop
!
!   Termination
    print *, " End of valid data"
end program temp_convert

C  90   100
F  20   32
*   0    0
```

3. The coefficients of successive orders of the binomial expansion are shown in the normal Pascal triangle form as

$$
\begin{array}{c}
1 \\
1\ 1 \\
1\ 2\ 1 \\
1\ 3\ 3\ 1 \\
1\ 4\ 6\ 4\ 1
\end{array}
$$

etc.

Write a program which reads an integer value limit and prints the coefficients of the first limit lines of this Pascal triangle.

4. Define a character variable of length 80. Write a program which reads a value for this variable. Assuming that each character in the variable is alphabetic, write code which sorts them into alphabetic order, and prints out the frequency of occurrence of each letter.

5. Write a program to read an integer value limit and print the first limit prime numbers, by any method.

6. Write a program which reads a value x, and calculates and prints the corresponding value x/(1.0+x). The case x=-1.0 should produce an error message and be followed by an attempt to read a new value of x.

7. Given a chain of entries of the type entry of Section 2.13, modify the code in Figure 4.5 (Section 4.4) so that it removes the entry with index 10, and makes the previous entry point to the following entry.

5. Program units and procedures

5.1 Introduction

As we saw in the previous chapter, it is possible to write a complete F program as a single unit, but it is preferable to break the program down into manageable units. Each such *program unit* corresponds to a program task that can be readily understood and, ideally, can be written, compiled, and tested independently. We will discuss the two kinds of program unit, the main program and module.

A complete program must, as a minimum, include one *main program*. This may contain statements of the kinds that we have met so far in examples, but normally its most important statements are invocations or *calls* to subsidiary programs known as *subprograms* and contained in *modules*. A subprogram defines a *function* or a *subroutine*. They differ in that a function returns a single object and does not alter the values of its arguments (so that it represents a function in the mathematical sense), whereas a subroutine usually performs a more complicated task, returning several results through its arguments and by other means. Functions and subroutines are known collectively as *procedures*.

A procedure may also be *intrinsic*, that is, it may be defined as part of the language (see Chapter 8); and it may be *external*, that is, defined by means other than F (for example, C, Fortran 77, or Fortran 90).

If a module contains a subprogram, it is called the *host* of that subprogram. Besides containing a collection of subprograms, a module may contain data definitions, derived type definitions, and interface blocks (Section 5.10). This collection may be expected to provide facilities associated with some particular task, such as providing matrix arithmetic, a library facility, or a data base. It may sometimes be large.

In this chapter, we will describe program units and the statements that are associated with them.

5.2 Main program

Every complete program must have one, and only one, main program. Optionally, it may contain calls to subprograms. A main program has the following form:

```
program program-name
    [specification-stmts]
    [executable-stmts]
end program program-name
```

The *program-name* may be any valid F name such as model. The end program statement has two purposes. It acts as a signal to the compiler that it has reached the end of the program unit and, when executed, it causes the complete program to stop.

A main program without calls to subprograms is usually used only for short tests, as in

```
program test
    print *, "Hello world!"
end program test
```

The specification statements define the environment for the executable statements. So far, we have met the type declaration statement (integer, real, complex, logical, character, and type(*type-name*)) that specifies the type and other properties of the entities that it lists. We will meet other specification statements in this chapter and in Chapter 7.

The executable statements specify the actions that are to be performed. So far, we have met the assignment statement; the pointer assignment statement; the if, do, and case constructs; and the read and print statements. We will meet other executable statements in this and later chapters. Execution of a program always commences with the first executable statement of the main program.

5.3   The stop statement

Another way to stop program execution is to execute a stop statement

```
stop
```

This statement is an executable statement that may appear in the main program or any subprogram. A well-designed program normally returns control to the main program for program termination, so the stop statement should appear there.

5.4   Subprograms

Subprograms are called from a main program or other subprograms and usually perform a well-defined task within the framework of a complete program. Apart from the leading statement, they have a form that is very like that of a main program:

```
subroutine-stmt
    [specification-stmts]
    [executable-stmts]
end subroutine subroutine-name
```

or

> *function-stmt*
>   [*specification-stmts*]
>   [*executable-stmts*]
> end function *function-name*

The effect of executing an end subroutine or end function statement in a subprogram is to return control to the caller, rather than to stop execution.

The simplest form of subprogram defines a subroutine without any arguments and has a *subroutine-stmt* of the form

subroutine *subroutine-name* ()

Such a subprogram is useful when a program consists of a sequence of distinct phases, in which case the main program consists of a sequence of call statements that invoke the subroutines as in the example

```
program game         ! Main program to control a card game
   use cards_module ! The subprograms are defined in a module
   :
   call shuffle ()   ! First shuffle the cards.
   call deal ()      ! Now deal them.
   call play ()      ! Play the game.
   call display ()   ! Display the result.
end program game     ! Cease execution.
```

But how do we handle the flow of information between the subroutines? How does play know which cards deal has dealt? There are, in fact, two methods by which information may be passed. The first is via data held in a module (Section 5.5) and this is used here; the second is via arguments (Section 5.6) in the procedure calls.

5.5 Modules

The module provides a means of packaging subprograms, global data, derived types and their associated operations, and interface blocks (Section 5.10). Everything associated with some task (such as interval arithmetic, see later in this section) may be collected into a module and accessed whenever it is needed. Those parts that are associated with the internal working and are of no interest to the user may be made 'invisible' to the user, which allows the internal design to be altered without the need to alter the program that uses it and prevents accidental alteration of internal data. We expect F libraries to consist of sets of modules.

Modules have the form shown in Figure 5.1, and the module cards_module of the previous section is an example of a module containing only subprograms. In another simple form, the body consists only of data specifications.

Figure 5.1

```
module module-name
     [specification-stmts]
[contains
   subprograms]
end module module-name
```

For example

```
module state
    integer, dimension(52), public :: cards
end module state
```

might hold the state of play of the game. It would be accessed by the statement

```
use state
```

appearing at the beginnings of the main program game and of the module cards_module containing the subprograms shuffle, deal, play, and display. The array cards is set by shuffle to contain the integer values 1 to 52 in a random order, where each integer value corresponds to a pre-defined playing card. For instance, 1 might stand for the ace of clubs, 2 for the two of clubs, etc. up to 52 for the king of spades. The array cards is changed by the subroutines deal and play, and finally accessed by subroutine display.

A further example of global data in a module would be the definitions of the values of the kind type parameters that might be required throughout a program (Sections 2.6.1 and 2.6.2). They can be placed in a module and used wherever they are required. On a processor that supports all the kinds listed, an example might be:

```
module numeric_kinds
     ! named constants for 4, 2, and 1 byte integers:
     integer, parameter, public ::                          &
          i4b = selected_int_kind(9),                       &
          i2b = selected_int_kind(4),                       &
          i1b = selected_int_kind(2)
     ! and for single, double and quadruple precision reals:
     integer, parameter, public ::                          &
          sp = kind(1.0),                                   &
          dp = selected_real_kind(2*precision(1.0_sp)), &
          qp = selected_real_kind(2*precision(1.0_dp))
end module numeric_kinds
```

The public attribute that we have placed in these modules will be explained in Section 7.4.

A very useful role for modules is to contain definitions of types and their associated operators. For example, a module might contain the type interval of Section 3.8, as shown in Figure 5.2. Given this module, any program unit needing this type and its operators need only include the statement

```
use interval_arithmetic
```

at the head of its specification statements.

Figure 5.2

```
module interval_arithmetic
    public :: operator(+), add_intervals
    type, public :: interval
        real :: lower, upper
    end type interval
    interface operator(+)
        module procedure add_intervals
    end interface
    :
contains
    function add_intervals(a,b) result (c)
        type(interval), intent(in) :: a, b
        type(interval)             :: c
        c%lower = a%lower + b%lower ! Production code would
        c%upper = a%upper + b%upper ! allow for roundoff.
    end function add_intervals
    :
end module interval_arithmetic
```

A subprogram always has access to other entities of the module, including the ability to call other subprograms of the module, rather as if it contained a use statement for the module.

A module may contain use statements that access prior modules. It must not access the same module in two use statements, directly or indirectly (when an accessed module itself has a use statement). Further details are given in Section 7.5.

It is possible within a module to specify that some of the entities are private to it and cannot be accessed from other program units. Also there are forms of the use statement that allow access to only part of a module and forms that allow renaming of the entities accessed. These features will be explained in Sections 7.4 and 7.7. For the present, we assume that the whole module is accessed without any renaming of the entities in it (which explains the appearance of public in our examples).

5.6   Arguments of procedures

Procedure arguments provide an alternative means for subprograms to access data. Returning to our card game example, instead of placing the array cards in a module, we might declare it in the main program and pass it as an actual argument to each subprogram, as shown in Figure 5.3.

Figure 5.3

```
  program game          ! Main program to control a card game
    use cards_module
    integer, dimension(52) :: cards
    call shuffle(cards)       ! First shuffle the cards.
    call deal(cards)          ! Now deal them.
    call play(cards)          ! Play the game.
    call display(cards)       ! Display the result.
  end program game            ! Cease execution.
```

Each subroutine receives cards as a dummy argument. For instance, shuffle has the form shown in Figure 5.4. (The intent attribute seen in the examples of this section will be explained in Section 5.8.)

Figure 5.4

```
  subroutine shuffle(cards)
     ! Subroutine that places the values 1 to 52 in cards
     ! in random order.
     integer, dimension(:), intent(out) :: cards
     ! Statements that fill cards
     :
  end subroutine shuffle     ! Return to caller.
```

We can, of course, imagine a card game in which deal is going to deal only three cards to each of four players. In this case, it would be a waste of time for shuffle to prepare a deck of 52 cards when only the first 12 cards are needed. This can be achieved by requesting shuffle to limit itself to a number of cards that is transmitted in the calling sequence thus:

```
  call shuffle(3*4, cards)
```

Inside shuffle, the algorithm to fill cards would be contained in a do construct with this number of iterations, as shown in Figure 5.5.

We have seen how it is possible to pass an array and a constant expression to and from a subprogram. An actual argument may be any variable or expression (or a procedure name, see Section 5.11). Each dummy argument of the called procedure must agree with the corresponding actual argument in type, type parameters,

Figure 5.5

```
subroutine shuffle(ncards, cards)
    integer, intent(in) :: ncards
    integer, dimension(:), intent(out) :: cards
    integer ::  icard
    do icard = 1, ncards
        :
        cards(icard) = ...
    end do
end subroutine shuffle
```

and rank. In the case of an array, the rank is the number of colons in the declaration of the dummy array (see Section 6.3) and the shape is taken from that of the actual argument. However, the names do not have to be the same. For instance, if two decks had been needed, we might have written the code shown in Figure 5.6. The important point is that subprograms can be written independently of one

Figure 5.6

```
program game
    use cards_module
    integer, dimension(52) :: acards, bcards
    call shuffle(acards)        ! First shuffle the a deck.
    call shuffle(bcards)        ! Next shuffle the b deck.
    :
end program game
```

another, the association of the dummy arguments with the actual arguments occurring each time the call is executed. We can imagine shuffle being used in other programs which use other names. In this manner, libraries of modules may be built up.

Being able to have different names for actual and dummy arguments provides a useful flexibility, but it should only be used when it is actually needed. When the same name can be used, the code is more readable.

As the type of an actual argument and its corresponding dummy argument must agree, care must be taken when using component selection within an actual argument. Thus, supposing the type definitions point and triangle of Figure 2.1 (Section 2.9) are available in a module def, we might write the code shown in Figure 5.7.

Figure 5.7

```
      use def
      type(triangle) :: t
      :
      call sub(t%a)
      :
  subroutine sub(p)
      use def
      type(point), intent(inout) :: p
```

5.6.1 Pointer arguments

A dummy argument is permitted to have the attribute pointer. In this case, the actual argument must also have the attribute pointer. When the subprogram is invoked, the rank of the actual argument must match that of the dummy argument, and its pointer association status is passed to the dummy argument. On return, the actual argument normally takes its pointer association status from that of the dummy argument, but it becomes undefined if the dummy argument is associated with a target that becomes undefined when the return is executed (for example, if the target is a local variable that does not have the save attribute, Section 7.6). The intent attribute would be ambiguous in this context, since it might refer to the pointer association status alone or to both the pointer association status and the value of its target; it is not allowed to be specified.

A pointer actual argument is also permitted to correspond to a non-pointer dummy argument. In this case, the pointer must have a target and the target is associated with the dummy argument, as in

```
      :
      subroutine find (c)
         real, intent(inout), dimension(:,:) :: c
         :
      end subroutine find
      :
      real, pointer, dimension(:,:) :: a
      :
      allocate ( a(80,80) )
      call find (a)
```

5.6.2 Restrictions on actual arguments

There are two important restrictions on actual arguments, which are designed to allow the compiler to optimize on the assumption that the dummy arguments are distinct from each other and from other entities that are accessible within the procedure. For example, a compiler may arrange for an array to be copied to a local variable on entry, and copied back on return. While an actual argument is associated with a dummy argument:

i) Action that affects the allocation status or pointer association status of the argument or any part of it (any pointer assignment, allocation, deallocation, or nullification) must be taken through the dummy argument. If this is done, then throughout the execution of the procedure, the argument may be referenced only through the dummy argument.

ii) Action that affects the value of the argument or any part of it must be taken through the dummy argument unless

   a. the dummy argument has the `pointer` attribute,

   b. the part is all or part of a pointer subobject, or

   c. the dummy argument has the `target` attribute, the dummy argument does not have intent `in`, and the actual argument is a target other than an array section with a vector subscript.

If this is done, then throughout the execution of the procedure, the argument may be referenced only through the dummy argument unless a., b., or c. holds.

An example of i) is a pointer that is nullified (Section 6.5.4) while still associated with the dummy argument. As an example of ii), consider

```
call modify(a(1:5), a(3:9))
```

Here, a(3:5) may not be changed through either dummy argument since this would violate the rule for the other argument. However, a(1:2) may be changed through the first argument and a(6:9) may be changed through the second. Another example is an actual argument that is an object being accessed from a module; here, the same object must not be accessed from the module by the procedure and redefined.

5.6.3   Arguments with the target attribute

In most circumstances, an implementation is permitted to make a copy of an actual argument on entry to a procedure and copy it back on return. This may be desirable on efficiency grounds, particularly when the actual argument is not held in contiguous storage. In any case, if a dummy argument has neither the `target` nor `pointer` attribute, any pointers associated with the actual argument do not become associated with the corresponding dummy argument but remain associated with the actual argument.

However, copy in / copy out is not allowed when

i) a dummy argument has the `target` attribute and

ii) the actual argument is a target other than an array section with a vector subscript.

In this case, the dummy and actual arguments must have the same shape, any pointer associated with the actual argument becomes associated with the dummy argument on invocation, and any pointer associated with the dummy argument on return remains associated with the actual argument.

When a dummy argument has the `target` attribute, but the actual argument is not a target or is an array section with a vector subscript, any pointer associated with the dummy argument obviously becomes undefined on return.

In other cases where the dummy argument has the `target` attribute, whether copy in / copy out occurs is processor dependent. No reliance should be placed on the pointer associations with such an argument after the invocation.

5.7   The return statement

We saw in Section 5.2 that if the last executable statement in a main program is executed, the end `program` statement is executed and the program stops. Similarly, if the last executable statement in a subprogram is executed, the end `subroutine` or end `function` statement is executed and control returns to the point of invocation. Just as the `stop` statement is an executable statement that provides an alternative means of stopping execution, so the `return` statement provides an alternative means of returning control from a subprogram. It has the form

```
return
```

It must not appear among the executable statements of a main program.

5.8   Argument intent

In Figure 5.5, the dummy argument `cards` was used to pass information out from `shuffle` and the dummy argument `ncards` was used to pass information in. This was declared with the intent `out` and intent `in` attributes, respectively. A third possibility is for a dummy argument to be used for both purposes, in which case intent `inout` must be specified. All arguments other than pointers and procedures (Section 5.11) are required to have declared intent. The requirement to specify intent is good for documentation, and it allows compilers to make more checks at compile time.

If a dummy argument is specified with intent `in`, it must not be redefined by the procedure, say by appearing on the left-hand side of an assignment or by being passed on as an actual argument to a procedure that redefines it. For intent `inout`, the corresponding actual argument must be a variable because the expectation is that it will be redefined by the procedure. For intent `out`, the corresponding actual argument must again be a variable; in this case, it becomes undefined on entry to the procedure because the intention is that it be used only to pass information out.

For a function, the dummy arguments (other than pointers and procedures) must have intent in. If a subroutine specifies defined assignment (Section 3.9), the first argument must have intent out or inout, and the second argument must have intent in.

If a dummy argument has the pointer attribute, its intent is not allowed to be specified. This is because of the ambiguity of whether the intent applies to the target data object or to the pointer association.

5.9 Functions

Functions are similar to subroutines in many respects, but they are invoked within an expression and return a value that is used within the expression. For example, the subprogram in Figure 5.8 returns the distance between two points in space and the statement

```
if (distance(a, c) > distance(b, c) ) then
```

invokes the function twice in the logical expression that it contains.

Figure 5.8

```
function distance(p, q) result (d)
    real, intent(in), dimension(:) :: p, q
    real :: d
    d = sqrt( (p(1)-q(1))**2 + (p(2)-q(2))**2 +    &
                    (p(3)-q(3))**2 )
    ! The intrinsic function sqrt is defined in Section 8.4.
    end function distance
```

Note the type declaration for the function result. The result behaves just like a dummy argument with intent out. It is initially undefined, but once defined it may appear in an expression and it may be redefined.

It is not permissible to write functions that change the values of their arguments, modify values in modules, rely on saved local data (Section 7.6), or perform input-output operations other than with the print or read * statement (or, see Chapter 9, the formatted read or formatted write statement for an internal file or for the unit designated with an asterisk).[1] These are all known as *side-effects* and conflict with good programming practice. Where they are needed, a subroutine should be used. It is reassuring to know that when a function is called, nothing else goes on 'behind the scenes', and it may be very helpful to an optimizing compiler. Because these restrictions do not apply to subroutines, it is not permissible to call a subroutine from a function except as a defined assignment (Section 3.9), and procedure dummy arguments of functions (Section 5.11) must be functions. Any subroutine called from a function, either by a defined assignment or indirectly,

---
[1]Note, however, that a function is permitted to contain a stop statement.

must obey all the rules for functions except that the first argument may have intent out or inout. The limited forms of input-output allowed in an F function are intended only for diagnostic purposes and should be avoided as far as possible.

A function result may be an array, in which case it must be declared as such. It may also be a pointer,[2] which is very useful when the size of the result depends on a calculation in the function itself. The result is initially undefined. Within the function, it must become associated or defined as disassociated. We expect the function reference usually to be such that a pointer assignment takes place for the result, that is, the reference occurs as the right-hand side of a pointer assignment (Section 3.12) or as a pointer component of a structure constructor. For example, the statements

```
use data_handler
real, dimension(100) :: x
real, pointer, dimension(:) :: y
 :
y => compact(x)
```

might be used to reference the pointer function in Figure 5.9 in the module data_handler. If the reference occurs as a primary of an expression, the result

---

Figure 5.9

```
function compact(x) result (c)
! A procedure to remove duplicates from the array x
    real, intent(in), dimension(:) :: x
    real, pointer, dimension(:) :: c
    integer :: n
    :                   ! find the number of distinct values, n
    allocate(c(n))
    :                   ! copy the distinct values into c
end function compact
```

---

must be associated with a target that is defined, and the value of the target is used for the evaluation of the expression.

The value returned by a non-pointer function must always be defined.

As well as being a scalar or array value of intrinsic type, a function result may also be a scalar or array value of a derived type, as we have seen already in Section 3.8. When the function is invoked, the function value must be used as a whole, that is, it is not permitted to be qualified by substring, array-subscript, array-section, or structure-component selection.

Although this is not very useful, a function is permitted to have an empty argument list. In this case, the brackets are obligatory both within the function statement and at every invocation.

---

[2]However, it is not possible for a pointer to have a function as its target. In other words, *dynamic binding*, or association of a pointer with a function at run time, is not available.

5.9.1   Prohibition of side-effects

The prohibition of side-effects in functions assists an optimizing compiler. The processor is not required to evaluate all the operands of an expression, or to evaluate entirely each operand, if the value of the expression can be determined otherwise. For example, in evaluating

```
x>y .or. l(z)   ! x, y, and z are real; l is a logical function
```

the function reference need not be made if x is greater than y. Similarly, the processor is not required to evaluate any subscript or substring expressions for an array of zero size or character object of zero character length.

5.10   Procedure interfaces

A call to a subprogram must either be from another statement in a subprogram of the module or from a statement following a use statement for the module. In both cases, the compiler will know all about the subprogram. In particular, it will know about its *interface*, that is whether it defines a function or a subroutine, the names and properties of the arguments, and the properties of the result if it defines a function. This, for example, permits the compiler to check whether the actual and dummy arguments match in the way that they should. We say that the interface is *explicit*. Similarly, intrinsic procedures (Chapter 8) always have explicit interfaces.

When compiling a call to an external (non-F) procedure, the compiler normally does not have a mechanism to access its code. To make the interface explicit in this case, too, the programmer must provide an interface block of the form

```
interface
    interface-body
    [interface-body]...
end interface
```

The syntax of the *interface-body* is that of a subprogram without any declarations of local variables and without any executable statements. The interface block is placed in a sequence of specification statements in a module.

5.11   Procedures as arguments

So far, we have taken the actual arguments of a procedure invocation to be variables and expressions, but another possibility is for them to be procedures. Such a dummy argument is called a *dummy procedure* and is declared with an interface block of the same form as for an external procedure (previous section).

Just as the type and shape of actual and dummy data objects must agree, so must the properties of the actual and dummy procedures. Normally, the *interface-body* is an exact copy of the subprogram's header, the specifications of its arguments and function result, and its end subroutine or end function statement. However,

- the names of the procedure, its arguments, and its result may be changed, and

- the information may be given by a different combination of statements.

Any dummy procedure must itself be declared with an interface block. Any variable declared must be a dummy argument or function result. It would make no sense to specify an intent attribute (Section 5.8) for a dummy procedure, and this is not permitted.

Let us consider the case of a library subprogram to perform function minimization. It needs to receive the user's function, just as the subroutine shuffle in Figure 5.5 needs to receive the required number of cards. The library code might look like the code in Figure 5.10. Notice the way the procedure argument is de-

---

Figure 5.10

```
module lib_minimum
public :: minimum
contains
   function minimum(a, b, func) result(m) ! Returns the minimum
         ! value of the function func(x) in the interval (a,b)
      real, intent(in) :: a, b
      interface
         function func(x) result(funcx)
            real, intent(in) :: x
            real :: funcx
         end function func
      end interface
      real :: m
      real :: f,x
      :
      f = func(x)    ! invocation of the user function.
      :
   end function minimum
end module lib_minimum
```

---

clared by an interface block playing a similar role to that of the type declaration statement for a data object. Such an interface block is required.

On the user side, the code may look like that in Figure 5.11. Notice that the structure is rather like a sandwich: user-written code invokes the library code which in turn invokes user-written code.

Figure 5.11

```
      module m_fun
      public :: fun
      contains
         function fun(x) result(f)
            real, intent(in) :: x
            real :: f
            :
         end function fun
      end module m_fun
      program main
         use m_fun
         use lib_minimum
         real :: f
         f = minimum(1.0, 2.0, fun)
         :
   end program main
```

The procedure that is passed must be a module procedure and its specific name must be passed when it also has a generic name (Section 5.16).

5.12   Keyword and optional arguments

In practical applications, argument lists can get long and many of the arguments may often not be needed. For example, a subroutine for constrained minimization might have the form

```
subroutine min_con(n, f, x, upper, lower,                          &
                equalities, inequalities, convex, xstart)
```

On many calls, there may be no upper bounds, or no lower bounds, or no equalities, or no inequalities, or it may not be known whether the function is convex, or a sensible starting point may not be known. All the corresponding dummy arguments may be declared optional. For instance, the bounds might be declared by the statement

```
real, optional, dimension(:), intent(in) :: upper,lower
```

If the first four arguments are the only wanted ones, we may use the statement

```
call min_con(n, f, x, upper)
```

but usually the wanted arguments are scattered. In this case, we may follow a (possibly empty) ordinary positional argument list for leading arguments by a keyword argument list, as in the statement

```
call min_con(n, f, x, equalities=q, xstart=x0)
```

The keywords are the dummy argument names and there must be no further positional arguments after the first keyword argument. In the dummy argument list, the non-optional arguments must precede the optional arguments.

This example also illustrates the merits of both positional and keyword arguments as far as readability is concerned. A small number of leading positional arguments (for example, n, f, x) are easily linked in the reader's mind to the corresponding dummy arguments. Beyond this, the keywords are very helpful to the reader in making these links. We recommend their use for long argument lists even when there are no gaps caused by optional arguments that are not present.

A non-optional argument must appear exactly once, either in the positional list or in the keyword list. An optional argument may appear at most once, either in the positional list or in the keyword list. An argument must not appear in both lists.

The called subprogram needs some way to detect whether an argument is present so that it can take appropriate action when it is not. This is provided by the intrinsic function present (see Section 8.2). For example

```
present(xstart)
```

returns the value .true. if the current call has provided a starting point and .false. otherwise. When it is absent, the subprogram might use a random number generator to provide a starting point.

A slight complication occurs if an optional dummy argument is used within the subprogram as an actual argument in a procedure invocation. For example, our minimization subroutine might start by calling a subroutine that handles the corresponding equality problem by the call

```
call min_eq(n, f, x, equalities, convex, xstart)
```

In such a case, an absent optional argument is also regarded as absent in the second-level subprogram. For instance, when convex is absent in the call of min_con, it is regarded as absent in min_eq too. Such absent arguments may be propagated through any number of levels of calls. An absent argument further supplied as an actual argument must be specified as a whole, and not as a sub-object. Furthermore, an absent pointer is not permitted to be associated with a non-pointer dummy argument (the target is doubly absent).

5.13　Scope of names

If a name is declared in the main program, the name may be used to refer to the entity there. This is our first encounter with *scope*. The scope of the name is the main program. In the case of a subprogram, any interface bodies for dummy arguments are not included in the scope; rather, they have their own scope. This rule has been adopted so that they can be written without regard to where there are inserted. Thus, an interface body can 'knock a hole' in the scope of a subprogram.

In the case of a module, holes in the scope are created by subprograms, derived-type definitions, and interface bodies for external procedures. This leads us to regard each module as consisting of a set of non-overlapping scoping units. A *scoping unit* is one of the following:

- a main program,

- a derived-type definition,

- a procedure interface body, excluding any interface bodies contained within it,

- a subprogram, excluding any interface bodies contained within it, or

- a module, excluding derived-type definitions, interface bodies, and subprograms contained within it.

An example containing four scoping units is shown in Figure 5.12.

Figure 5.12

```
module scope1              ! scope 1
    public :: scope3       ! scope 1
    type, public :: scope2 ! scope 2
        :                  ! scope 2
    end type scope2        ! scope 2
    :                      ! scope 1
contains                   ! scope 1
    subroutine scope3 (a)  ! scope 3
        interface          ! scope 3
            :              ! scope 4
        end interface      ! scope 3
        :                  ! scope 3
    end subroutine scope3  ! scope 3
end module scope1          ! scope 1
```

Once an entity has been declared in a scoping unit, its name may be used to refer to it in that scoping unit. An entity declared in another scoping unit is always a different entity even if it has the same name and exactly the same properties. Each is known as a *local* entity. This is very helpful to the programmer, who does not have to be concerned about the possibility of accidental name clashes. Note that this is true for derived types, too. Even if two derived types (declared in separate modules) have the same name and the same components, entities declared with them are treated as being of different types.

A use statement of the form

use *module-name*

is regarded as a re-declaration of all the module entities inside the local scoping unit, with exactly the same names and properties. The module entities are said to be accessible by *use association*. Names of entities in the module may not be used for local entities (but see Section 7.7 for a description of further facilities provided by the use statement when greater flexibility is required).

In the case of a derived-type definition or a subprogram, the name of an entity in the host (including an entity accessed by use association) is similarly treated as being automatically re-declared with the same properties, provided no entity with this name is declared locally, is a local dummy argument or function result, or is accessed by use association. The host entity is said to be accessible by *host association*. For example, in the subroutine inner of Figure 5.13, x is accessible by host association, but y is a separate local variable and the y of the host is inaccessible. We note that inner calls f, another procedure of the module.

Figure 5.13

```
module outer
    public        :: inner,f
    real, public :: x, y
    :
contains
    subroutine inner ()
        real :: y
        y = f(x) + 1.0
        :
    end subroutine inner
    function f(z) result (r)
        real, intent(in) :: z
        real :: r
        :
    end function f
end module outer
```

Note that a subprogram does not have access to the local entities of any other subprogram of the module.

Host association does not extend to interface blocks. This allows an interface body to be constructed without reference to where it will be inserted.

Within a scoping unit, each named data object, procedure, derived type, and named do construct, must have a distinct name, with the one exception of generic names of procedures (to be described in Section 5.16). Within a type definition, each component of the type, and each derived type or named constant accessed by host association, must have a distinct name. Apart from these rules, names may be re-used. For instance, a name may be used for the components of two types, or the arguments of two procedures referenced with keyword calls.

The names of program units and external procedures are *global*, that is, available anywhere in a complete program. Each must be distinct from the others and from any of the local entities of the program unit.

At the other extreme, the do variable of an implied-do in an array constructor (Section 6.13) has a scope that is just the implied-do.

5.14 Direct recursion

Normally, a subprogram may not invoke itself, either directly or indirectly through a sequence of other invocations. However, if the leading statement is prefixed recursive, this is allowed. Figure 5.14 illustrates the use of a recursive function to calculate $n! = n(n - 1) \ldots (1)$.

Figure 5.14

```
recursive function factorial(n) result(res)
    integer, intent(in) :: n
    integer :: res
    if(n==1) then
        res = 1
    else
        res = n*factorial(n-1)
    end if
end function factorial
```

Just as in Figure 5.14, any recursive procedure that calls itself directly must contain a conditional test that terminates the sequence of calls at some point, otherwise it will call itself indefinitely.

Each time a recursive procedure is invoked, a fresh set of local data objects is created, which ceases to exist on return. They consist of all data objects declared in its specification statements, but excepting those with the save attribute (see Section 7.6).

5.15 Indirect recursion

A procedure may also be invoked by indirect recursion, that is, one procedure may call another which then calls the first. Note that the rules on ordering of modules (end of Section 5.5) require that they be all in the same module.

To illustrate that this may be useful, suppose we wish to perform a two-dimensional integration but have only the procedure for one-dimensional integration shown in Figure 5.15. For example, suppose that it is desired to integrate a

Figure 5.15

```
recursive function integrate(f, bounds) result (res)
   ! Integrate f(x) from bounds(1) to bounds(2)
   interface
      function f(x) result (r)
         real, intent(in) :: x
         real :: r
      end function f
   end interface
   real, dimension(:), intent(in) :: bounds
   real :: res
   :
end function integrate
```

function f of x and y over a rectangle. We might write an F function to receive the value of x as an argument and the value of y from the host module itself by host association, as shown in Figure 5.16.

Figure 5.16

```
module func
   public                      :: f
   real, public                :: yval
   real, dimension(2), public :: xbounds, ybounds
contains
   function f(xval) result(r)
      real, intent(in) :: xval
      real :: r
      r = ...       ! Expression involving xval and yval
   end function f
end module func
```

We can then integrate over x for a particular value of y, as shown in Figure 5.17, and over the whole rectangle thus

```
volume = integrate(fy, ybounds)
```

Note that integrate calls fy, which in turn calls integrate.

Figure 5.17

```
function fy(y) result(r)
   use func
   use integrate_module
   real, intent(in) :: y
   real :: r
   yval = y
   r = integrate(f, xbounds)
end function fy
```

5.16 Overloading and generic interfaces

It is sometimes very convenient to overload a procedure name, that is, call several procedures by the same generic name. For example, in a module containing procedures with the specific names sgamma and dgamma, the interface block

```
interface gamma
   module procedure sgamma, dgamma
end interface
```

permits both the functions sgamma and dgamma to be invoked using the generic name gamma.

A specific name for a procedure may not be the same as its generic name. However, a generic name may be the same as another accessible generic name. In such a case, all the procedures that have this generic name may be invoked through it. This capability is important, since a module may need to extend the intrinsic functions such as sin to a new type such as interval (Section 3.8).

Another form of overloading occurs when an interface block specifies a defined operation (Section 3.8) or a defined assignment (Section 3.9) to *extend* an intrinsic operation or assignment. The scope of the defined operation or assignment is the module that contains the interface block. If an intrinsic operator is extended, the number of arguments must be consistent with the intrinsic form (for example, it is not possible to define a unary *).

The general form of the generic interface block is thus

```
interface [generic-spec]
   module procedure procedure-name-list
   [module procedure procedure-name-list]...
end interface
```

where *generic-spec* is

generic-name, operator(*defined-operator*), or assignment(=).

All the procedures must be accessible module procedures (as shown in the complete module in Figures 5.19 & 5.20 below). No procedure name may be given a particular *generic-spec* more than once in the interface blocks within a module.

If operator is specified on the interface statement, all the procedures in the block must be functions with one or two non-optional arguments (which must have intent in).[3] If assignment is specified, all the procedures must be subroutines with two non-optional arguments, the first having intent out or inout and the second intent in. In order that invocations are always unambiguous, if two procedures have the same generic operator and the same number of arguments or both define assignment, one must have a dummy argument that corresponds by position in the argument list to a dummy argument of the other that has a different type, different kind type parameter, or different rank.

All procedures that have a given generic name must be subroutines or all must be functions, including the intrinsic ones when an intrinsic procedure is extended. Any two non-intrinsic procedures with the same generic name must differ sufficiently for any invocation to be unambiguous. The rule is that either

i) one of them has more non-optional dummy arguments of a particular data type, kind type parameter, and rank than the other has dummy arguments (including optional dummy arguments) of that data type, kind type parameter, and rank; or

ii) at least one of them must have a non-optional dummy argument that both

   - corresponds by position in the argument list to a dummy argument that is not present in the other, is present with a different type or kind type parameter, or is present with a different rank, and

   - corresponds by name to a dummy argument that is not present in the other, is present with a different type or kind type parameter, or is present with a different rank.

For case (ii), both rules are needed in order to cater for both keyword and positional dummy argument lists. For instance, the interface in Figure 5.18 is invalid because the two functions are always distinguishable in a positional call, but not on a keyword call such as f(i=int,x=posn). When an intrinsic procedure is extended, the intrinsic name must be declared on an intrinsic statement (Section 8.1.3) and the dummy arguments of each procedure must differ from the arguments of the intrinsic procedure sufficiently for every invocation to be unambiguous.

There are many scientific applications in which it is useful to keep a check on the sorts of quantities involved in a calculation. For instance, in dimensional analysis, whereas it might be sensible to divide length by time to obtain velocity, it is not sensible to add time to velocity. There is no intrinsic way to do this, but we conclude this section with an outline example, Figures 5.19 & 5.20, of how it might be achieved using derived types.

---

[3]Since intent must not be specified for a pointer dummy argument (Section 5.6.1), this implies that if an operand of derived data type also has the pointer attribute, it is the value of its target that is passed to the function defining the operator, and not the pointer itself. The pointer status is inaccessible within the function.

Figure 5.18

```
!  Example of a broken overloading rule
   module broken
      public :: f, fxi, fix
      interface f
         module procedure fxi, fix
      end interface
   contains
      function fxi(x,i) result (r)
         real, intent(in) :: x
         integer, intent(in) ::  i
         real :: r
         :
      end function fxi
      function fix(i,x) result (r)
         integer, intent(in) ::  i
         real, intent(in) :: x
         real :: r
         :
      end function fix
   end module broken
```

Note that definitions for operations between like entities are also required, as shown by time_plus_time. Similarly, any intrinsic function that might be required, here sqrt, must be overloaded appropriately. Of course, this can be avoided if the components of the variables are referenced directly, as in

```
t%seconds = t%seconds + 1.0
```

5.17   Assumed character length

A character dummy argument must be declared with an asterisk for the value of the length type parameter, and takes the value from the actual argument. For example, a subroutine to sort the elements of a character array might be written thus

```
subroutine sort(chars)
   character(len=*), dimension(:), intent(inout) :: chars
   :
end subroutine sort
```

If the length of the associated actual argument is needed within the procedure, the intrinsic function len (Section 8.6.1) may be invoked, as in Figure 5.21.

Figure 5.19

```
module sorts
    public :: operator(/), operator(+)
    public :: length_by_time, time_plus_time, sqrt_metres_squared
    intrinsic sqrt
    type, public :: time
        real :: seconds
    end type time
    type, public :: velocity
        real :: metres_per_second
    end type velocity
    type, public :: length
        real :: metres
    end type length
    type, public :: length_squared
        real :: metres_squared
    end type length_squared
    interface operator(/)
        module procedure length_by_time
    end interface
    interface operator(+)
        module procedure time_plus_time
    end interface
    interface sqrt
        module procedure sqrt_metres_squared
    end interface
contains
    function length_by_time(s, t) result (res)
        type(length), intent(in) :: s
        type(time), intent(in)    :: t
        type(velocity)            :: res
        res%metres_per_second = s%metres / t%seconds
    end function length_by_time
    function time_plus_time(t1, t2)  result (res)
        type(time), intent(in)    :: t1, t2
        type(time)                :: res
        res%seconds = t1%seconds + t2%seconds
    end function time_plus_time
    function sqrt_metres_squared(12) result (res)
        type(length_squared), intent(in) :: 12
        type(length)                     :: res
        res%metres = sqrt(12%metres_squared)
    end function sqrt_metres_squared
end module sorts
```

Figure 5.20

```
program test
   use sorts
   type(length)          :: s, l
   type(length_squared)  :: s2
   type(velocity)        :: v
   type(time)            :: t
   s  = length(10.0)
   s2 = length_squared(10.0)
   t  = time(3.0)
   v = s / t
! Note: v = s + t    or    v = s * t  would be illegal
   t = t + time(1.0)
   l = sqrt(s2)
   print *, v, t, l
end program test
```

Figure 5.21

```
function count_letter (letter, string) result(c)
   character (len=*), intent(in) :: letter, string
   integer :: c
   integer :: i
!  Count the number of occurrences of letter in string
   c = 0
   do i = 1, len(string)
      if (string(i:i) == letter(1:1)) then
         c = c + 1
      end if
   end do
end function count_letter
```

5.18   Order of statements

We have now met examples of all the different classes of statement which the
F language contains. Each time a new class of statement has been introduced,
some mention has been made of the position in which it may appear, and these
are summarized for main programs, subroutines, and functions in Figures 5.22,
5.23, and 5.24. We defer the ordering of statements in a module to Section 7.5.

Figure 5.22 Order of statements in a main program.

```
program program-name
    [use-statement] ...
    [intrinsic-statement] ...
    [local-entity-definition] ...
    [executable-construct] ...
end program program-name
```

Figure 5.23 Order of statements in a subroutine.

```
[recursive] subroutine subroutine-name([dummy-argument-list])
    [use-statement] ...
    [intrinsic-statement] ...
    [dummy-argument-definition] ...
    [local-entity-definition] ...
    [executable-construct] ...
end subroutine subroutine-name
```

Figure 5.24 Order of statements in a function.

```
[recursive] function function-name([dummy-argument-list]) &
                result(result-name)
    [use-statement] ...
    [intrinsic-statement] ...
    [dummy-argument-definition] ...
      result-definition
    [local-entity-definition] ...
      executable-construct
    [executable-construct] ...
end function function-name
```

5.19 Summary

A program consists of a sequence of program units. It must contain exactly one main program but may contain any number of modules. We have described both kinds of program unit. Modules contain data definitions, type definitions, interface blocks, and subprograms, all of which may be accessed in other program units with the use statement.

Subprograms define procedures, which may be functions or subroutines. They may also be defined intrinsically (Chapter 8) and external procedures may be defined by means other than F, provided each has an interface block in a module. We have explained how information is passed between program units and to procedures through argument lists and through the use of modules. Procedures may be called recursively provided they are correspondingly specified.

The interface to a procedure is always explicit, which allows keyword calls to be made, and the procedure to have optional arguments. Interface blocks permit module procedures to be invoked as operations or assignments, or by a generic name. The character lengths of dummy arguments are assumed.

We have also explained about the scope of F names, and introduced the concept of a scoping unit.

Many of the features are not in Fortran 77: modules, the interface block, optional and keyword arguments, argument intent, pointer dummy arguments and function results, recursion, and overloading. These are powerful additions to the language, particularly in the construction of large programs and libraries.

5.20 Exercises

1. A subroutine receives as arguments an array of values, x, and the number of elements in x, n. If the mean and variance of the values in x are estimated by

$$\text{mean} = \frac{1}{n} \sum_{i=1}^{n} x(i)$$

and

$$\text{variance} = \frac{1}{n-1} \sum_{i=1}^{n} (x(i) - \text{mean})^2$$

write a subroutine which returns these calculated values as arguments. The subroutine should check for invalid values of n (≤ 1).

2. A subroutine matrix_mult multiplies together two matrices A and B, whose dimensions are $i \times j$ and $j \times k$, respectively, returning the result in a matrix C dimensioned $i \times k$. Write matrix_mult, given that each element of C is defined by

$$C(m, n) = \sum_{\ell=1}^{j} (A(m, \ell) \times B(\ell, n))$$

The matrices should appear as arguments to matrix_mult.

3. The subroutine random_number (Section 8.14.2) returns a random number in the range 0.0 to 1.0, that is

```
call random_number(r)    ! 0≤r<1
```

Using this function, write the subroutine shuffle of Figure 5.4.

4. A character string consists of a sequence of letters. Write a function to return that letter of the string which occurs earliest in the alphabet, for example, the result of applying the function to "DGUMVETLOIC" is "C".

5. Write a procedure to calculate the volume of a cylinder of radius r and length ℓ, $\pi r^2 \ell$, using as the value of π the result of acos(-1.0), and reference it in a main program.

6. Choosing a simple card game of your own choice, and using the random number procedure (Section 8.14.2), write subroutines deal and play of Section 5.4, using data in a module to communicate between them.

7. Objects of the intrinsic type character are of a fixed length. Write a module containing a definition of a variable length character string type, of maximum length 80, and also the procedures necessary to:

   i) assign a character variable to a string;

  ii) assign a string to a character variable;

 iii) return the length of a string;

 iv) concatenate two strings.

6. Array features

6.1 Introduction

In an era when many computers have the hardware capability to perform operations on *vectors* of operands, it is self-evident that a numerically based language such as F should have matching notational facilities. Such facilities provide not only a notational convenience for the programmer, but provide too an opportunity to extend the power of the language to manipulate arrays. In addition, a concise syntax makes the presence of array manipulation obvious to compilers which, especially on vector processors, are able to generate well-optimized object code. However, to achieve this gain new optimization techniques are required, for instance the ability to recognize that two or more consecutive array statements may, in some cases, be processed in a single loop at the object code level. These techniques are being progressively introduced.[1]

Arrays were introduced in Sections 2.10 to 2.13, their use in simple expressions and in assignments was explained in Sections 3.10 and 3.11, and they were used as procedure arguments in Chapter 5. These descriptions were deliberately restricted because F contains a very full set of array features whose complete description would have unbalanced those chapters. The purpose of this chapter is to describe the array features in detail, but without anticipating the descriptions of the array intrinsic procedures of Chapter 8; the rich set of intrinsic procedures should be regarded as an integral part of the array features.

6.2 Zero-sized arrays

It might be thought that an array would always have at least one element. However, such a requirement would force programs to contain extra code to deal with certain natural situations. For example, the code in Figure 6.1 solves a lower-triangular set of linear equations. When i has the value n, the sections have size zero, which is just what is required.

F allows arrays to have zero size in all contexts. Whenever a lower bound exceeds the corresponding upper bound, the array has size zero.

---

[1] A fuller discussion of this topic can be found in *Optimizing Supercompilers for Supercomputers*, M. Wolfe (Pitman, 1989).

Figure 6.1

```
do i = 1,n
   x(i) = b(i) / a(i, i)
   b(i+1:n) = b(i+1:n) - a(i+1:n, i) * x(i)
end do
```

There are few special rules for zero-sized arrays because they follow the usual rules, though some care may be needed in their interpretation. For example, two zero-sized arrays of the same rank may have different shapes. One might have shape (0,2) and the other (0,3) or (2,0). Such arrays of differing shapes are not conformable and therefore may not be used together as the operands of a binary operation. However, an array is always conformable with a scalar so the statement

zero-sized-array = scalar

is valid and the scalar is 'broadcast to all the array elements', making this a 'do nothing' statement.

A zero-sized array is regarded as being defined always, because it has no values that can be undefined.

6.3   Assumed-shape arrays

The shape of a non-pointer dummy argument array is taken automatically to be that of the corresponding actual array argument. Such an array is said to be an *assumed-shape* array. The shape is declared by the dimension attribute, and each dimension has the form

    [*lower-bound*] :

where *lower-bound* is an integer expression that may depend on module data or the other arguments (see Section 7.11 for the exact rules). If *lower-bound* is omitted, the default value is 1. Note that it is the shape that is passed, and not the upper and lower bounds. For example, if the actual array is a, declared thus:

```
real, dimension(0:10, 0:20) :: a
```

and the dummy array is da, declared thus:

```
real, dimension(:, :) :: da
```

then a(i,j) corresponds to da(i+1,j+1); to get the natural correspondence, the lower bound must be declared:

```
real, dimension(0:, 0:) :: da
```

A dummy array with the pointer attribute is not regarded as an assumed-shape array because its shape is not necessarily assumed.

6.4 Automatic objects

A procedure with dummy arguments that are arrays whose size varies from call to call may also need local arrays whose size varies. A simple example is the array work in the subroutine to interchange two arrays that is shown in Figure 6.2.

Figure 6.2

```
subroutine swap(a, b)
   real, dimension(:), intent(inout) :: a, b
   real, dimension(size(a)) :: work
              ! size provides the size of an array,
              ! and is defined in Section 8.11.2.
   work = a
   a = b
   b = work
end subroutine swap
```

Arrays whose extents vary in this way are called *automatic arrays*, and are examples of *automatic data objects*. These are data objects whose declarations depend on the value of non-constant expressions, and are not dummy arguments. Implementations are likely to bring them into existence when the procedure is called and destroy them on return, maintaining them on a stack. The non-constant expressions are limited to be specification expressions (Section 7.11).

The other way that automatic objects arise is through varying character length. The variable word2 in

```
subroutine example(word1)
   character(len = *), intent(inout) :: word1
   character(len = len(word1)) :: word2
```

is an example. A fuller example is shown in Figure 6.3.

An array bound or the character length of an automatic object is fixed for the duration of each execution of the procedure and does not vary if the value of the specification expression varies or becomes undefined.

An automatic object must not have the save attribute (Section 7.6).

6.5 Heap storage

There is an underlying assumption in F that the processor supplies a mechanism for managing heap storage. The statements described in this section are the user interface to that mechanism.

Figure 6.3

```
module example
    public :: double
contains
    function double(a) result(da)
        character (len=*), intent(in) :: a
        character (len=2*len(a)) :: da
        da = a//a
    end function double
end module example
program loren
    use example
    character (len = *), parameter :: a = "just a simple test"
    print *, double(a)
end program loren
```

6.5.1 Allocatable arrays

Sometimes an array is required to be of a size that is known only after some data have been read or some calculations performed. An array with the `pointer` attribute might be used for this purpose, but this is really not appropriate if the other properties of pointers are not needed. Instead, an array that is not a dummy argument or function result may be given the `allocatable` attribute by a statement such as

```
real, dimension(:, :), allocatable :: a
```

Such an array is called *allocatable*. Its rank is specified when it is declared, but the bounds are undefined until an `allocate` statement such as

```
allocate(a(n, 0:n+1))      ! n of type integer
```

has been executed for it. Its initial allocation status is 'not currently allocated' and it becomes allocated following successful execution of an `allocate` statement.

An important example is shown in Figure 6.4. The array `work` is placed in a module and is allocated at the beginning of the main program to a size that depends on input data. The array is then available throughout program execution in any subprogram that has a `use` statement for `work_array`.

When an allocatable array `a` is no longer needed, it may be deallocated by execution of the statement

```
deallocate (a)
```

following which the array is 'not currently allocated'. The `deallocate` statement is described in more detail in Section 6.5.3.

Figure 6.4

```
module work_array
    integer, public :: n
    real, dimension(:,:,:), allocatable, public :: work
end module work_array
program main
    use work_array
    read *, n
    allocate(work(n, 2*n, 3*n))
    :
```

If it is required to make any change to the bounds of an allocatable array, the array must be deallocated and then allocated afresh. Allocating an allocatable array that is already allocated, or deallocating an allocatable array that is not currently allocated, is an error.

An allocatable array that does not have the save attribute (Section 7.6) may have a third allocation state: undefined. Since an undefined allocatable array may not be referenced in any way, we recommend avoiding this state. It occurs on return from a subprogram if the array is local to the subprogram or local to a module that is currently accessed only by the subprogram, and the array is allocated. To avoid this situation, such an allocatable array must be explicitly deallocated before such a return.

If a variable-sized array component of a structure is required, unfortunately, an array pointer must be used (see Section 6.11). The prohibition on allocatable arrays here was made to keep the feature simple.

6.5.2   The allocate statement

We mentioned in Section 2.13 that the allocate statement can also be used to give fresh storage for a pointer target directly. A pointer becomes associated (Section 3.3) following successful execution of the statement. The general form of the allocate statement is

allocate(*allocation-list* [,stat=*stat*])

where *allocation-list* is a list of allocations of the form

allocate-object [(*array-bounds-list*)]

each *array-bound* has the form

[*lower-bound*:] *upper-bound*

and *stat* is a scalar integer variable that must not be part of an object being allocated.

If the `stat=` specifier is present, *stat* is given either the value zero after a successful allocation or a positive value after an unsuccessful allocation (for example, if insufficient storage is available). After an unsuccessful execution, each array that was not successfully allocated retains its previous allocation or pointer association status. If `stat=` is absent and the allocation is unsuccessful, program execution stops.

Each *allocate-object* is an allocatable array or a pointer. It may have zero character length and in the case of a pointer may be a structure component.

Each *lower-bound* and each *upper-bound* is a scalar integer expression. The default value for the lower bound is 1. The number of *array-bound*s in a list must equal the rank of the *allocate-object*. They determine the array bounds, which do not alter if the value of a variable in one of the expressions changes subsequently. An array may be allocated to be of size zero, and it may have zero character length.

The bounds of all the arrays being allocated are regarded as undefined during the execution of the `allocate` statement, so none of the expressions that specify the bounds may depend on any of the bounds. For example,

```
allocate (a(size(b)), b(size(a)))    ! illegal
```

or even

```
allocate (a(n), b(size(a)))          ! illegal
```

is not permitted, but

```
allocate (a(n))
allocate (b(size(a)))
```

is valid. This restriction allows the processor to perform the allocations in a single `allocate` statement in any order.

In contrast to the case with an allocatable array, a pointer may be allocated a new target even if it is currently associated with a target. In this case, the previous association is broken. If the previous target was created by allocation, it becomes inaccessible unless another pointer is associated with it. We expect linked lists normally to be created by using a single pointer in an `allocate` statement for each node of the list, using pointer components of the allocated object at the node to hold the links from the node. We illustrate this by the addition of an extra nonzero element to the sparse vector held as a chain of entries of the type

```
type, public :: entry
    real :: value
    integer :: index
    type(entry), pointer :: next
end type entry
```

of Section 2.13. The code in Figure 6.5 adds the new entry at the front of the chain. Note the importance of the last statement being a pointer assignment: the assignment

```
first = current
```

would overwrite the old leading entry by the new one.

Figure 6.5

```
type(entry), pointer :: first, current
real :: fill
integer :: fill_index
:
allocate (current)
current = entry (fill, fill_index, first)
first => current
```

6.5.3   The deallocate statement

When an allocatable array or pointer target is no longer needed, its storage may be recovered by using the deallocate statement. Its general form is

    deallocate (*allocate-object-list* [,stat=*stat*])

where each *allocate-object* is an allocatable array that is allocated or a pointer that is associated with the whole of a target that was allocated through a pointer in an allocate statement. Here *stat* is a scalar integer variable that must not be deallocated by the statement nor depend on an object that is deallocated by the statement. If stat= is present, *stat* is given either the value zero after a successful execution or a positive value after an unsuccessful execution (for example, if a pointer is disassociated). After an unsuccessful execution, each array that was not successfully deallocated retains its previous allocation or pointer association status. If stat= is absent and the deallocation is unsuccessful, program execution stops.

A pointer becomes disassociated (Section 3.3) following successful execution of the statement. If there is more than one object in the list, there must be no dependencies among them, to allow the processor to deallocate the objects one by one in any order.

A danger in using the deallocate statement is that storage may be deallocated while pointers are still associated with the targets it held. Such pointers are left 'dangling' in an undefined state, and must not be reused until they are again associated with an actual target.

In order to avoid an accumulation of unused and unusable storage, all explicitly allocated storage should be explicitly deallocated when it is no longer required. This explicit management is required in order to avoid a potentially significant overhead on the part of the processor in handling arbitrarily complex allocation and reference patterns. Note also that the processor is not required to recover storage allocated through a pointer but no longer accessible through this or any other pointer. This might be important where, for example, a pointer function is referenced within an expression – the programmer cannot rely on the compiler to arrange for deallocation. To ensure that there is no memory leakage, it is necessary to use functions on the right-hand side of assignments, as in the example compact in Section 5.9, and to deallocate the pointer on the left-hand side (there, y) when it is no longer needed.

6.5.4   The nullify statement

A pointer may be explicitly disassociated from its target by executing a nullify statement. Its general form is

    nullify(*pointer-object-list*)

There must be no dependencies among the objects, in order to allow the processor to nullify the objects one by one in any order. The statement is also useful for giving the disassociated status to an undefined pointer. An advantage of nullifying pointers rather than leaving them undefined is that they may then be tested by the intrinsic function associated (Section 8.2). For example, the end of the chain of Figure 6.5 will be flagged as a disassociated pointer if the statement

    nullify(first)

is executed initially to create a zero-length chain. Because often there are other ways to access a target (for example, through another pointer), the nullify statement does not deallocate the targets. If deallocation is also required, a deallocate statement should be executed instead.

6.6   Elemental operations and assignments

We saw in Section 3.10 that an intrinsic operator can be applied to conformable operands, to produce an array result whose element values are the values of the operation applied to the corresponding elements of the operands. Such an operation is called *elemental*.

It is not essential to use operator notation to obtain this effect. Many of the intrinsic procedures (Chapter 8) are elemental and have scalar dummy arguments that may be called with array actual arguments provided all the array arguments have the same shape. For a function, the shape of the result is the shape of the array arguments. For example, we may find the square roots of all the elements of a real array thus:

    a = sqrt(a)

For a subroutine, if any argument is array-valued, all the arguments with intent out or inout must be arrays. If a procedure that references an elemental function has an optional array-valued dummy argument that is absent, that dummy argument must not be used in the elemental reference unless another array of the same rank is associated with an non-optional argument of the elemental function (to ensure that the rank does not vary from call to call).

Similarly, an intrinsic assignment may be used to assign a scalar to all the elements of an array, or to assign each element of an array to the corresponding element of an array of the same shape (Section 3.11). Such an assignment is also called *elemental*.

If a similar effect is desired for a defined operator, a function must be provided for each rank or pair of ranks for which it is needed. For example, the module in Figure 6.6 provides summation for scalars and rank-one arrays of intervals (Section 3.8). We leave it as an exercise for the reader to add definitions for mixing scalars and rank-one arrays.

Similarly, elemental versions of defined assignments must be provided explicitly.

Figure 6.6

```
module interval_addition
    public :: operator(+), add00, add11
    type, public :: interval
        real :: lower, upper
    end type interval
    interface operator(+)
        module procedure add00, add11
    end interface
contains
    function add00 (a, b) result(c)
        type (interval), intent(in) :: a, b
        type (interval)             :: c
        c%lower = a%lower + b%lower  ! Production code would
        c%upper = a%upper + b%upper  ! allow for roundoff.
    end function add00
    function add11 (a, b) result(c)
        type (interval), dimension(:), intent(in) :: a,b
        type (interval), dimension(size(a))       :: c
        c%lower = a%lower + b%lower  ! Production code would
        c%upper = a%upper + b%upper  ! allow for roundoff.
    end function add11
end module interval_addition
```

6.7 Array-valued functions

We mentioned in Section 5.9 that a function may have an array-valued result, and have used this language feature in Figure 6.6 where the interpretation is obvious.

The shape is specified within the function definition by the dimension attribute for the function result. Unless the function result is a pointer, the bounds must be explicit expressions and they are evaluated on entry to the function. For another example, see the declaration of the function result in Figure 6.7.

Figure 6.7

```
function mult(a, b) result(c)
   type(matrix), dimension(:,:), intent(in) :: a
   type(matrix), dimension(:), intent(in) :: b
   type(matrix), dimension(size(a, 1)) :: c
                ! size is defined in Section 8.11.2
   integer :: j, n
   c = 0.0     ! A defined assignment from a real
               ! scalar to a rank-one matrix.
   n = size(a, 1)
   do j = 1, size(a, 2)
      c = c + a(1:n, j) * b(j)
            ! Uses defined operations for addition of
            ! two rank-one matrices and multiplication
            ! of a rank-one matrix by a scalar matrix.
   end do
end function mult
```

An array-valued function is not necessarily elemental. For example, at the end of Section 3.10 we considered the type

```
type, public :: matrix
   real :: element
end type matrix
```

Its scalar and rank-one operations might be as for reals, but for multiplying a rank-two array by a rank-one array, we might use the module function shown in Figure 6.7 to provide matrix by vector multiplication.

6.8   The where construct

It is often desired to perform an array operation only for certain elements, say those whose values are positive. The where construct provides this facility. A simple example is

```
where ( a > 0.0 )  ! a is a real array
   a = 1.0/a
end where
```

which reciprocates the positive elements of a and leaves the rest unaltered. The general form for a single assignment is

```
where (logical-array-expr)
    array-variable = expr
end where
```

The logical array expression *logical-array-expr* must have the same shape as *array-variable*. It is evaluated first and then just those elements of *expr* that correspond to elements of *logical-array-expr* that have the value true are evaluated and are assigned to the corresponding elements of *array-variable*. All other elements of *array-variable* are left unaltered. The assignment must not be a defined assignment.

A single logical array expression may be used for a sequence of array assignments all of the same shape. The general form of this construct is

```
where (logical-array-expr)
    array-assignments
end where
```

The logical array expression *logical-array-expr* is first evaluated and then each array assignment is performed in turn, under the control of this mask. If any of these assignments affect entities in *logical-array-expr*, it is always the value obtained when the where statement is executed that is used as the mask.

Finally, the where construct may take the form

```
where (logical-array-expr)
    array-assignments
elsewhere
    array-assignments
end where
```

Here, the assignments in the first block of assignments are performed in turn under the control of *logical-array-expr* and then the assignments in the second block are performed in turn under the control of .not.*logical-array-expr*. Again, if any of these assignments affect entities in *logical-array-expr*, it is always the value obtained when the where statement is executed that is used as the mask. A simple example of this where construct is

```
where (pressure <= 1.0)
    pressure = pressure + inc_pressure
    temp = temp + 5.0
elsewhere
    raining = .true.
end where
```

where pressure, inc_pressure, temp, and raining are arrays of the same shape.

If a where construct masks an elemental function reference, the function is called only for the wanted elements. For example,

```
where ( a > 0 )
    a = log(a)       ! log is defined in Section 8.4
end where
```

would not lead to erroneous calls of log for negative arguments.

This masking applies to all elemental function references except any that are within an argument of a non-elemental function reference. The masking does not extend to array arguments of such a function. In general, such arguments have a different shape so that masking would not be possible, but the rule applies in such a case as

```
where (a > 0)
    a = a/sum(log(a)) ! sum is defined in Section 8.10
end where
```

Here the logarithms of each of the elements of a are summed, and the statement will fail if they are not all positive.

If a non-elemental function reference or an array constructor is masked, it is fully evaluated before the masking is applied.

6.9 Array elements

In Section 2.10, we restricted the description of array elements to simple cases. In general, an array element is a scalar of the form

> *part-ref* [*%part-ref*] ...

where *part-ref* is

> *part-name*[(*subscript-list*)]

The last *part-ref* must have a *subscript-list*. The number of subscripts in each list must be equal to the rank of the array or array component, and each subscript must be a scalar integer expression whose value is within the bounds of its dimension of the array or array component. To illustrate this, take the type

```
type, public :: triplet
    real :: u
    real, dimension(3)   :: du
    real, dimension(3,3) :: d2u
end type triplet
```

which was considered in Section 2.10. An array may be declared of this type:

```
type(triplet), dimension(10,20,30) :: tar
```

and

```
tar(n,2,n*n)            ! n of type integer
```

is an array element. It is a scalar of type triplet and

```
tar(n, 2, n*n) % du
```

is a real array with

    tar(n, 2, n*n) % du(2)

as one of its elements.

   If an array element is of type character, it may be followed by a substring reference:

   (*substring-range*)

for example,

    page (k*k) (i+1:j-5) ! i, j, k of type integer.

By convention, such an object is called a substring rather than an array element.

   Notice that it is the array *part-name* that the subscript list qualifies. It is not permitted to apply such a subscript list to an array designator unless the designator terminates with an array *part-name*. An array section, a function reference, or an array expression in parentheses must not be qualified by a subscript list.

6.10   Array subobjects

Array sections were introduced in Section 2.10 and provide a convenient way to access a regular subarray such as a row or a column of a rank-two array:

    a(i, 1:n)   ! Elements 1 to n of row i
    a(1:m, j)   ! Elements 1 to m of column j

For simplicity of description, we did not explain that one or both bounds may be omitted when the corresponding bound of the array itself is wanted, and that a stride other than one may be specified:

    a(i, :)   ! The whole of row i
    a(i, 1:n:3) ! Elements 1, 4, ... of row i

   Another form of section subscript is a rank-one integer expression. All the elements of the expression must be defined with values that lie within the bounds of the parent array's subscript. For example,

    v((/ 1, 7, 3, 2 /))

is a section with elements v(1), v(7), v(3), and v(2), in this order. Such a subscript is called a *vector subscript*. If there are any repetitions in the values of the elements of a vector subscript, the section is called a *many-one section* because more than one element of the section is mapped onto a single array element. For example

    v((/ 1, 7, 3, 7 /))

has elements 2 and 4 mapped onto v(7). A many-one section must not appear on the left of an assignment statement because there would be several possible values for a single element. For instance, the statement

```
v( (/ 1, 7, 3, 7 /) ) = (/ 1, 2, 3, 4 /)      ! Illegal
```

is not allowed because the values 2 and 4 cannot both be stored in v(7). The extent is zero if the vector subscript has zero size.

When an array section with a vector subscript is an actual argument, it is regarded as an expression and the corresponding dummy argument must have intent in. We expect compilers to make a copy as a temporary regular array on entry. Also, an array section with a vector subscript is not permitted to be a pointer target, since allowing them would seriously complicate the mechanism that compilers would otherwise have to establish for pointers. For similar reasons, such an array section is not permitted to be an internal file (Section 9.6).

The general form of a subobject is

part-ref [*%part-ref*] ... [(*substring-range*)]

where *part-ref* now has the form

part-name [(*section-subscript-list*)]

where the number of section subscripts in each list must be equal to the rank of the array or array component. Each *section-subscript* is either a *subscript* (Section 6.9), a rank-one integer expression (vector subscript), or a *subscript-triplet* of the form

[*lower*] : [*upper*] [: *stride*]

where *lower*, *upper*, and *stride* are scalar integer expressions. If *lower* is omitted, the default value is the lower bound for this subscript of the array. If *upper* is omitted, the default value is the upper bound for this subscript of the array. If *stride* is omitted, the default value is one. The stride may be negative so that it is possible to take, for example, the elements of a row in reverse order by specifying a section such as

```
a(i, 10:1:-1)
```

The extent is zero if *stride*>0 and *lower*>*upper*, or if *stride*<0 and *lower*<*upper*. The value of *stride* must not be zero.

Normally, we expect the values of both *lower* and *upper* to be within the bounds of the corresponding array subscript. However, all that is required is that each value actually used to select an element is within the bounds. Thus,

```
a(1, 2:11:2)
```

is legal even if the upper bound of the second dimension of a is only 10.

The *subscript-triplet* specifies a sequence of subscript values, *lower, lower + stride, lower + 2*stride,...*

going as far as possible without going beyond *upper* (above it when *stride*>0 or below it when *stride*<0). The length of the sequence for the *i*-th *subscript-triplet* determines the *i*-th extent of the array that is formed.

The rank of a *part-ref* with a *section-subscript-list* is the number of vector subscripts and subscript triplets that it contains. So far in this section, all the examples have been of rank one; by contrast, the ordinary array element

```
a(1,7)
```

is an example of a *part-ref* of rank zero, and the section

```
a(:,1:7)
```

is an example of a *part-ref* of rank two. The rank of a *part-ref* without a *section-subscript-list* is the rank of the object or component. It is not permissible for more than one *part-ref* to be arrays; for example, it is not permitted to write

```
tar % du   ! Illegal
```

for the array `tar` of Section 6.9. The reason for this is that if `tar%du` were considered to be an array, its element (1,2,3,4) would correspond to

```
tar(2,3,4)%du(1)
```

which would be too confusing a notation.

The *part-ref* with nonzero rank determines the rank and shape of the subobject. If any of its extents is zero, the subobject itself has size zero. It is called an array section if the final *part-ref* has a *section-subscript-list* or another *part-ref* has a nonzero rank.

A *substring-range* may be present only if the last *part-ref* is of type character and is either a scalar or has a *section-subscript-list*. By convention, the resulting object is called a section rather than a substring. It is formed from the unqualified section by taking the specified substring of each element. Note that, if c is a rank-one character array,

```
c(i:j)
```

is the section formed from elements i to j; if substrings of all the array elements are wanted, we may write the section

```
c(:)(k:l)
```

An array section that ends with a component name is also called a *structure component*. Note that if the component is scalar, the section cannot be qualified by a trailing subscript list or section subscript list. Thus, using the example of Section 6.9,

```
tar % u
```

is such an array section and

```
tar (1, 2, 3) % u
```

is a component of a valid element of `tar`. The form

```
tar % u (1, 2, 3)   ! not permitted
```

is not allowed.

Additionally, a *part-name* to the right of a *part-ref* with nonzero rank must not have the `pointer` attribute. This is because such an object would represent an array of pointers and require a very different implementation mechanism from that needed for an ordinary array. For example, consider the array

```
type(entry), dimension(n) :: rows  ! n of type integer
```

for the type `entry` defined near the end of Section 6.5.2. If we were allowed to write the object `rows%next`, it would be interpreted as another array of size n and type `entry`, but its elements are likely to be stored without any regular pattern (each having been separately given storage by an `allocate` statement) and indeed some will be null if any of the pointers are disassociated. Note that there is no problem over accessing individual pointers such as `rows(i)%next`.

6.11   Arrays of pointers

Although arrays of pointers as such are not allowed in F, the equivalent effect can be achieved by creating a type containing a pointer component. For example, a lower-triangular matrix may be held by using a pointer for each row. Consider the type

```
type, public :: row
    real, dimension(:), pointer :: r
end type row
```

and the arrays

```
type(row), dimension(n) :: s, t    ! n of type integer
```

Storage for the rows can be allocated thus

```
do i = 1, n                ! i of type integer.
    allocate (t(i)%r(1:i)) ! Allocate row i of length i.
end do
```

The array assignment

```
s = t
```

would then be equivalent to the pointer assignments

```
s(i)%r => t(i)%r
```

for all the components.

A type containing just a pointer component is useful also when constructing a linked list that is more complicated than the chain described in Section 2.13. For instance, if a variable number of links are needed at each entry, the recursive type entry of Figure 2.3 might be expanded to the pair of types:

```
type, public :: ptr
    type(entry), pointer :: point
end type ptr
type, public :: entry
    real :: value
    integer :: i
    type(ptr), pointer, dimension(:) :: children
end type entry
```

After appropriate allocations and pointer associations, it is then possible to refer to the index of child j of node as

```
node%children(j)%point%i
```

6.12   Pointers as aliases

If an array section without vector subscripts, such as

```
table(m:n, p:q)
```

is wanted frequently while the integer variables m, n, p, and q do not change their values, it is convenient to be able to refer to the section as a named array such as

```
window
```

Such a facility is provided in F by pointers and the pointer assignment statement. Here window would be declared thus

```
real, dimension(:, :), pointer :: window
```

and associated with table, which must of course have the target or pointer attribute, by the execution of the statement

```
window  => table(m:n, p:q)
```

If, later on, the size of window needs to be changed, all that is needed is another pointer assignment statement. Note, however, that the subscript bounds for window in this example are (1:n-m+1, 1:q-p+1) since they are as provided by the functions lbound and ubound (Section 8.11.2).

The facility provides a mechanism for subscripting or sectioning arrays such as

```
tar % u
```

where `tar` is an array and `u` is a scalar component, discussed in the previous section. Here we may perform the pointer association

```
taru => tar % u
```

if `taru` is a rank-three pointer of the appropriate type. Subscripting as in

```
taru(1, 2, 3)
```

is then permissible. Here the subscript bounds for `taru` will be those of `tar`.

6.13 Array constructors

The syntax that we introduced in Section 2.10 for array constants may be used to construct more general rank-one arrays. The general form of an *array-constructor* is

```
(/ array-constructor-value-list /)
```

where each *array-constructor-value* is one of *expr* or *constructor-implied-do*. The array thus constructed is of rank one with its sequence of elements formed from the sequence of scalar expressions and elements of the array expressions in array-element order. A *constructor-implied-do* has the form

```
(array-constructor-value-list, variable = expr1, expr2 [,expr3])
```

where *variable* is a named integer scalar variable, and *expr1, expr2*, and *expr3* are scalar integer expressions. Its interpretation is as if the *array-constructor-value-list* had been written

```
max ( (expr2 - expr1 + expr3)/expr3, 0 )
```

times, with *variable* replaced by *expr1, expr1+expr3*, ..., as for the do construct (Section 4.5). A simple example is

```
(/ (i,i=1,10) /)
```

which is equal to

```
(/ 1, 2, 3, 4, 5, 6, 7, 8, 9, 10 /)
```

Note that the syntax permits nesting of one *constructor-implied-do* inside another, as in the example

```
(/ ((i,i=1,3), j=1,3) /)
```

which is equal to

```
(/ 1, 2, 3, 1, 2, 3, 1, 2, 3 /)
```

and the nesting of structure components within array constructors (and vice versa), for instance, for the type in Section 6.7,

```
(/ (matrix(0.0), i = 1, 100) /)
```

The sequence may be empty, in which case a zero-sized array is constructed.
The scope of the *variable* is the *constructor-implied-do*. Other array constructors, or even other parts of the same constructor, may refer to another variable
having the same name.   Each such variable is available only within its own
constructor-implied-do and is unavailable outside array constructs. It must neither be initialized nor saved and it must be neither a dummy argument, a function
result, a pointer, nor accessed by use or host association.
   The type and type parameters of an array constructor are those of the first
expr, and each *expr* must have the same type and type parameters. If every *expr,*
expr1, expr2, and *expr3* is a constant expression, the array constructor is a constant
expression.
   An array of rank greater than one may be constructed from an array constructor
by using the intrinsic function reshape (Section 8.12.3). For example,

```
reshape( source = (/ 1,2,3,4,5,6 /), shape = (/ 2,3 /) )
```

has the value

```
    1   3   5
    2   4   6
```

6.14   Mask arrays

Logical arrays are needed for masking in where constructs (Section 6.8), and they
play a similar role in many of the array intrinsic functions (Chapter 8). Often,
such arrays are large, and there may be a worthwhile storage gain from using non-
default logical types, if available. For example, some processors may use bytes to
store elements of logical arrays whose kind value is 1, and bits to store elements
of logical arrays whose kind value is 0.   Unfortunately, there is no *portable*
facility to specify such arrays, since there is no intrinsic function comparable to
selected_int_kind and selected_real_kind.
   Logical arrays are formed implicitly in certain expressions, usually as compiler-
generated temporary variables. In

```
where (a > 0.0)
    a = 2.0 * a
end where
```

a > 0.0 is a logical array. In such a case, an optimizing compiler can be expected
to choose a suitable kind type parameter for the temporary array.

6.15   Summary

We have explained that arrays may have zero size and that no special rules are needed for them. A non-pointer dummy array assumes its shape from the corresponding actual argument. Storage for an array may be allocated automatically on entry to a procedure and automatically deallocated on return, or the allocation may be controlled in detail by the program. Functions may be array-valued either through the mechanism of an elemental reference that performs the same calculation for each array element (for intrinsic functions only), or through the truly array-valued function. Array assignments may be masked through the use of the where construct. Structure components may be arrays if the parent is an array or the component is an array, but not both. A subarray may either be formulated directly as an array section, or indirectly by using pointer assignment to associate it with a pointer. An array may be constructed from a sequence of expressions. A logical array may be used as a mask.

Basically, the whole of the contents of this chapter represents features that are not in Fortran 77, and is a hallmark of the language. The intrinsic functions are an important part of the array features of F and will be described in Chapter 8.

We conclude this chapter with a complete program, Figures 6.9 & 6.10, that illustrates the use of array expressions, array assignments, allocatable arrays, automatic arrays, and array sections. The module linear contains a subroutine for solving a set of linear equations, and this is called from a main program that prompts the user for the problem and then solves it.

6.16   Exercises

1. Given the array declaration

```
real, dimension(50,20) :: a
```

write array sections representing

   i) the first row of a;

   ii) the last column of a;

   iii) every second element in each row and column;

   iv) as for (iii) in reverse order in both dimensions;

   v) a zero-sized array.

2. Write a where construct to double the value of all the positive elements of an array z.

3. Write an array declaration for an array j which is to be completely defined by the statement

```
j = (/ (3, 5, i=1,5), 5,5,5, (i, i =  5,3,-1 ) /)
```

Figure 6.9

```
module linear
   public :: solve
   integer, parameter, public :: kind10=selected_real_kind(10)

contains
   subroutine solve(a, piv_tol, b, ok)
   ! arguments
      real(kind=kind10), intent(inout), dimension(:,:) :: a
                         ! The matrix a.
      real(kind=kind10), intent(in) :: piv_tol
                         ! Smallest acceptable pivot.
      real(kind=kind10), intent(inout), dimension(:) :: b
                         ! The right-hand side vector on
                         ! entry. Overwritten by the solution.
      logical, intent(out)       :: ok
                         ! True after a successful entry
                         ! and false otherwise.

   ! Local variables
      integer :: i    ! Row index.
      integer :: j    ! Column index.
      integer :: n    ! Matrix order.
      real(kind=kind10), dimension(size(b)) :: row
                         ! Automatic array needed for workspace;
                         ! size is described in Section 8.11.2.
      real(kind=kind10) :: element ! Workspace variable.

      n = size(b)
      ok = size(a, 1) == n .and. size(a, 2) == n
      if (.not.ok) then
         return
      end if

      do j = 1, n
!     Update elements in column j.
         do i = 1, j - 1
            a(i+1:n, j) = a(i+1:n, j) - a(i,j) * a(i+1:n, i)
         end do
!     Find pivot and check its size (using maxval just to
!     obtain a scalar).
         i = maxval(maxloc(abs(a(j:n, j)))) + j - 1
            ! maxval and maxloc are in Sections 8.10.1 and 8.13.
         if (abs(a(i, j)) < piv_tol) then
            ok = .false.
            return
         end if
```

Figure 6.10

```
!     If necessary, apply row interchange
      if (i/=j) then
          row = a(j, :)
          a(j, :) = a(i, :)
          a(i, :) = row
          element = b(j)
          b(j) = b(i)
          b(i) = element
      end if
!     Compute elements j+1 : n of j-th column.
      a(j+1:n, j) = a(j+1:n, j)/a(j, j)
      end do
!  Forward substitution
      do i = 1, n-1
          b(i+1:n) = b(i+1:n) - b(i)*a(i+1:n, i)
      end do
!   Back-substitution
      do j = n, 1, -1
          b(j) = b(j)/a(j, j)
          b(1:j-1) =  b(1:j-1) - b(j)*a(1:j-1, j)
      end do
   end subroutine solve
end module linear

program main
   use linear
   integer :: i, n
   real(kind=kind10), allocatable, dimension(:,:) :: a
   real(kind=kind10), allocatable, dimension(:) ::  b
   logical :: ok
   print *, " Matrix order?"
   read *,  n
   allocate ( a(n, n), b(n) )
   do i = 1, n
      write(unit=*, fmt="(a, i2, a)") " Elements of row ", i, " of a?"
          ! Edit descriptors are described in Section 9.11
      read *, a(i,:)
      write(unit=*, fmt="(a, i2, a)") " Component ", i, " of b?"
      read *, b(i)
   end do
   call solve(a, maxval(abs(a))*1.0e-10, b, ok)
   if (ok) then
      write(unit=*, fmt="(/,a,/,(5f12.4))") " Solution is", b
   else
      print *, " The matrix is singular"
   end if
end program main
```

4. Classify the following arrays:

```
subroutine example(n, a, b)
    real, dimension(:)              :: a
    real, dimension(0:)            :: b
    real, pointer, dimension(:, :) :: d
    real, dimension(n, 10)         :: w
```

5. Write a declaration and a pointer assignment statement suitable to reference as an array all the third elements of component du in the elements of the array tar having all three subscript values even (Section 6.9).

6. Given the array declarations

```
integer, dimension(100, 100), target :: l, m, n
integer, dimension(:, :), pointer     :: ll, mm, nn
```

rewrite the statements

```
l(j:k+1, j-1:k) = l(j:k+1, j-1:k) + l(j:k+1, j-1:k)
l(j:k+1, j-1:k) = m(j:k+1, j-1:k) + n(j:k+1, j-1:k) + n(j:k+1, j:k+1)
```

as they could appear following execution of the statements

```
ll => l(j:k+1, j-1:k)
mm => m(j:k+1, j-1:k)
nn => n(j:k+1, j-1:k)
```

7. Complete Exercise 1 of Chapter 4 using array syntax instead of do constructs.

8. Write a module to maintain a data structure consisting of a linked list of integers, with the ability to add and delete members of the list, efficiently.

9. Write a module that contains the example in Figure 6.7 (Section 6.7) as a module procedure and supports the defined operations and assignments that it contains.

7. Specification statements

7.1 Introduction

In the preceding chapters we have learnt the elements of the F language, how they may be combined into expressions and assignments, how we may control the logic flow of a program, how to divide a program into manageable parts, and have considered how arrays may be processed. We have seen that this knowledge is sufficient to write programs, when combined with a rudimentary print statement and with the program and end program statements.

Already in Chapters 2 to 6, we met some specification statements when declaring the type and other properties of data objects, but to ease the reader's task we did not always explain all the details. In this chapter we fill this gap. To begin with, however, it is necessary to recall the place of specification statements in a programming language. A program is processed by a computer in (usually) three stages. In the first stage, *compilation*, the source code (text) of the program is read and processed by a program known as a *compiler* which analyses it, and generates a file containing *object code*. Each program unit of the complete program is usually processed separately. The object code is a translation of the source code into a form which can be understood by the computer hardware, and contains the precise instructions as to what operations the computer is to perform. In the second stage of processing, the object code is placed in the relevant part of the computer's storage system by a program often known as a loader which prepares it for the next stage; during this second stage, the separate program units are linked to one another, that is joined to form a complete executable program. The third stage consists of the *execution*, whereby the coded instructions are performed and the results of the computations made available.

During the first stage, the compiler requires information about the entities involved. This information is provided at the beginning of each program unit or subprogram by specification statements. The description of most of these is the subject of this chapter. The specification statements associated with procedure interfaces, including interface blocks and the interface statement were explained in Chapter 5.

7.2   Named constants and constant expressions

Inside a program, we often need to define a constant or set of constants. For instance, in a program requiring repeated use of the speed of light, we might use a real variable c that is given its value by the statement

```
c = 2.99792458
```

A danger in this practice is that the value of c may be overwritten inadvertently, for instance because another programmer re-uses c as a variable to contain a different quantity, failing to notice that the name is already in use.

Another situation which can arise is that the program contains specifications such as

```
real, dimension(10) :: x, y, z
integer, dimension(10, 10) :: mesh
integer, dimension(100) ::  ipoint
```

where all the dimensions are 10 or 10^2. Such specifications may be used extensively, and 10 may even appear as an explicit constant, say as a parameter in a do-construct which processes these arrays:

```
do i = 1, 10
```

Later, it may be realised that the value 20 rather than 10 is required, and the new value must be substituted everywhere the old one occurs, an error-prone undertaking.

Yet another case was met in Section 2.6, where a named constant was needed for the kind type parameter values.

In order to deal with all of these situations, F contains what are known as *named constants*. These may never appear on the left-hand side of an assignment statement, but may be used in expressions in any way in which a literal constant may be used. A type declaration statement with the parameter attribute is used to specify such a constant:

```
real, parameter :: c = 2.99792458
```

The value is protected, as c is now the name of a constant and may not be used as a variable name in the same scoping unit. Similarly, we may write

```
integer, parameter                   :: length = 10
real, dimension(length)              :: x, y, z
integer, dimension(length, length) :: mesh
integer, dimension(length**2)        :: ipoint
:
do i = 1, length
```

which has the clear advantage that in order to change the value of 10 to 20 only a single line need be modified, and the new value is then correctly propagated.

In this example, the expression length**2 appeared in one of the array bound specifications. This is a particular example of a constant expression. A *constant expression* is an expression in which each operation is intrinsic, and each primary is

   i) a constant or a subobject of a constant,

   ii) an array constructor whose expressions (including bounds and strides) have primaries that are constant expressions,

   iii) a structure constructor whose components are constant expressions,

   iv) an elemental intrinsic function reference whose arguments are constant expressions,

   v) a transformational intrinsic function reference whose arguments are constant expressions,

   vi) a reference to an inquiry function (Section 8.1.2) other than present, associated, or allocated, where each argument is either a constant expression or a variable whose type parameters or bounds inquired about are neither assumed, defined by an expression that is not constant, defined by an allocate statement, nor defined by a pointer assignment,

   vii) an implied-do variable whose bounds and strides are constant expressions, or

   viii) a constant expression enclosed in parentheses,

and where each subscript, section subscript, and substring bound is a constant expression.

Because the values of named constants are expected to be evaluated at compile time, the expressions permitted for their definition are restricted in their form. An *initialization expression* is a constant expression in which

   i) the exponentiation operator must have an integer power,

   ii) an elemental intrinsic function must have arguments and results of type integer or character, and

   iii) of the transformational functions, only repeat, reshape, selected_int_kind, selected_real_kind, and trim are permitted.

If an initialization expression invokes an inquiry function for a type parameter or an array bound of an object, the type parameter or array bound must be specified in a prior specification statement or to the left in the same specification statement.

In the definition of a named constant we may use any initialization expression, and the constant becomes defined with the value of the expression according to the rules of intrinsic assignment. This is illustrated by the example:

```
integer, parameter :: length=10, long=selected_real_kind(12)
real, parameter    :: lsq = length**2
```

Note from this example that it is possible in one statement to define several named constants, in this case two, separated by commas.

A named constant may be an array, as in the case

```
real, dimension(3), parameter :: field = (/ 0.0, 10.0, 20.0 /)
```

and it may be of derived type, as in the case

```
type(posn), parameter :: a = posn(1.0,2.0,0)
```

for the type

```
type, public :: posn
   real    :: x, y
   integer :: z
end type posn
```

Note that a subobject of a constant need not necessarily have a constant value. For example, if i is an integer variable, field(i) may have the value 0.0, 10.0, or 20.0. Note also that a constant may not be a pointer, allocatable array, dummy argument, or function result, since these are always variables.

Any named constant used in an initialization expression must either be accessed from the host, be accessed from a module, be declared in a preceding statement, or be declared to the left of its use in the same statement. An example using a constant expression including a named constant that is defined in the same statement is

```
integer, parameter :: apple = 3, pear = apple**2
```

Finally, there is an important point concerning the definition of a scalar named constant of type character. Its length may be specified as an asterisk and taken directly from its value, which obviates the need to count the length of a character string, and makes modifications to its definition much easier. An example of this is

```
character(len=*), parameter :: string = "No need to count"
```

Unfortunately, there *is* a need to count when a character array is defined using an array constructor, since all the elements must be of the same length:

```
character(len=7), parameter, dimension(2) ::            &
                   c=(/"Metcalf", "Reid   "/)
```

would not be correct if the three blanks in "Reid   " were removed.

The parameter attribute is an important means whereby constants may be protected from overwriting, and programs modified in a safe way. It should be used for these purposes on every possible occasion.

7.3 Initial values for variables

A variable that is specified in a module or one of its subprograms may be assigned an initial value. This is done by adding the save attribute (Section 7.6) to its type declaration statement, and following the name of the variable by an initialization expression (Section 7.2), as in the examples:

```
real, save                :: a = 0.0
real, save, dimension(3) :: b = (/ 0.0, 1.2, 4.5 /)
```

The initial value is defined by the value of the corresponding expression according to the rules of intrinsic assignment. Although this feature is not available in a main program, the same effect may be achieved with assignment statements at the start of the executable code.

No variable that is given an initial value may be a dummy argument, accessed by use or host association, a pointer, an allocatable array, an automatic object, or a function result.

7.4 The public and private attributes

Modules (Section 5.5) permit specifications to be 'packaged' into a form that allows them to be accessed elsewhere in the program. So far, we have assumed that all the entities in the module are to be accessible, that is have the public attribute, but sometimes it is desirable to limit the access. For example, several procedures in a module may need access to a work array containing the results of calculations that they have performed. If access is limited to only the procedures of the module, there is no possibility of an accidental corruption of these data by another procedure and design changes can be made within the module without affecting the rest of the program. In cases where entities are not to be accessible outside their own module, they may be given the private attribute.

These two attributes must be specified for data objects in the module with the public and private attributes on type declaration statements, as in

```
real, public     :: x, y, z
integer, private :: u, v, w
```

For procedures and defined operators, they must be specified in public and private statements, as in

```
public  :: x, y, z, operator(.add.)
private :: u, v, w, assignment(=), operator(*)
```

which have the general forms

```
public  :: access-id-list
private :: access-id-list
```

where *access-id* is a name or a *generic-spec* (Section 5.16).

Note that if a procedure has a generic identifier, the accessibility of its specific name is independent of the accessibility of its generic identifier. One may be `public` while the other is `private`, which means that it is accessible only by its specific name or only by its generic identifier.

Thus, to make a generic procedure name accessible but the corresponding specific names inaccessible, we might write

```
module example
    private :: specific_int, specific_real
    public  :: generic_name
    interface generic_name
        module procedure specific_int, specific_real
    end interface
contains
    subroutine specific_int(i)
        :
    subroutine specific_real(a)
        :
end module example
```

An entity with a type must not have the `public` attribute if its type has the `private` attribute (because there is virtually nothing one can do with such an entity without access to its type). If a module procedure has a dummy argument or function result of private type, the procedure must be given the attribute `private` and must not have a generic identifier that is `public`. The `public` and `private` attributes may appear only in the specifications of a module. The use of the `private` statement for components of derived types in this context will be described in Section 7.8.

7.5   Accessing one module from another

One module may access another, but F has been designed so that no entity is acccessed by more than one route through use statements. A module with use statements will usually have the statement

```
private
```

immediately following the use statements. This directly prevents the entities accessed from other modules being accessed through this module. The ordering of the statements of such a module is specified in Figure 7.1.

Alternatively, a module may take the form shown in Figure 7.2. Such a module defines nothing new. Rather, it makes available, as a new module, some or all of the entities in the accessed modules. Any scoping unit accessing the module must not access the accessed modules directly or through another route. We imagine module libraries being written as sets of small modules that are accessed as a collection by this mechanism. This keeps all the modules of modest size.

Figure 7.1 Order of statements in a module without a `public` statement.

```
module module-name
    [use-statement] ...
    [private]        ! Must be present if there are any use
                     ! statements.
    [access-statement] ...
                     ! public/private for module procedures and
                     ! generic identifiers.
    [intrinsic-statement] ...    ! Section 8.1.3.
    [module-entity-definition] ... ! Derived-type definition,
           ! type declaration statement, or interface block.
[contains]
    subprogram       ! function or subroutine.
    [subprogram] ... ! There must be at least one subprogram
                     ! if there is a contains statement.
end module module-name
```

Figure 7.2 Order of statements in a module with a `public` statement.

```
module module-name
    use-statement
    [use-statement] ...
    public
end module module-name
```

As an example of this concept, consider a module `vector` for rank-one real arrays. Another module `matrix` uses `vector` to provide facilities for rank-two real arrays. If both are needed, they may be merged as shown in Figure 7.3.

Figure 7.3

```
module both
    use vector
    use matrix
    public
end module both
```

7.6   The save attribute

Let us suppose that we wish to retain the value of a local variable in a subprogram, for example to count the number of times the subprogram is entered. We might write a section of code as in Figure 7.4. In this example, the local variables, a and counter, are initialized to zero, and it is assumed that their current values are available each time the subroutine is called. This is not necessarily the case. F allows the computer system being used to 'forget' a new value, the variable becoming undefined on each return unless it has the save attribute. In Figure 7.4, it is sufficient to change the declaration of a to

```
real, save :: a
```

to be sure that its value is always retained between calls.

Figure 7.4

```
subroutine anything(x)
   real, intent(in) :: x
   real :: a                       ! Needs a save attribute.
   integer, save :: counter = 0 ! Initialize the counter.
   :
   counter = counter + 1
   if (counter==1) then
      a = 0.0
   else
      a = a + x
   end if
   :
```

A similar situation arises with the use of variables in modules (Section 5.5). On return from a subprogram that accesses a variable in a module, the variable becomes undefined unless the main program accesses the module, another subprogram in execution accesses the module, or the variable has the save attribute.

If a variable that becomes undefined has a pointer associated with it, the pointer's association status becomes undefined.

The save attribute must not be specified for a dummy argument, a function result, or an automatic object (Section 6.4). It may be specified for a pointer, in which case the pointer association status is saved. It may be specified for an allocatable array, in which case the allocation status and value are saved. A saved variable in a recursive subprogram is shared by all instances of the subprogram.

The save attribute is not permitted to appear in the declaration statements in a main program. The variables of the main program automatically behave as if they have the save attribute, since there is no return statement in a main program.

7.7   The use statement

In Section 5.5, we introduced the use statement in its simplest form

```
use module-name
```

which provides access to all the public named data objects, derived types, interface blocks, procedures, and generic identifiers in the module named. Any use
statements must precede other specification statements in a scoping unit.

If access is needed to two or more modules that have been written independently, the same name may be used in more than one module. This is the main
reason for permitting accessed entities to be renamed by the use statement. Renaming is also available to resolve a name clash between a local entity and an
entity accessed from a module, though our preference is to use a text editor or
other tool to change the local name. With renaming, the use statement has the
form

use *module-name,* *rename-list*

where each *rename* has the form

local-name => *use-name*

and refers to a public entity in the module that is to be accessed by a different local
name.

As an example,

```
use stats_lib, sprod => prod
use maths_lib
```

makes all the public entities in both stats_lib and maths_lib accessible. If
maths_lib contains an entity called prod, it is accessible by its own name while
the entity prod of stats_lib is accessible as sprod.

A name clash is permissible only for a generic name that is required. Here,
all generic interfaces accessed by the name are treated as a single concatenated
interface block. This is true also for defined operators and assignments, where
no renaming facility is available. In all these cases, any two procedures having
the same generic identifier must differ as explained in Section 5.16. We imagine
that this will usually be exactly what is needed. For example, we might access
modules for interval arithmetic and matrix arithmetic, both needing the functions
sqrt, sin, etc., the operators +, -, etc., and assignment, but for different types.

For cases where only a subset of the names of a module is needed, the only
option is available, having the form

use *module-name,* only : *only-list*

where each *only* has the form

access-id

or

[*local-name* =>] *use-name*

where each *access-id* is a public entity in the module, and is either a *use-name* or
a *generic-spec* (Section 5.16). This provides access to an entity in a module only

if the entity is public and is specified as a *use-name* or *access-id*. Where a *use-name* is preceded by a *local-name*, the entity is known locally by the *local-name*. An example of such a statement is

```
use stats_lib, only : sprod => prod, mult
```

which provides access to prod by the local name sprod and to mult by its own name.

Only one use statement for a given module is allowed and an entity must not appear more than once as a *use-name*.

An only list will be rather clumsy if almost all of a module is wanted. The effect of an 'except' clause can be obtained by renaming unwanted entities. An example is

```
use blas, except_this_one => gemm
```

where blas is the name of the module and gemm is the name of the unwanted procedure.

When a module contains use statements, the entities accessed are treated as entities in the module, except that they normally have the private attribute, so are not accessible through a use statement for the module. Only in the simple case explained in Section 7.5 do they have the public attribute.

Of course, all the local names of entities accessed from modules must differ from each other and from names of local entities. If a local entity is accidentally given the same name as an accessible entity from a module, this will be noticed at compile time.

7.8　Derived-type definitions

When derived types were introduced in Section 2.9, some simple example definitions were given, but the full generality was not included. An example illustrating more features is

```
type, public :: lock
   private
   integer, pointer, dimension(:) :: key
   logical :: state
end type lock
```

A derived-type definition is permitted only in the scoping unit of a module and has the general form

```
type, access :: type-name
     [ private ]
     component-def-stmt
     [component-def-stmt] ...
end type type-name
```

where *access* is either `public` or `private`. If *access* is `private`. the `private` statement must not be present. Each *component-def-stmt* has the form

type [,*component-attr-list*] :: *component-name-list*

where *type* specifies the type and type parameters (Section 7.10), and each *component-attr* is either `pointer` or `dimension`(*extent-list*). If the *type* is a derived type and the `pointer` attribute is not specified, the type must be previously defined in the module or accessible there by use association. If the `pointer` attribute is specified, the type may also be the one being defined (for example, the type `entry` of Section 2.13), or one defined elsewhere in the module.

A *type-name* must not be the same as the name of any intrinsic type or a derived type accessed from a module.

The bounds of an array component are declared by an *extent-list* where each *extent* is

:

for a pointer component (see example in Section 6.11) or

[*lower-bound*:] *upper-bound*

for a non-pointer component, and *lower-bound* and *upper-bound* are constant expressions that are restricted to specification expressions (Section 7.11). Similarly, the character length of a component of type character must be a constant specification expression.

The *access* qualifier on a type statement may be `public` or `private` and specifies the accessibility of the type. If it is `private`, then the type name, the structure constructor for the type, any entity of the type, and any procedure with a dummy argument or function result of the type are all inaccessible outside the host module. If a `private` statement appears for a type with `public` accessibility, the components of the type are inaccessible in any scoping unit accessing the module, so that neither component selection nor structure construction are available there. Also, if any component is of a derived type that is `private`, the type being defined must be `private` or have `private` components.

We can thus distinguish three levels of access:

i) all `public`, where the type and all its components are accessible;

ii) a `public` type with `private` components, where the type is accessible but its components are hidden;

iii) all `private`, where both the type and its components are used only within the host module, and are hidden to an accessing procedure.

Case ii) has, where appropriate, the advantage of enabling changes to be made to the type without in any way affecting the code in the accessing procedure. Case iii) offers this advantage and has the additional merit of not cluttering the name space of the accessing procedure. The use of `private` accessibility for the components or for the whole type is thus recommended whenever possible.

We note that even if two derived-type definitions are identical in every respect, entities of those two types are regarded as being of different types.

7.9   The type declaration statement

We have already met many simple examples of the declarations of named entities by `integer`, `real`, `complex`, `logical`, `character`, and `type`(*type-name*) statements. The general form is

>   *type* [, *attribute*] ... :: *object-list*

where *type* specifies the type and type parameters (Section 7.10), *attribute* is one of the following

`parameter`	`dimension`(*extent-list*)
`public`	`intent`(*inout*)
`private`	`optional`
`pointer`	`save`
`target`	`allocatable`

and each *object* is

>   *object-name* [= *initialization-expr*]

No attribute may appear more than once in a given type declaration statement. If the statement specifies a `parameter` attribute, =*initialization-expr* must appear. If =*initialization-expr* appears for one or more objects, `save` or `parameter` must be specified (in a main program only `parameter` but not `save` may appear).

If a pointer attribute is specified, the `target`, `intent`, and `allocatable` attributes must not be specified. The `target` and `parameter` attributes may not be specified for the same entity.

If an object is specified with the `intent` or `parameter` attribute, this is shared by all its subobjects. The `pointer` attribute is not shared in this manner, but note that a derived-data type component may itself be a pointer. However, the `target` attribute is shared by all its subobjects, except for any that are pointer components.

The `allocatable`, `parameter`, or `save` attribute must not be specified for a dummy argument or function result. The `intent` and `optional` attributes may be specified only for dummy arguments, the `intent` attribute being required for them.

7.10   Type and type parameter specification

We have used *type* to represent one of the following

```
integer [(kind = kind-value)]
real [(kind = kind-value)]
complex [(kind = kind-value)]
character (len = len-value)
logical [(kind = kind-value)]
type (type-name)
```

in the component definition statement (Section 7.8) and the type declaration statement (Section 7.9). A *kind-value* must be a scalar named integer constant and must have a value that is valid on the processor being used.

For a scalar named constant, a *len-value* may be specified as an asterisk, in which case the value is assumed from that of the constant itself. For a dummy argument of a subprogram, the *len-value* must be specified as an asterisk, and the value is assumed from that of the associated actual argument. In both cases, the len intrinsic function (Section 8.6.1) is available if the actual length is required directly, for instance as a do construct iteration count. A combined example is

```
function line(char_arg) result(res)
    character(len=*), intent(in) :: char_arg
    character(len=len(char_arg)) :: res
    character(len=*), parameter  :: char_const = "page"
    if ( len(char_arg) < len(char_const) ) then
        :
```

A *len-value* that is not an asterisk must be a specification expression (next section). Negative values declare character entities to be of zero length.

7.11 Specification expressions

Non-constant scalar integer expressions may be used to specify the array bounds (examples in Section 6.4) and character lengths of data objects in a subprogram, and of function results. Such an expression may depend only on data values that are defined on entry to the subprogram. Any variable referenced must not have its type and type parameters specified later in the same sequence of specification statements.

Intrinsic function references are limited to:

i) an elemental function reference for which the arguments and result are of type integer or character,

ii) a reference to repeat, trim, or reshape for which the arguments are of type integer or character,

iii) a reference to selected_int_kind or selected_real_kind,

iv) a reference to an inquiry function other than present, associated, or allocated, provided the quantity inquired about does not depend on an allocation or on a pointer assignment.

Array constructors and derived-type constructors are permitted, but references to non-intrinsic procedures are not permitted. The expression may reference an inquiry function for an array bound or for a type parameter of an entity which either is accessed by use or host association, or is specified earlier in the same specification sequence, but not later in the sequence.[1] An element of an array specified in the same specification sequence can be referenced only if the bounds of the array are specified earlier in the sequence.[2] Such an expression is called a *specification expression*.

An array whose bounds are declared using specification expressions is called an *explicit-shape array*.

The bounds and character lengths are not affected by any redefinitions or undefinitions of variables in the expressions during execution of the procedure. A variety of possibilities are shown in Figure 7.5.

Figure 7.5

```
subroutine sample(arr, value, string)
    use definitions                          ! Contains the real a
    real, dimension(:,:), intent(out) :: arr ! Assumed-shape array
    integer, intent(in)               :: value
    character(len=*), intent(in)      :: string ! Assumed length
    real, dimension(ubound(arr, 1)+5) :: x      ! Automatic array
    character(len=value+len(string))  :: cc     ! Automatic object
    integer, parameter :: pa2 =     &
                          selected_real_kind(2*precision(a))
    real(kind=pa2) :: z         ! Precision of z is twice that of a
    :
```

7.12   Summary

In this chapter, most of the specification statements of F have been described. The following concepts have been introduced: named constants, constant expressions, data initialization, control of the accessibility of entities in modules, saving data between procedure calls, selective access of entities in a module, renaming entities accessed from a module, and specification expressions that may be used when specifying data objects and function results.

---

[1]This avoids such a case as

```
character (len=len(a)) ::  fun
character (len=len(fun)) ::  a
```

[2]This avoids such a case as

```
integer, parameter, dimension (j(1):j(1)+1) ::  i = (/0,1/)
integer, parameter, dimension (i(1):i(1)+1) ::  j = (/1,2/)
```

The features described here that are not in Fortran 77 are initialization and spec-ification expressions; the attributes: public, private, pointer, allocatable, target, intent, and optional; and the use statement. The type declaration state-ment has been much extended.

Figure 7.6

```
module sort              ! To sort postal addresses by zip code.
    public  :: selection_sort
    private :: swap
    integer, parameter, private :: string_length = 30
    type, public :: address
        character(len = string_length) :: name, street, town
        character(len=2)                :: state
        integer                         :: zip_code
    end type address
contains
    recursive subroutine selection_sort (array_arg)
        type (address), dimension (:), intent (inout)           &
                                         :: array_arg
        integer                          :: current_size
        integer, dimension (1)           :: big
            ! Result of maxloc (Section 8.13) is array valued
        current_size = size (array_arg)
        if (current_size > 0) then
            big = maxloc (array_arg(:) % zip_code)
            call swap (array_arg(big(1)), array_arg(current_size))
            call selection_sort (array_arg(1: current_size - 1))
        end if
    end subroutine selection_sort
    subroutine swap (i, j)
        type (address), intent (inout) :: i, j
        type (address)   :: temp
        temp = i
        i = j
        j = temp
    end subroutine swap
end module sort
```

We conclude this chapter with a complete program, Figures 7.6 and 7.7, that uses a module to sort US-style addresses (name, street, town, and state with a numerical zip code) by order of zip code. It illustrates the interplay between many of the features described so far, but note that it is not a production code since the sort routine is not very efficient and the full range of US addresses is not handled.

Figure 7.7

```
program zippy
   use sort
   integer, parameter                        :: array_size = 100
   type (address), dimension (array_size) :: data_array
   integer                                   :: i, n, ios
   do i = 1, array_size
      read (unit=*,fmt="(/,a,/,a,/,a,/,a2,i8)", iostat=ios) &
           data_array(i)      ! For iostat= see Section 9.7;
      if (ios/=0) then
         exit
      end if
      write (unit=*,fmt="(/,a,/,a,/,a,/,a2,i8)") data_array(i)
   end do                       ! For editing see Section 9.12.
   n = i - 1
   call selection_sort (data_array(1: n))
   write (unit=*,fmt= "(/,/,a)") "after sorting:"
   do i = 1, n
      write (unit=*,fmt= "(/,a,/,a,/,a,/,a2,i8)") data_array(i)
   end do
end program zippy
```

Suitable test data are:

```
Prof. James Bush,
206 Church St. SE,
Minneapolis,
MN 55455

J. E. Dougal,
Rice University,
Houston,
TX 77251

Jack Finch,
104 Ayres Hall,
Knoxville,
TN 37996
```

7.13 Exercises

1. Write suitable type statements for the following quantities:

i) an array to hold the number of counts in each of the 100 bins of a histogram numbered from 1 to 100;

ii) an array to hold the temperature to two significant decimal places at points, on a sheet of iron, equally spaced at 1cm intervals on a rectangular grid 20cm square, with points in each corner, (the melting point of iron is 1530° C);

iii) an array to describe the state of 20 on/off switches;

iv) an array to contain the information destined for a printed page of 44 lines each of 70 letters or digits.

2. Explain the difference between the following pair of declarations

```
real, save :: i = 3.1
```

and

```
real, parameter :: i = 3.1
```

What is the value of i in each case?

3. Write type declaration statements which initialize:

i) all the elements of an integer array of length 100 to the value zero.

ii) all the odd elements of the same array to 0 and the even elements to 1.

iii) the elements of a real 10×10 square array to 1.0 .

iv) a character string to the digits 0 to 9.

4. i) Write a type declaration statement that declares and initializes a variable of derived type person (Section 2.9).

ii) Write a type declaration statement that declares and initializes a variable of type entry (Section 2.13).

5. Which of the following are initialization expressions:

i) kind(x), for x of type real

ii) selected_real_kind(6, 20)

iii) 1.7**2

iv) 1.7**2.0

v) (1.7, 2.3)**(-2)

vi) (/ (7*i, i=1, 10) /)

vii) person("Reid", 25*2.0, 22**2)

viii) entry(1.7, 1, null_pointer)

8. Intrinsic procedures

8.1 Introduction

In a language that has a clear orientation towards scientific applications there is an obvious requirement for the most frequently required mathematical functions to be provided as part of the language itself, rather than expecting each user to code them afresh. When provided with the compiler, they are normally coded to be very efficient and will have been well tested over the complete range of values that they accept. It is difficult to compete with the high standard of code provided by the vendors.

The efficiency of the intrinsic procedures when handling arrays on vector or parallel computers is likely to be particularly marked because a single call may cause a large number of individual operations to be performed, during the execution of which advantage may be taken of the specific nature of the hardware.

Another feature of a substantial number of the intrinsic procedures is that they extend the power of the language by providing access to facilities that are not otherwise available in the language. Examples are inquiry functions for the presence of an optional argument, the parts of a floating-point number, and the length of a character string.

There are some hundred intrinsic procedures in all, a particularly rich set. They fall into distinct groups, which we describe in turn. A list in alphabetical order, with one-line descriptions, is given in Appendix A.

The names of the intrinsic procedures are reserved words that may not be used in other contexts.

8.1.1 Keyword calls

The procedures may be called with keyword actual arguments, using the dummy argument names as keywords. This facility is not very useful for those with a single non-optional argument, but is useful for those with several optional arguments. For example

```
call date_and_time (date=d)
```

returns the date in the scalar character variable d. The rules for positional and keyword argument lists were explained in Section 5.12. In this chapter, the dummy arguments that are optional are indicated with square brackets. We have taken some 'poetic licence' with this notation, which might suggest to the reader that the positional form is permitted following an absent argument (this is not the case).

8.1.2   Categories of intrinsic procedures

There are four categories of intrinsic procedures:

i) *Elemental procedures* are specified for scalar arguments, but may also be applied to conforming array arguments. In order that the rank always be known at compile time, at least one of the array arguments must correspond to a non-optional argument of the elemental procedure. In the case of an elemental function, each element of the result, if any, is as would have been obtained by applying the function to corresponding elements of each of the array arguments. In the case of an elemental subroutine (of which F has only one – mvbits) with an array argument, each argument of intent out or inout must be an array, and each element is as would have resulted from applying the subroutine to corresponding elements of each of the array arguments.

ii) *Inquiry functions* return properties of their principal arguments that do not depend on their values; indeed, for named variables, their values may be undefined.

iii) *Transformational functions* are functions that are neither elemental nor inquiry; they usually have array arguments and an array result whose elements depend on many of the elements of the arguments.

iv) *Non-elemental subroutines.*

8.1.3   The intrinsic statement

A name may be specified to be that of an intrinsic procedure in an intrinsic statement, which has the general form

intrinsic *intrinsic-name-list*

where *intrinsic-name-list* is a list of intrinsic procedure names. A name must not appear more than once in the intrinsic statements of a scoping unit. This statement is required for a name that appears as a generic name on the interface block of an intrinsic procedure that is being extended (Section 5.16).

8.1.4   Argument intents

The functions do not change the values of their arguments. In fact, the non-pointer arguments all have the intent in. For the subroutines, the intents vary from case to case (see the descriptions given later in the chapter).

8.2 Inquiry functions for any type

The following are inquiry functions whose arguments may be of any type:

associated (pointer [,target]), when target is absent, returns the value
true if the pointer pointer is associated with a target and false otherwise.
The pointer association status of pointer must not be undefined. If target
is present, it must have the same type, type parameters, and rank as pointer.
The value is true if pointer is associated with target, and false otherwise.
In the array case, true is returned only if the shapes are identical and
corresponding array elements, in array element order, are associated with
each other. If the character length or array size is zero, false is returned. A
different bound, as in the case of associated(p,a) following the pointer
assignment p => a(:) when lbound(a) = 0, is insufficient to cause false
to be returned. The argument target may itself be a pointer, in which case
its target is compared with the target of pointer; the pointer association
status of target must not be undefined and if either pointer or target is
disassociated, the result is false .

present (a) may be called in a subprogram that has an optional dummy argument a. It returns the value true if the corresponding actual argument is
present in the current call to it, and false otherwise. If an absent dummy
argument is used as an actual argument in a call of another subprogram, it
is regarded as also absent in the called subprogram.

There is an inquiry function whose argument may be of any intrinsic type:

kind (x) has type default integer and value equal to the kind type parameter
value of x.

8.3 Elemental numeric functions

There are 15 elemental functions for performing simple numerical tasks, many of
which perform type conversions for some or all types of arguments.

8.3.1 Elemental functions that may convert

If kind is present in the following elemental functions, it must be a named constant
and provide a kind type parameter that is supported on the processor.

abs (a) returns the absolute value of an argument of type integer, real, or complex. The result is of type integer if a is of type integer and otherwise it is
real. It has the same kind type parameter as a.

aimag (z) returns the imaginary part of the complex value z. The type is real
and the kind type parameter is that of z.

aint (a [,kind]) truncates a real value a towards zero to produce a real that is a whole number. The value of the kind type parameter is the value of the argument kind if it is present, or that of the default real otherwise.

anint (a [,kind]) returns a real whose value is the nearest whole number to the real value a. The value of the kind type parameter is the value of the argument kind, if it is present, or that of the default real otherwise.

ceiling (a) returns the least default integer greater than or equal to its real argument.

cmplx (x [,y][,kind]) converts x or (x, y) to complex type with the value of the kind type parameter being the value of the argument kind if it is present or that of the default complex otherwise. If y is absent, x may be of type integer, real, or complex. If y is present, it must be of type integer or real and x must be of type integer or real.

floor (a) returns the greatest default integer less than or equal to its real argument.

int (a [,kind]) converts to integer type with the value of the kind type parameter being the value of the argument kind, if it is present, or that of the default integer otherwise. The argument a may be

- integer, in which case int(a)=a,
- real, in which case the value is truncated towards zero, or
- complex, in which case the real part is truncated towards zero.

nint (a [,kind]) returns the integer value that is nearest to the real a. If kind is present, the value of the kind type parameter of the result is the value of kind, otherwise it is that of the default integer type.

real (a [,kind]) converts to real type with the value of the kind type parameter being that of kind if it is present. If kind is absent, the kind type parameter is that of default real when a is of type integer or real, and is that of a when a is type complex. The argument a may be of type integer, real, or complex. If it is complex, the imaginary part is ignored.

8.3.2   Elemental functions that do not convert

The following are elemental functions whose result is of type and kind type parameter that are those of the first or only argument. For those having more than one argument, all arguments must have the same type and kind type parameter.

conjg (z) returns the conjugate of the complex value z.

max (a1, a2 [,a3,...]) returns the maximum of two or more integer or real values.

`min (a1, a2 [,a3,...])` returns the minimum of two or more integer or real values.

`modulo (a, p)` returns a modulo p when a and p are both integer or both real, that is `a-floor(a/p)*p` in the real case, and `a-floor(a÷p)*p` in the integer case, where ÷ represents ordinary mathematical division. If p=0, the result is processor dependent.

`sign (a, b)` returns the absolute value of a times the sign of b. The arguments a and b must be both integer or both real. If b=0, its sign is taken as positive.

8.4 Elemental mathematical functions

The following are elemental functions that evaluate elementary mathematical functions. The type and kind type parameter of the result are those of the first argument, which is usually the only argument.

`acos (x)` returns the arc cosine (inverse cosine) function value for real values x such that $|x| \leq 1$, expressed in radians in the range $0 \leq \mathrm{acos}(x) \leq \pi$.

`asin (x)` returns the arc sine (inverse sine) function value for real values x such that $|x| \leq 1$, expressed in radians in the range $-\frac{\pi}{2} \leq \mathrm{asin}(x) \leq \frac{\pi}{2}$.

`atan (x)` returns the arc tangent (inverse tangent) function value for real x, expressed in radians in the range $-\frac{\pi}{2} \leq \mathrm{atan}(x) \leq \frac{\pi}{2}$.

`atan2 (y, x)` returns the arc tangent (inverse tangent) function value for pairs of reals, x and y, of the same type and type parameter. The result is the principal value of the argument of the complex number (x, y), expressed in radians in the range $-\pi < \mathrm{atan2}(y, x) \leq \pi$. The values of x and y must not both be zero.

`cos (x)` returns the cosine function value for an argument of type real or complex that is treated as a value in radians.

`cosh (x)` returns the hyperbolic cosine function value for a real argument x.

`exp (x)` returns the exponential function value for a real or complex argument x.

`log (x)` returns the natural logarithm function for a real or complex argument x. In the real case, x must be positive. In the complex case, x must not be zero, and the imaginary part w of the result lies in the range $-\pi < w \leq \pi$.

`log10 (x)` returns the common (base 10) logarithm of a real argument whose value must be positive.

`sin (x)` returns the sine function value for a real or complex argument that is treated as a value in radians.

sinh (x) returns the hyperbolic sine function value for a real argument.

sqrt (x) returns the square root function value for a real or complex argument *x*. If *x* is real, its value must be not be negative. In the complex case, the real part of the result is not negative, and when it is zero the imaginary part of the result is not negative.

tan (x) returns the tangent function value for a real argument that is treated as a value in radians.

tanh (x) returns the hyperbolic tangent function value for a real argument.

8.5   Elemental character and logical functions

8.5.1   Character-integer conversions

The following are elemental functions for conversions from a single character to an integer, and vice-versa.

char (i) is of type character and length one. It returns the character in position *i* in the ASCII collating sequence. The value of *i* must be in the range $0 \le i \le 127$.

ichar (c) is of type default integer and returns the position of the character c in the ASCII collating sequence.

8.5.2   String-handling elemental functions

The following are elemental functions that manipulate strings. The arguments string, substring, and set are always of type character.

adjustl (string) adjusts left to return a string of the same length by removing all leading blanks and inserting the same number of trailing blanks.

adjustr (string) adjusts right to return a string of the same length by removing all trailing blanks and inserting the same number of leading blanks.

index (string, substring [,back]) has type default integer and returns the starting position of substring as a substring of string, or zero if it does not occur as a substring. If back is absent or present with value false, the starting position of the first such substring is returned; the value 1 is returned if substring has zero length. If back is present with value true, the starting position of the last such substring is returned; the value len(string)+1 is returned if substring has zero length.

len_trim(string) returns a default integer whose value is the length of string without trailing blank characters.

scan (string, set [,back]) returns a default integer whose value is the position of a character of string that is in set, or zero if there is no such character. If the logical back is absent or present with value false, the position of the leftmost such character is returned. If back is present with value true, the position of the rightmost such character is returned.

verify (string, set [,back]) returns the default integer value 0 if each character in string appears in set, or the position of a character of string that is not in set. If the logical back is absent or present with value false, the position of the left-most such character is returned. If back is present with value true, the position of the rightmost such character is returned.

8.5.3 Logical conversion

The following elemental function converts from a logical value with one kind type parameter to another.

logical (1 [,kind]) returns a logical value equal to the value of the logical 1. The value of the kind type parameter of the result is the value of kind if it is present or that of default logical otherwise. If kind is present, it must be a named constant and provide a kind type parameter that is supported on the processor.

8.6 Non-elemental string-handling functions

8.6.1 String-handling inquiry function

len (string) is an inquiry function that returns a scalar default integer holding the number of characters in string if it is scalar, or in an element of string if it is array valued. The value of string need not be defined.

8.6.2 String-handling transformational functions

There are two functions that cannot be elemental because the length type parameter of the result depends on the value of an argument.

repeat (string, ncopies) forms the string consisting of the concatenation of ncopies copies of string, where ncopies is of type integer and its value must not be negative. Both arguments must be scalar.

trim (string) returns string with all trailing blanks removed. The argument string must be scalar.

8.7   Numeric inquiry and manipulation functions

8.7.1   Models for integer and real data

The numeric inquiry and manipulation functions are defined in terms of a model set of integers and a model set of reals for each kind of integer and real data type implemented. For each kind of integer, it is the set

$$i = s \times \sum_{k=1}^{q} w_k \times r^{k-1}$$

where s is ± 1, q is a positive integer, r is an integer exceeding one (usually 2), and each w_k is an integer in the range $0 \le w_k < r$. For each kind of real, it is the set

$$x = 0$$

and

$$x = s \times b^e \times \sum_{k=1}^{p} f_k \times b^{-k}$$

where s is ± 1, p and b are integers exceeding one, e is an integer in a range $e_{min} \le e \le e_{max}$, and each f_k is an integer in the range $0 \le f_k < b$ except that f_1 is also nonzero.

Values of the parameters in these models are chosen for the processor so as best to fit the hardware with the proviso that all model numbers are representable. Note that it is quite likely that there are some machine numbers that lie outside the model. For example, many computers represent the integer $-r^q$ and the IEEE Standard for Binary Floating-point Arithmetic contains reals with $f_1 = 0$ (called denormalized numbers) and register numbers with increased precision and range.

8.7.2   Numeric inquiry functions

There are nine inquiry functions that return values from the models associated with their arguments. Each has a single argument that may be scalar or array-valued and each returns a scalar result. The value of the argument need not be defined.

digits (x), for real or integer x, returns the default integer whose value is the number of significant digits in the model that includes x, that is p or q.

epsilon (x), for real x, returns a real result with the same type parameter as x that is almost negligible compared with the value one in the model that includes x, that is b^{1-p}.

huge (x), for real or integer x, returns the largest value in the model that includes x. It has the type and type parameter of x. The value is

$$(1 - b^{-p})b^{e_{max}}$$

or

$$r^{q-1}$$

maxexponent (x), for real x, returns the default integer e_{max}, the maximum exponent in the model that includes x.

minexponent (x), for real x, returns the default integer e_{min}, the minimum exponent in the model that includes x.

precision (x), for real or complex x, returns a default integer holding the equivalent decimal precision in the model representing real numbers with the same type parameter value as x. The value is

$$\text{int}((p-1) * \log10(b)) + k,$$

where k is 1 if b is an integral power of 10 and 0 otherwise.

radix (x), for real or integer x, returns the default integer that is the base in the model that includes x, that is b or r.

range (x), for integer, real, or complex x, returns a default integer holding the equivalent decimal exponent range in the models representing integer or real numbers with the same type parameter value as x. The value is int(log10(*huge*)) for integers and

$$\text{int}(\min(\log10(huge), -\log10(tiny)))$$

for reals, where *huge* and *tiny* are the largest and smallest positive numbers in the models.

tiny (x), for real x, returns the smallest positive number

$$b^{e_{min}-1}$$

in the model that includes x. It has the type and type parameter of x.

8.7.3 Elemental functions to manipulate reals

There are seven elemental functions whose first or only argument is of type real and that return values related to the components of the model values associated with the actual value of the argument.

exponent (x) returns the default integer whose value is the exponent part e of x when represented as a model number. If x=0, the result has value zero.

fraction (x) returns a real with the same type parameter as x whose value is the fractional part of x when represented as a model number, that is $x\,b^{-e}$.

nearest (x, s) returns a real with the same type parameter as x whose value is the nearest different machine number in the direction given by the sign of the real s. The value of s must not be zero.

rrspacing (x) returns a real with the same type parameter as x whose value is the reciprocal of the relative spacing of model numbers near x, that is $| x \, b^{-e} | b^p$.

scale (x, i) returns a real with the same type parameter as x, whose value is $x \, b^i$, where b is the base in the model for x, and i is of type integer.

set_exponent (x, i) returns a real with the same type parameter as x, whose fractional part is the fractional part of the model representation of x and whose exponent part is i, that is $x \, b^{i-e}$.

spacing (x) returns a real with the same type parameter as x whose value is the absolute spacing of model numbers near x. It is b^{e-p} if x is nonzero and this result is within range; otherwise, it is tiny(x).

8.7.4   Transformational functions for kind values

There are two functions that return the least kind type parameter value that will meet a given numeric requirement. they have scalar arguments and results, so are classified as transformational.

selected_int_kind (r) returns the default integer scalar that is the kind type parameter value for an integer data type able to represent all integer values n in the range $-10^r < n < 10^r$, where r is a scalar integer. If more than one is available, a kind with least decimal exponent range is chosen (and least kind value if several have least decimal exponent range). If no corresponding kind is available, the result is -1.

selected_real_kind ([p][, r]) returns the default integer scalar that is the kind type parameter value for a real data type with decimal precision (as returned by the function precision) at least p, and decimal exponent range (as returned by the function range) at least r. If more than one is available, a kind with the least decimal precision is chosen (and least kind value if several have least decimal precision). Both p and r are scalar integers; at least one of them must be present. If no corresponding kind value is available, the result is -1 if sufficient precision is unavailable, -2 if sufficient exponent range is unavailable, and -3 if both are unavailable.

8.8   Bit manipulation procedures

There are eleven procedures for manipulating bits held within integers. They are based on those in the US Military Standard MIL-STD 1753. They differ only in that here they are elemental, where appropriate, whereas the original procedures accepted only scalar arguments.

These intrinsics are based on a model in which an integer holds s bits w_k, $k = 0, 1, \ldots, s - 1$, in a sequence from right to left, based on the non-negative value

$$\sum_{k=0}^{s-1} w_k \times 2^k$$

This model is valid only in the context of these intrinsics. It is identical to the model for integers in Section 8.7.1 when r is an integral power of 2 and $w_{s-1} = 0$, but when $w_{s-1} = 1$ the models do not correspond, and the value expressed as an integer may vary from processor to processor.

8.8.1 Inquiry function

bit_size (i) returns the number of bits in the model for bits within an integer of the same type parameter as i. The result is a scalar integer having the same type parameter as i.

8.8.2 Elemental functions

btest (i, pos) returns the default logical value true if bit pos of the integer i has value 1 and false otherwise. pos must be an integer with value in the range $0 \leq pos < bit\_size(i)$.

iand (i, j) returns the logical and of all the bits in i and corresponding bits in j, according to the truth table

i	1	1	0	0
j	1	0	1	0
iand(i, j)	1	0	0	0

The arguments i and j must have the same type parameter value, which is the type parameter value of the result.

ibclr (i, pos) returns an integer, with the same type parameter as i, and value equal to that of i except that bit pos is cleared to 0. The argument pos must be an integer with value in the range $0 \leq pos < bit\_size(i)$.

ibits (i, pos, len) returns an integer, with the same type parameter as i, and value equal to the len bits of i starting at bit pos right adjusted and all other bits zero. The arguments pos and len must be integers with non-negative values such that $pos+len \leq bit\_size(i)$.

ibset (i, pos) returns an integer, with the same type parameter as i, and value equal to that of i except that bit pos is set to 1. The argument pos must be an integer with value in the range $0 \leq pos < bit\_size(i)$.

ieor (i, j) returns the logical exclusive or of all the bits in i and corresponding bits in j, according to the truth table

i	1	1	0	0
j	1	0	1	0
ieor(i, j)	0	1	1	0

The arguments i and j must have the same type parameter value, which is the type parameter value of the result.

ior (i, j) returns the logical inclusive or of all the bits in i and corresponding bits in j, according to the truth table

i	1	1	0	0
j	1	0	1	0
ior(i, j)	1	1	1	0

The arguments i and j must have the same type parameter value, which is the type parameter value of the result.

ishft (i, shift) returns an integer, with the same type parameter as i, and value equal to that of i except that the bits are shifted shift places to the left (-shift places to the right if shift is negative). Zeros are shifted in from the other end. The argument shift must be an integer with value satisfying the inequality |shift| ≤ bit_size(i).

ishftc (i, shift [, size]) returns an integer, with the same type parameter as i, and value equal to that of i except that the size rightmost bits (or all the bits if size is absent) are shifted circularly shift places to the left (-shift places to the right if shift is negative). The argument shift must be an integer with absolute value not exceeding the value of size (or bit_size(i) if size is absent).

not (i) returns the logical complement of all the bits in i, according to the truth table

i	0	1
not(i)	1	0

8.8.3 Elemental subroutine

call mvbits (from, frompos, len, to, topos) copies the sequence of bits in from that starts at position frompos and has length len to to, starting at position topos. The other bits of to are not altered. The arguments from, frompos, len, and topos are all integers with intent in, and they must have values that satisfy the inequalities: frompos+len ≤ bit_size(from), len ≥ 0, frompos ≥ 0, topos+len ≤ bit_size(to), and topos ≥ 0. The argument to is an integer with intent inout; it must have the same kind type parameter as from. The same variable may be specified for from and to.

8.9 Vector and matrix multiplication functions

There are two transformational functions that perform vector and matrix multiplications. They each have two arguments that are both of numeric type (integer, real, or complex) or both of logical type. The result is of the same type and type parameter as for the multiply or and operation between two such scalars. The functions sum and any, used in the definitions, are defined in Section 8.10.1.

dot_product (vector_a, vector_b) requires two arguments each of rank one and the same size. If vector_a is of type integer or type real, it returns sum(vector_a * vector_b); if vector_a is of type complex, it returns sum(conjg(vector_a) * vector_b); and if vector_a is of type logical, it returns any(vector_a .and. vector_b).

matmul (matrix_a, matrix_b) performs matrix multiplication. For numeric arguments, three cases are possible:

  i) matrix_a has shape (n, m) and matrix_b has shape (m, k). The result has shape (n, k) and element (i, j) has the value sum(matrix_a(i, :) * matrix_b(:, j)).

  ii) matrix_a has shape (m) and matrix_b has shape (m, k). The result has shape (k) and element (j) has the value sum(matrix_a * matrix_b(:, j)).

  iii) matrix_a has shape (n,m) and matrix_b has shape (m). The result has shape (n) and element (i) has the value sum(matrix_a(i, :) * matrix_b).

For logical arguments, the shapes are as for numeric arguments and the values are determined by replacing 'sum' and "*" in the above expressions by 'any' and '.and.'.

8.10 Transformational functions that reduce arrays

There are seven transformational functions that perform operations on arrays such as summing their elements.

8.10.1 Single argument case

In their simplest form, these functions have a single array argument and return a scalar result. All except count have a result of the same type and type parameter as the argument.

all (mask) returns the value true if all elements of the logical array mask are true or mask has size zero, and otherwise returns the value false.

any (mask) returns the value true if any of the elements of the logical array mask is true, and returns the value false if no elements are true or if mask has size zero.

count (mask) returns the default integer value that is the number of elements of the logical array mask that have the value true.

maxval (array) returns the maximum value of an element of an integer or real array. If array has size zero, it returns the negative value of largest magnitude supported by the processor.

minval (array) returns the minimum value of an element of an integer or real array. If array has size zero, it returns the largest positive value supported by the processor.

product (array) returns the product of the elements of an integer, real, or complex array. It returns the value one if array has size zero.

sum (array) returns the sum of the elements of an integer, real, or complex array. It returns the value zero if array has size zero.

8.10.2 Optional argument dim

All these functions have an optional second argument dim that is a scalar integer. If this is present, the operation is applied to all rank-one sections that span right through dimension dim to produce an array of rank reduced by one and extents equal to the extents in the other dimensions. For example, if a is a real array of shape (4,5,6), sum(a,dim=2) is a real array of shape (4,6) and element (i, j) has value sum($a(i,:,j)$).

As the rank of the result depends on whether dim is specified, the corresponding actual argument must not itself be an optional dummy argument.

8.10.3 Optional argument mask

The functions maxval, minval, product, and sum have a third optional argument, a logical array mask. If this is present, it must have the same shape as the first argument and the operation is applied to the elements corresponding to true elements of mask; for example, sum(a, mask = a>0) sums the positive elements of the array a. The argument mask affects only the value of the function and does not affect the evaluation of arguments that are array expressions.

8.11 Array inquiry functions

There are five functions for inquiries about the bounds, shape, size and allocation status of an array of any type. Because the result depends only the array properties, the value of the array need not be defined.

8.11.1   Allocation status

allocated (array) returns a scalar default logical. When the allocatable array
array is currently allocated, the value is true; otherwise it is false. If the
allocation status of array is undefined, the result is undefined.

8.11.2   Bounds, shape, and size

The following functions enquire about the bounds of an array. In the case of an
allocatable array, it must be allocated; and in the case of a pointer, it must be
associated with a target. An array section or an array expression is taken to have
lower bounds 1 and upper bounds equal to the extents (like an assumed-shape
array with no specified lower bounds).

lbound (array [,dim]), when dim is absent, returns a rank-one default integer
array holding the lower bounds. When dim is present, it must be a scalar
integer and the result is a scalar default integer holding the lower bound
in dimension dim. As the rank of the result depends on whether dim is
specified, the corresponding actual argument must not itself be an optional
dummy argument.

shape (source) returns a rank-one default integer array holding the shape of the
array or scalar source. In the case of a scalar, the result has size zero.

size (array [,dim]) returns a scalar default integer that is the size of the array
array or extent along dimension dim if the scalar integer dim is present.

ubound (array [,dim]) is similar to lbound except that it returns upper bounds.

8.12   Array construction and manipulation functions

There are eight functions that construct or manipulate arrays of any type.

8.12.1   The merge elemental function

merge (tsource, fsource, mask) is an elemental function.   The argument
tsource may have any type and fsource must have the same type and
type parameters. The argument mask must be of type logical. The result
is tsource if mask is true and fsource otherwise.

The principal application of merge is when the three arguments are arrays
having the same shape, in which case tsource and fsource are merged under the
control of mask. Note, however, that tsource or fsource may be scalar in which
case the elemental rules effectively broadcast it to an array of the correct shape.

8.12.2   Packing and unpacking arrays

The transformational function pack packs into a rank-one array those elements
of an array that are selected by a logical array of conforming shape, and the
transformational function unpack performs the reverse operation. The elements
are taken in array element order.

pack (array, mask [,vector]), when vector is absent, returns a rank-one
array containing the elements of array corresponding to true elements of
mask in array element order; mask may be scalar with value true, in which
case all elements are selected. If vector is present, it must be a rank-one
array of the same type and type parameters as array and size at least equal
to the number t of selected elements; the result has size equal to the size n
of vector; if $t < n$, elements i of the result for $i > t$ are the corresponding
elements of vector.

unpack (vector, mask, field) returns an array of the type and type parameters of vector and shape of mask. The argument mask must be a logical
array and vector must be a rank-one array of size at least the number of
true elements of mask. The argument field must be of the same type and
type parameters as vector and must either be scalar or be of the same shape
as mask. The element of the result corresponding to the ith true element of
mask, in array-element order, is the ith element of vector; all others are
equal to the corresponding elements of field if it is an array or to field if
it is a scalar.

8.12.3   Reshaping an array

The transformational function reshape allows the shape of an array to be changed,
with possible permutation of the subscripts.

reshape (source, shape [,pad] [,order]) returns an array with shape given
by the rank-one integer array shape, and type and type parameters those
of the array source. The size of shape must be constant, and its elements
must not be negative. If pad is present it must be an array of the same type
and type parameters as source. If pad is absent or of size zero, the size
of the result must not exceed the size of source. If order is absent, the
elements of the result, in array element order, are the elements of source
in array element order followed by copies of pad in array-element order.
If order is present, it must be a rank-one integer array of the same size as
shape and with a value that is a permutation of $(1, 2, \ldots, n)$; the elements
$r(s_1, \ldots, s_n)$ of the result, taken in subscript order for the array having
elements $r(s_{\text{order}(1)}, \ldots, s_{\text{order}(n)})$, are those of source in array element
order followed by copies of pad in array-element order. For example,
if order has the value (/3,1,2/), the elements $r(1,1,1)$, $r(1,1,2)$, $\ldots$,
$r(1,1,k)$, $r(2,1,1)$, $r(2,1,2)$, $\ldots$ correspond to the elements of source
and pad in array-element order.

8.12.4 Transformational function for replication

spread (source, dim, ncopies) returns an array of type and type parameters those of source and of rank increased by one. The argument source may be scalar or array-valued. The arguments dim and ncopies are integer scalars. The result contains max(ncopies, 0) copies of source, and element $(r_1, \ldots, r_{n+1})$ of the result is source$(s_1, \ldots, s_n)$ where $(s_1, \ldots, s_n)$ is $(r_1, \ldots, r_{n+1})$ with subscript dim omitted (or source itself if it is scalar).

8.12.5 Array shifting functions

cshift (array, shift [,dim]) returns an array of the same type, type parameters, and shape as array. The argument dim is an integer scalar. If dim is omitted, it is as if it were present with the value 1. The argument shift is of type integer and must be scalar if array is of rank one. If shift is scalar, the result is obtained by shifting every rank-one section that extends across dimension dim circularly shift times. The direction of the shift depends on the sign of shift and may be determined from the case with shift=1 and array of rank one and size m, when element i of the result is array$(i+1)$, $i = 1, 2, \ldots, m - 1$ and element m is array(1). If shift is an array, it must have shape that of array with dimension dim omitted, and it supplies a separate value for each shift.

eoshift (array, shift [,boundary] [,dim]) is identical to cshift except that an end-off shift is performed and boundary values are inserted into the gaps so created. The argument boundary may be omitted when array has intrinsic type, in which case the value zero is inserted for the integer, real, and complex cases; false in the logical case; and blanks in the character case. If boundary is present, it must have the same type and type parameters as array; it may be scalar and supply all needed values or it may be an array whose shape is that of array with dimension dim omitted and supply a separate value for each shift.

8.12.6 Matrix transpose

The transpose function performs a matrix transpose for any array of rank two.

transpose (matrix) returns an array of the same type and type parameters as the rank-two array matrix. Element (i, j) of the result is matrix(j, i).

8.13 Transformational functions for geometric location

There are two transformational functions that find the locations of the maximum and minimum values of an integer or real array.

maxloc (array [,mask]) returns a rank-one default integer array of size equal
to the rank of array. Its value is the sequence of subscripts of an element
of maximum value (among those corresponding to true values of the conforming logical array mask if it is present), as though all the declared lower
bounds of array were 1. If there is more than one such element, the first in
array element order is taken.

minloc (array [,mask]) returns a rank-one default integer array of size equal
to the rank of array. Its value is the sequence of subscripts of an element
of minimum value (among those corresponding to true values of the conforming logical array mask if it is present), as though all the declared lower
bounds of array were 1. If there is more than one such element, the first in
array element order is taken.

8.14   Non-elemental intrinsic subroutines

There are four non-elemental intrinsic subroutines, which were chosen to be subroutines rather than functions because of the need to return information through
the arguments.

8.14.1   Real-time clock

There are two subroutines that return information from the real-time clock, the
first based on the ISO standard IS 8601 (Representation of dates and times). It
is assumed that there is a basic system clock that is incremented by one for each
clock count until a maximum count_max is reached and on the next count is set to
zero. Default values are returned on systems without a clock. All the arguments
have intent out.

call date_and_time ([date] [,time] [,zone] [,values]) returns the following (with default values blank or -huge(0), as appropriate, when there
is no clock):

date is a scalar character variable holding the date in the form *ccyymmdd*,
corresponding to century, year, month, and day.

time is a scalar character variable holding the time in the form *hhmmss.sss*,
corresponding to hours, minutes, seconds, and milliseconds.

zone is a scalar character variable that is set to the difference between
local time and Coordinated Universal Time (UTC, also known as
Greenwich Mean Time) in the form *Shhmm*, corresponding to sign,
hours, and minutes. For example, a processor in New York in winter
would return the value -0500.

values is a rank-one default integer array holding the sequence of values: the
year, the month of the year, the day of the month, the time difference

in minutes with respect to UTC, the hour of the day, the minutes of the hour, the seconds of the minute, and the milliseconds of the second.

call system_clock ([count][,count_rate][,count_max]) returns the following:

count is a scalar default integer holding a processor-dependent value based on the current value of the processor clock, or -huge(0) if there is no clock. On the first call, the processor may set an initial value that may be zero.

count_rate is a scalar default integer holding the number of clock counts per second, or zero if there is no clock.

count_max is a scalar default integer holding the maximum value that count may take, or zero if there is no clock.

8.14.2 Random numbers

A sequence of pseudorandom numbers is generated from a seed that is held as a rank-one array of integers. The subroutine random_number returns the pseudorandom numbers and the subroutine random_seed allows an inquiry to be made about the size or value of the seed array, and the seed to be reset. The subroutines provide a portable interface to a processor-dependent sequence.

call random_number (harvest) returns a pseudorandom number from the uniform distribution over the range $0 \le x < 1$ or an array of such numbers. harvest has intent out, may be a scalar or an array, and must be of type real.

call random_seed ([size] [,put] [,get]) has the following arguments:

size has intent out and is a scalar default integer that the processor sets to the size n of the seed array.

put has intent in and is a default integer array of rank one and size n that is used by the processor to reset the seed. A processor may set the same seed value for more than one value of put.

get has intent out and is a default integer array of rank one and size n that the processor sets to the current value of the seed.

No more than one argument may be specified; if no argument is specified, the seed is set to a processor-dependent value.

8.15 Summary

In this chapter, we introduced the four categories of intrinsic procedures, explained the intrinsic statement, and gave detailed descriptions of all the procedures. None of the procedures of Sections 8.2, 8.6.2, and 8.7 to 8.14 were present in Fortran 77 nor, within Sections 8.3 to 8.5, were any of ceiling, floor, modulo, adjustl, adjustr, len_trim, scan, verify, and logical. The function len has become an inquiry function. The remaining functions were present in Fortran 77, but in F have been generalized to handle kind type parameters (where appropriate), have become elemental, and several have additional optional arguments.

8.16 Exercises

1. Write a program to calculate the real or imaginary roots of the quadratic equation

$$ax^2 + bx + c = 0$$

for any values of a, b, and c. The program should read these three values and print the results. Use should be made of the appropriate intrinsic functions.

2. Repeat Exercise 1 of Chapter 5, avoiding the use of do constructs.

3. Given the rules explained in Sections 3.12 and 8.2, what are the values printed by the following program?

```
program main
    real, target, dimension(3:10) :: a
    real, pointer, dimension(:)   :: p1, p2
    p1 => a(3:9:2)
    p2 => a(9:3:-2)
    print *, associated(p1, p2)
    print *, associated(p1, p2(4:1:-1))
end program main
```

4. In the following program, two pointer assignments, one to an array the other to an array section, are followed by a subroutine call. Bearing in mind the rules given in Sections 3.12, 6.3, and 8.11.2, what values does the program print?

```
module mystery
public :: what
contains
    subroutine what (x, y)
        real, intent(in), dimension(:) :: x, y
        print *, lbound (x), lbound (y)
    end subroutine what
end module mystery
program main
    use mystery
    real, target, dimension(5:10)  :: a
    real, pointer, dimension(:)    :: p1, p2
    p1 => a
    p2 => a(:)
    print *, lbound (a), lbound (a(:))
    print *, lbound (p1), lbound (p2)
    call what (a, a(:))
end program main
```

9. Data transfer

9.1 Introduction

The F language has, in comparison with most other high-level programming languages, a particularly rich set of facilities for input/output (I/O). However, I/O is an area of F into which not all programmers need to delve very deeply. For most small-scale programs it is sufficient to know how to read a few data records containing input variables, and how to transmit to a terminal or printer the results of a calculation. In large-scale data processing, on the other hand, the programs often have to deal with huge streams of data to and from many disc, tape, and cartridge files; in these cases it is essential that great attention be paid to the way in which the I/O is designed and coded, as otherwise both the execution time and the real time spent in the program can suffer dramatically. The term *file* is used for a collection of data on one of these devices and a file is always organized into a sequence of *records*.

This chapter begins by discussing the various forms of formatted I/O, that is I/O which deals with records that do not use the internal number representation of the computer, but rather a character string which can be displayed for visual inspection by the human eye. It is also the form usually needed for transmitting data between different kinds of computers. The so-called *edit descriptors*, which are used to control the translation between the internal number representation and the external format, are then explained. Finally, the topics of unformatted (or binary) I/O and direct-access files are covered.

9.2 Number conversion

The ways in which numbers are stored internally by a computer are the concern of neither the F language nor this book. However, if we wish to output values – to display them on a terminal or to print them – then their internal representations must be converted into a character string which can be read in a normal way. For instance, the contents of a given computer word may be (in hexadecimal) be1d7dbf and correspond to the value -0.000450. For our particular purpose, we may wish to display this quantity as, say, -4.5E-04. The conversion from the internal representation to the external form is carried out according to the information specified by an edit descriptor contained in a *format specification*.

These will both be dealt with fully later in this chapter; for the moment, it is sufficient to give a few examples. For instance, to print an integer value in a field of 10 characters width, we would use the edit descriptor i10, where i stands for integer conversion, and 10 specifies the width of the output field. To print a real quantity in a field of 10 characters, five of which are reserved for the fractional part of the number, we specify f10.5. The edit descriptor f stands for floating-point (real) conversion, 10 is the total width of the output field and 5 is the width of the fractional part of the field. If the number given above were to be converted according to this edit descriptor, it would appear as *bb*-0.00045, where *b* represents a blank. To print a character variable in a field of 10 characters, we would specify a10, where a stands for alphanumeric conversion.

A format specification consists of a list of edit descriptors enclosed in parentheses, and is coded as a character expression, for instance

```
"(i10, f10.3, a10)"
```

To print the scalar variables j, b, and c, of types integer, real, and character respectively, we may then write

```
print "(i10, f10.3, a10)", j,b,c
```

The part of the statement designating the quantities to be printed is known as the *output list* and forms the subject of the following section.

9.3   I/O lists

The quantities to be read or written by a program are specified in an I/O list. For output, they may be expressions but for input must be variables. Examples are shown in Figure 9.1, where we note the use of a *repeat count* in front of those edit descriptors that are required repeatedly. A repeat count must be a positive integer literal constant and not have a kind type parameter. Function references are permitted in an I/O list, provided they do not themselves cause further I/O to occur.

Figure 9.1

```
integer              :: i
real, dimension(10) :: a
character(len=20)    :: word
print "(i10)",      i
print "(10f10.3)", a
print "(3f10.3)",  a(1),a(2),a(3)
print "(a10)",     word(5:14)
print "(2f10.3)",  a(1)*a(2)+i, sqrt(a(3))
```

In all these examples, except the last one, the expressions consist of single variables and would be equally valid in input statements using the read statement, for example

```
read "(i10)", i
```

Such statements may be used to read values which are then assigned to the variables in the input list.

If an array appears as an item, it is treated as if the elements were specified in array element order. For example, the third of the print statements in Figure 9.1 could have been written

```
print "(3f10.3)", a(1:3)
```

However, no element of the array may appear more than once in an input item. Thus, the case in Figure 9.2 is not allowed.

Figure 9.2

```
        integer, dimension(10) :: j
        integer, dimension(3)  :: k
        :
        k = (/ 1, 2, 1 /)
        read "(3i10)", j(k)      ! Illegal because j(1) appears twice
```

If an allocatable array appears as an item, it must be currently allocated.

Any pointers in an I/O list must be associated with a target, and transfer takes place between the file and the targets.

An item of derived type is treated as if the components were specified in the same order as in the type declaration. This rule is applied repeatedly for components of derived type, so that it is as if we specified the list of items of intrinsic type that constitute its ultimate components. For example, if p and t are of the types point and triangle of Figure 2.1, the statement

```
read "(8f10.5)", p, t
```

has the same effect as the statement

```
read "(8f10.5)", p%x, p%y, t%a%x, t%a%y, t%b%x,          &
                 t%b%y, t%c%x, t%c%y
```

Each ultimate component must be accessible (not, for example, be a private component of a public type).

An object in an I/O list is not permitted to be of a derived type that has a pointer component at any level of component selection. One reason for this restriction is because of the problems associated with recursive data structures. For example, supposing chain is a data object of the type entry of Figure 2.3 (in Section 2.13) and is set up to hold a chain of length three, then it has as its ultimate components `chain%i`, `chain%next%i`, `chain%next%next%i`, and `chain%next%next%next`, the last of which is a disassociated pointer.

Note that a zero-sized array may occur as an item in an I/O list. Such an item corresponds to no actual data transfer.

9.4 Format definition

In the `print` and `read` statements of the previous section, the format specification was given each time in the form of a character constant immediately following the keyword. In fact, there are two ways in which a format specification may be given. They are:

i) As a character expression whose value commences with a format specification in parentheses:

```
character(len=*), parameter :: form="(f10.3)"
:
print form, q
```

or

```
character(len=1), dimension(7), save :: carray=      &
                 (/ "(","f","1","0",".","3",")" /)
:
print carray, q ! Elements of an array expression
                ! are concatenated.
```

or

```
character(len=4), dimension(10) :: carr1
character(len=3), dimension(10) :: carr2
integer         :: i, j
:
carr1(10) = "(f10"
carr2(3) = ".3)"
:
i = 10
j = 3
:
print carr1(i)//carr2(j), q
```

or, simply,

```
print "(f10.3)", q
```

From these examples it may be seen that it is possible to program formats in a flexible way, and particularly that it is possible to use arrays, expressions and also substrings in a way which allows a given format to be built up dynamically at execution-time from various components. Only spaces are permitted to follow the trailing right parenthesis. In the case of an array, its elements are concatenated in array element order. However, on input *no* component of the format specification may appear also in the input list, or be associated with it. This is because the whole format specification is required to be established *before* any I/O takes place. Further, no redefinition or undefinition of any characters of the format is permitted during the execution of the I/O statement.

ii) As an asterisk. This is a type of I/O known as *list-directed* I/O, in which the format is defined by the computer system at the moment the statement is executed, depending on both the type and magnitude of the entities involved. This facility is particularly useful for the input and output of small quantities of values, especially in temporary code which is used for test purposes, and which is removed from the final version of the program:

```
print *, "Square-root of q = ", sqrt(q)
```

This example outputs a character constant describing the expression which is to be output, followed by the value of the expression under investigation. On the terminal screen, this might appear as

```
Square-root of q = 4.392246
```

the exact format being dependent on the computer system used. Except for adjacent strings, values are separated by spaces or commas. Logical data are represented as T for true and F for false. The processor may represent a sequence of r identical values c by the form $r * c$. Further details of list-directed input/output are deferred until Section 9.9.

Blank characters are permitted as follows within a format specification with no effect on the interpretation: either side of a comma, either side of a parenthesis, after a repeat count (Section 9.11.1), or before a tab count (Section 9.11.3). They are not permitted elsewhere.

9.5 Unit numbers

Input/output operations are used to transfer data between the storage of an executing program and an external medium. There are many types of external media: the terminal, printer, disc drive, and magnetic cartridge are perhaps the most familiar. Whatever the device, an F program regards each one from which it reads or to which it writes as a *unit*, and each unit, with two exceptions, has associated with it a *unit number*. This number must not be negative and is often in the range 1 to 99. Thus we might associate with a disc drive from which we are reading the unit number 10, and to a magnetic cartridge drive to which we are writing the unit number 11. All program units of an executable program that refer to a particular unit number are referencing the same file.

There are two I/O statements, print and a variant of read, that do not reference any unit number; these are the statements that we have used so far in examples, for the sake of simplicity. A read statement without a unit number will normally expect to read from the terminal, unless the program is working in batch (non-interactive) mode in which case there will be a disc file with a reserved name from which it reads. A print statement will normally expect to output to the terminal, unless the program is in batch mode in which case another disc file with a reserved name will be used. Such files are usually suitable for subsequent output on a physical output device. The system may implicitly associate unit numbers with these default units.

Apart from these two special cases, all I/O statements must refer explicitly to a unit in order to identify the device to which or from which data are to be transferred. The unit may be given in one of three forms. These are shown in the following examples which use another form of the read containing a unit specifier, unit=u, and format specifier, fmt=fmt, in parentheses and separated by a comma, where *fmt* is a format specification as described in the previous section:

```
read (unit=u, fmt=fmt) list
```

The three forms of u are:

i) As a scalar integer expression that gives the unit number:

```
read (unit=4,      fmt="(f10.3)") q
read (unit=nunit, fmt="(f10.3)") q
read (unit=4*i+j, fmt="(f10.3)") a
```

where the value may be any nonnegative integer allowed by the system for this purpose.

ii) As an asterisk:

```
read (unit=*, fmt="(f10.3)") q
```

where the asterisk implies the standard input unit designated by the system, the same as that used for read without a unit number.

iii) As a character variable identifying an *internal file* (see next section).

9.6   Internal files

Internal files allow format conversion between various representations to be carried out by the program in a storage area defined within the program itself. There are two particularly useful applications, one to read data whose format is not properly known in advance, and the other to prepare output lists containing mixed character and numerical data, all of which has to be prepared in character form, perhaps to be displayed as a caption on a graphics display. The first application will now be described; the second will be dealt with in Section 9.8.

Imagine that we have to read a string of 30 digits, which might correspond to 30 one-digit integers, 15 two-digit integers or 10 three-digit integers. The information as to which type of data is involved is given by the value of an additional digit, which has the value 1, 2, or 3, depending on the number of digits each integer contains. An internal file provides us with a mechanism whereby the 30 digits can be read into a character buffer area. The value of the final digit can be tested separately, and 30, 15, or 10 values read from the internal file, depending on this value. The basic code to achieve this might read as follows (no error recovery or data validation is included, for simplicity):

```
integer, dimension(30)          :: ival
integer                         :: key
character(len=30)               :: buffer
character(len=6), dimension(3), parameter ::  &
                     form=(/ "(30i1)", "(15i2)","(10i3)" /)
read (unit=*, fmt="(a30,i1)")        buffer, key
read (unit=buffer, fmt=form (key)) ival (1:30/key)
```

Here, ival is an array which will receive the values, buffer a character variable of a length sufficient to contain the 30 input digits, and form a character array containing the three possible formats to which the input data might correspond. The first read statement reads 30 digits into buffer as character data, and a final digit into the integer variable key. The second read statement reads the data from buffer into ival, using the appropriate conversion as specified by the edit descriptor selected by key. After execution of this code, ival will contain 30/key values, their number and exact format not having been known in advance.

If an internal file is a scalar, it has a single record whose length is that of the scalar. If it is an array, its elements, in array element order, are treated as successive records of the file and each has length that of an array element. It may not be an array section with a vector subscript.

A record becomes defined when it is written. The number of characters sent must not exceed the length of the record. It may be less, in which case the rest of the record is padded with blanks. A record may be read only if it is defined (which need not only be by an output statement). Records are padded with blanks, if necessary.

An internal file is always positioned at the beginning of its first record prior to data transfer (the array section notation may be used to start elsewhere in an array). Of course, if an internal file is an allocatable array or pointer, it must be allocated or associated with a target. Also, no item in the input/output list may be in the file or associated with the file.

An internal file may be used for list-directed I/O (Section 9.9).

9.7   Formatted input

In the previous sections we have given complete descriptions of the ways that formats and units may be specified, using simplified forms of the read and print statements as examples. There are, in fact, two forms of the formatted read statement. Without a unit, it has the form

> read *fmt* [,*list*]

and with a unit it may take the form

> read (unit=*u*, fmt=*fmt* [,iostat=*ios*]) [*list*]

where *u* and *fmt* are the unit and format specifiers described in Sections 9.4 and 9.5; iostat= is an optional specifier which allows a user to specify how a read statement shall recover from various exceptional conditions; and *list* is a list of variables. The keyword items may be specified in any order, although the order given above is usual.

For simplicity of exposition, we have so far limited ourselves to formats that correspond to a single record in the file, but we will meet later in this chapter cases that lead to the input of a part of a record or of several successive records.

If the optional iostat= specifier is specified, then *ios* must be a scalar integer variable of default kind which, after execution of the read statement, has a negative value if an endfile condition was detected on the input device (Section 10.2.3), a positive value if an error was detected (for instance a parity error), or the value zero otherwise. The actual values assigned to *ios* in the event of an exception occurring are not defined by the standard, only the signs. If an exception occurs, execution will stop unless iostat is specified. An example of a read statement with its associated error recovery is given in Figure 9.3, in which error is a subroutine to deal with the exceptions. It will normally be system dependent.

Figure 9.3

```
      read (unit=nunit, fmt="(3f10.3)", iostat=ios) a,b,c
      if (ios == 0) then
   !    Successful read - continue execution.
      :
      :
   !
      else
   !    Error condition - take appropriate action.
         call error (ios)
      end if
      :
```

It is a good practice to include some sort of error recovery in all read statements which are included permanently in a program. On the other hand, input for test purposes is normally sufficiently well handled by the simple form of read without unit number, and without error recovery.

9.8 Formatted output

There are two types of formatted output statements, the print statement which has appeared in many of the examples so far in this chapter, and the write statement whose syntax is similar to that of the read statement:

> print *fmt* [,*list*]

and

> write (unit=*u*, fmt=*fmt* [,iostat=*ios*]) [*list*]

where all the components have the same meanings as described for the read statement (Section 9.7). An asterisk for *u* specifies the standard output unit, as used by print. If an error condition occurs on output, execution of the statement terminates and the file position becomes indeterminate.

An example of a write statement is

> write (unit=nout, fmt="(10f10.3)", iostat=ios) a

An example using an internal file is given in Figure 9.4, which builds a character string from numeric and character components. The final character string might be passed to another subroutine for output, for instance as a caption on a graphics display.

Figure 9.4

```
integer            :: day
real               :: cash
character(len=50)  :: line
  :
!   write into line
write (unit=line, fmt="(a, i2, a, f8.2, a)")                    &
      "Takings for day ", day, " are ", cash, " dollars"
```

In this example, we declare a character variable that is long enough to contain the text to be transferred to it. (The write statement contains a format specification with a edit descriptors without a field width. These assume a field width corresponding to the actual length of the character strings to be converted.) After execution of the write statement, line might contain the character string

> Takings for day 3 are 4329.15 dollars

and this could be used as a string for further processing.

The number of characters written to line must not exceed its length.

9.9　List-directed I/O

In Section 9.4, the list-directed output facility using an asterisk as format specifier was introduced. We assumed that the list was short enough to fit into a single record, but for long lists the processor is free to output several records. Character constants may be split between records, and complex constants that are as long as, or longer than, a record may be split after the comma that separates the two parts. Apart from these cases, a value always lies within a single record. For historical reasons (control of line and page feeds on line printers), the first character of each record is blank. Note that when a character constant is continued, the first character of the continuation record is blank. The only blanks permitted in a numeric constant are within a split complex constant after the comma.

This facility is equally useful for input, especially of small quantities of test data. On the input record, the various constants may appear in any of their usual forms, just as if they were being read under the usual edit descriptors, as defined in Section 9.11. Exceptions are that complex values must be enclosed in parentheses, character constants may be delimited, a blank must not occur except in a delimited character constant or in a complex constant before or after a numeric field, and the optional characters which are allowed in a logical constant (those other than t and f, see Section 9.11.2) must include neither a comma nor a slash.

Character constants that are enclosed quotation marks may be spread over as many records as necessary to contain them, except that a doubled quotation mark must not be split between records. Delimiters may be omitted for a character constant if

- it is of nonzero length;

- the constant does not contain a blank, comma, or slash;

- it is contained in one record;

- the first character is neither a quotation mark nor (for compatibilty with Fortran 90) an apostrophe; and

- the leading characters are not numeric followed by an asterisk.

In this case, the constant is terminated when a blank, comma, slash, or end of record is encountered, and quotation marks appearing within the constant must not be doubled.

Whenever a character value has a different length from the corresponding list item, the value is truncated or padded on the right with blanks, as in the character assignment statement.

It is possible to use a repeat count for a given constant, for example 6*10 to specify six occurrences of the integer value 10.

The (optionally repeated) constants are separated in the input by *separators*. A separator is one of the following, appearing other than in a character constant:

- a comma, optionally preceded and optionally followed by one or more contiguous blanks,

- a slash (/), optionally preceded and optionally followed by one or more contiguous blanks, or

- one or more contiguous blanks between two non-blank values or following the last non-blank value.

An end of record not within a character constant is regarded as a blank and, therefore, forms part of a separator. A blank embedded in a complex constant or delimited character constant is not a separator. An input record may be terminated by a slash separator, in which case all the following values in the record are ignored, and the input statement terminates.

If there are no values between two successive separators, or between the beginning of the first record and the first separator, this is taken to represent a *null value* and the corresponding item in the input list is left unchanged, defined or undefined as the case may be. A null value must not be used for the real or imaginary part of a complex constant, but a single null value may be used for the whole complex value. A series of null values may be represented by a repeat count without a constant: ,6*, . When a slash separator is encountered, null values are given to any remaining list items.

An example of this form of the read statement is:

```
integer                  :: i
real                     :: a
complex, dimension(2) :: field
logical                  :: flag
character(len=12)        :: title
character(len=4)         :: word
:
read *, i, a, field, flag, title, word
```

If this reads the input record

10*b*6.4*b*(1.0,0.0)*b*(2.0,0.0)*btbt*test/

(in which *b* stands for a blank, and blanks are used as separators), then i, a, field, flag, and title will acquire the values 10, 6.4, (1.0,0.0) and (2.0,0.0), .true. and test respectively, while word remains unchanged. For the input records

10,0.64e1,2*,.true.
"histogram*b*10"/val1

(in which commas are used as separators), the variables i, a, flag, and title will acquire the values 10, 6.4, .true., and histogram*b*10 respectively. The variables field and word remain unchanged, and the input string val1 is ignored as it follows a slash. (Note the quotation marks, which are required as the string contains a blank. Without delimiters, this string would appear to be a string followed by the integer value 10.) Because of this slash, the read statement does not continue with the next record and the list is thus not fully satisfied.

9.10   Non-advancing I/O

So far we have considered each read or write statement to perform the input or output of a complete record. There are, however, many applications, especially in screen management, where this would become an irksome restriction. What is required is the ability to read and write without always advancing the file position to ahead of the next record. This facility is provided by *non-advancing* I/O. To gain access to this facility, the optional advance= specifier must appear in the read or write statement and be associated with a scalar character expression *advance* which evaluates, after suppression of any trailing blanks and conversion of any upper-case letters to lower case, to the value no. The only other allowed value is yes which is the default value if the specifier is absent; in this case normal (advancing) I/O occurs.

An optional specifier is available for a non-advancing read statement:

> size=*size*

where *size* is a default integer scalar variable.

An advancing I/O statement always repositions the file after the last record accessed, but a non-advancing I/O statement performs no such repositioning and may therefore leave the file positioned within a record. If a non-advancing input statement attempts to transfer data from beyond the end of the *current* record, an end-of-record condition occurs. The iostat variable, if present, will then acquire a different negative value to the one indicating an end-of-file condition. In order to provide a means of controlling this process, the size= specifier, when present, sets *size* to the number of characters actually read. A full example is thus

```
character(len=3) :: key
integer          :: u, s, ios
  :
read(unit=u, fmt="(a3)", advance="no", size=s, iostat=ios) key
if (ios == 0) then
   :
else
! key is not in one record
   key(s+1:) = ""
   :
end if
```

As for error and end-of-file conditions, the program terminates when an end-of-record condition occurs if iostat= is not specified.

If encountering an end-of-record on reading results in the input list not being satisfied, blanks will be inserted as padding but not included in the size= count.

It is possible to perform normal and non-advancing I/O on the same record or file. For instance, a non-advancing read might read the first few characters of a record and a normal read the remainder.

A particular application of this facility is to write a prompt to a terminal screen and to read from the next character position on the screen without an intervening line-feed:

```
write (unit=*, fmt="(a)", advance="no")          &
                          "enter next prime number:"
read  (unit=*, fmt="(i10)") prime_number
```

Non-advancing I/O may be performed only on an external file, and may not be used for list-directed I/O. Note that, as for advancing input/output, several records may be processed by a single statement.

9.11   Edit descriptors

In the description of the possible forms of a format specification in Section 9.4, a few examples of the edit descriptors were given. As mentioned there, edit descriptors give a precise specification of how values are to be converted into a character string on an output device or internal file, or converted from a character string on an input device or internal file to internal representations.

Edit descriptors in a list are separated by commas, and only in the case where an input/output list is empty or specifies only zero-sized arrays may there be no edit descriptor at all in the format specification.

9.11.1   Repeat counts

Edit descriptors fall into two classes: *data* and *control*. The data edit descriptors may be preceded by a repeat count (a nonzero unsigned default integer literal constant), as in the example

```
10f12.3
```

Of the remaining edit descriptors, only the slash edit descriptor (Section 9.11.3) may have an associated repeat count. A repeat count may be applied to a group of edit descriptors, enclosed in parentheses:

```
print "(3(i5,f8.2))", i(1), a(1), i(2), a(2), i(3), a(3)
```

(for integer i and real a). This is equivalent to writing

```
print "(i5,f8.2,i5,f8.2,i5,f8.2)",i(1),a(1),i(2),a(2),i(3),a(3)
```

Repeat counts such as this may be nested:

```
print "(2(2i5,2f8.2))", i(1),i(2),a(1),a(2),i(3),i(4),a(3),a(4)
```

If a format specification without components in parentheses is used with an I/O list that contains more elements than the number of edit descriptors, taking account of repeat counts, then a new record will begin, and the format specification repeated. Further records begin in the same way until the list is exhausted. To print an array of 100 integer elements, 10 elements to a line, the following statement might be used:

```
print "(10i8)", (/ (i(j), j=1,100) /)
```

Similarly, when reading from an input file, new records would be read until the list is satisfied, a new record being taken from the input file each time the specification is repeated *even if the individual records contain more input data than specified by the format specification*. These superfluous data would be ignored. For example, reading the two records (*b* again stands for a blank)

```
bbb10bbb15bbb20
bbb25bbb30bbb35
```

under control of the read statement

```
    read "(2i5)", i,j,k,l
```

would result in the four integer variables i, j, k and l acquiring the values 10, 15, 25 and 30, respectively.

If a format contains components in parentheses, as in

```
    "(2i5, 3(i2,2(i1,i3)), 2(2f8.2,i2))"
```

whenever the format is exhausted, a new record is taken and format control reverts to the repeat factor preceding the left parenthesis corresponding to the last-but-one right parenthesis, here 2(2f8.2,i2), or to the parenthesis itself if it has no repeat factor. This we call *reversion*.

9.11.2   Data edit descriptors

For all the numeric edit descriptors, if the output field is too narrow to contain the number to be output, it is filled with asterisks. Embedded blanks in numeric input fields are treated as null characters which are squeezed out by moving the other characters in the input field to the right, and adding leading blanks to the field. If the field is totally blank, it is treated as zero.

Integer values may be converted by means of the i edit descriptor. This comes in a basic form, iw, which defines the width of a field, w, a nonzero unsigned default integer literal constant. The integer value will be read from or written to this field, adjusted to its right-hand side. If we again designate a blank position by *b* then the value −99 printed under control of the edit descriptor i5 will appear as *bb*-99, the sign counting as one position in the field.

For output, an alternative form of this edit descriptor allows the number of digits which are to be printed to be specified exactly, even if some are leading zeros.

The form i$w.m$ specifies the width of the field, w, and that at least m digits are to be output, where m is an unsigned default integer literal constant. The value 99 printed under control of the edit descriptor i5.3 would appear as bb099. The value of m is even permitted to be zero, but the field will be then filled with asterisks unless the value printed is 0. On input, i$w.m$ is interpreted in exactly the same way as iw.

Real values may be converted by either es or f edit descriptors. The f descriptor we have met in earlier examples. Its general form is f$w.d$, where w and d are unsigned default integer literal constants which define, respectively, the field width and the number of digits to appear after the decimal point in the output field. The decimal point counts as one position in the field. On input, if the input string has a decimal point, the value of d is ignored. Reading the input string b9.3729b with the edit descriptor f8.3 would cause the value 9.3729 to be transferred. All the digits are used, but roundoff may be inevitable because of the actual physical storage reserved for the value on the computer being used.

There are, in addition, two other forms of input string that are acceptable to the f edit descriptor. The first is an optionally signed string of digits without a decimal point. In this case, the d rightmost digits will be taken to be the fractional part of the value. Thus b-14629 read under control of the edit descriptor f7.2 will transfer the value -146.29. The second form is the standard default real form of literal constant, as defined in Section 2.6.2, and the variant in which the exponent is signed and e is omitted. In this case, the d part of the descriptor is again ignored. Thus the value 14.629e-2 (or 14.629-2), under control of the edit descriptor f9.1, will transfer the value 0.14629. The exponent letter may also be E, d, or D.

Values are rounded on output following the normal rules of arithmetic. Thus, the value 10.9336, when output under control of the edit descriptor f8.3, will appear as bb10.934, and under the control of f4.0 as b11.

The es (*scientific*) edit descriptor has two forms, es$w.d$ and es$w.dee$, and is more appropriate for numbers with a magnitude below about 0.01, or above 1000. The rules for these two forms for input are identical to those for the f$w.d$ edit descriptor. For output with the es$w.d$ form of the descriptor, a different character string will be transferred, containing a significand and an exponent field of four characters that consists of either E followed by a sign and two digits or of a sign and three digits. The absolute value of a nonzero significand is greater than or equal to 1 and less than 10. Thus, the value 0.0217 transferred under an es9.2 edit descriptor would appear as 2.17E-02 or 2.17-002. The form containing the exponent letter E is not used if the magnitude of the exponent exceeds 99. For instance, es10.4 would cause the value 1.234×10^{-150} to be transferred as the string b1.234-150.

In the second form of the es edit descriptor, es$w.dee$, e is an unsigned, nonzero default integer literal constant that determines the number of digits to appear in the exponent field. This form is obligatory for exponents whose magnitude is greater than 999. Thus the value 1.234×10^{1234} with the edit descriptor es12.4e4 is transferred as the string b1.234E+1234. An increasing number of computers are able to deal with these very large exponent ranges.

Complex values may be edited under control of pairs of f or es edit descriptors. The two descriptors do not need to be identical. The complex value (0.1,100.0) converted under control of f6.1,es8.1 would appear as *bbb*0.1*b*1.0E+02. The two descriptors may be separated by control edit descriptors (to be described in Section 9.11.3)

Logical values may be edited using the l*w* edit descriptor. This defines a field of width *w* which on input consists of optional blanks, optionally followed by a decimal point, followed by t or f (or T or F), optionally followed by additional characters. Thus a field defined by l7 permits the strings .true. and .false. to be input. The characters t or f will be transferred as the values true or false respectively. On output, the character T or F will appear in the right-most position in the output field.

Character values may be edited using the a edit descriptor in one of its two forms, either a or a*w*. In the first of the two forms, the width of the input or output field is determined by the actual width of the item in the I/O list. Thus, a character variable of length 10, containing the value STATEMENTS, when written under control of the a edit descriptor would appear in a field 10 characters wide. If, however, the first variable were converted under an a11 edit descriptor, it would be printed with a leading blank, *b*STATEMENTS. Under control of a8, the eight left-most characters only would be written: STATEMEN.

Conversely, with the same variable on input, an a11 edit descriptor would cause the 10 right-most characters in the 11 character-wide input field to be transferred: *b*STATEMENTS would be transferred as STATEMENTS. The a8 edit descriptor would cause the eight characters in the field to be transferred to the eight left-most positions in the variable, and the remaining two would be filled with blanks: STATEMEN would be transferred as STATEMEN*bb*.

Finally, values of *derived types* are edited by the appropriate sequence of edit descriptors corresponding to the intrinsic types of the ultimate components of the derived type. An example is:

```
type, public :: string
    integer   :: length
    character(len=20) :: word
end type string
type(string) :: text
read(unit=*, fmt="(i2, a)") text
```

9.11.3   Control edit descriptors

It is sometimes necessary to give other instructions to an I/O device than just the width of fields and how the contents of these fields are to be interpreted. For instance, it may be that one wishes to position fields at certain columns or to start a new record without issuing a new write command. For this type of purpose, the control edit descriptors provide a means of informing the processor which action has to be taken. Some of these edit descriptors contain information that is used as it is processed; one is like a switch which changes the conditions under which I/O takes place from the point where it is encountered, until the end of the processing of the I/O statement containing it (including reversions, Section 9.11.1). This latter descriptor we shall deal with first.

Control edit descriptors setting conditions

Negative numerical values are always written with **leading signs** on output. For positive quantities other than exponents, whether the signs are written depends on the processor. The ss (sign suppress) edit descriptor suppresses leading plus signs, that is the value 99 printed by i5 is *bbb*99 and 1.4 is printed by es10.2 as *bb*1.40E+00. To switch on plus sign printing, the sp (sign print) edit descriptors may be used: the same numbers written by sp,i5,es10.2 become *bb*+99 and *b*+1.40E+00. The s edit descriptor restores the option to the processor. An ss, sp, or s will remain in force for the remainder of the format specification, unless another ss, sp, or s edit descriptor is met. These edit descriptors provide complete control over sign printing, and are useful for producing coded outputs which have to be compared automatically, on two different computers.

Control edit descriptors for immediate processing

Tabulation in an input or output field can be achieved using the edit descriptors tn, tr$n$, and tl$n$, where n is a positive default integer literal constant. These state, respectively, that the next part of the I/O should begin at position n in the current record (where the *left tab limit* is position 1), or at n positions to the right of the current position, or at n positions to the left of the current position (the left tab limit if the current position is less than or equal to n). Let us suppose that, following an advancing read, we read an input record *bb*9876 with the following statement:

```
read (unit=*, fmt="(t3, i4, tl4, i1, i2)") i, j, k
```

The format specification will move a notional pointer firstly to position 3, whence i will be read. The variable i will acquire the value 9876, and the notional pointer is then at position 7. The edit descriptor tl4 moves it left four positions, back to position 3. The quantities j and k are then read, and they acquire the values 9 and 87, respectively. These edit descriptors cause replacement on output, or multiple reading of the same items in a record on input. On output, any gaps ahead of the last character actually written are filled with spaces.

If the current record is the first one processed by the I/O statement and follows non-advancing I/O that left the file positioned within a record, the next character is the left tab limit; otherwise, the first character of the record is the left tab limit.

The t edit descriptor never causes replacement of a character already in an output record, but merely cause a change in the position within the record such that such a replacement might be caused by a subsequent edit descriptor.

New records may be started at any point in a format specification by means of the slash (/) edit descriptor. This edit descriptor, although described here, may in fact have repeat counts; to skip, say, three records one can write either /,/,/ or 3/. On input, a new record will be started each time a / is encountered, even if the contents of the current record have not all been transferred. Reading the two records

        *bbb*99*bbb*10
        *bb*100*bbb*11

with the statement

        read "(i5,i3,/,i5,i3,i2)", i, j, k, l, m

will cause the values 99, 0, 100, 0 and 11 to be transferred to the five integer variables, respectively.

The result of writing with a format containing a sequence of, say, four slashes, as represented by

        print "(i5,4/,i5)", i, j

is to separate the two values by three blank records (the last slash starts the record containing j); if i and j have the values 99 and 100, they would appear as

        *bbb*99
        b
        b
        b
        *bb*100

A slash edit descriptor written to an internal file will cause the following values to be written to the next element of the character array specified for the file. Each such element corresponds to a record, and the number of characters written to a record must not exceed its length.

Colon editing is a means of terminating format control if there are no further items in an I/O list. Consider the following output statement, for an integer array l:

        print "(i5, :, /, i5, :, /, i5)", (/ (l(i), i=1,n) /)

If n has the value 3, then three values are printed on separate lines. If n has the value 1 then, without the colons, one value would be printed followed by a blank line:

        59
        b

The colon, however, stops the processing of the format, so that this blank line is not printed. It has no effect if there are further items in the I/O list.

9.12   Unformatted I/O

The whole of this chapter has so far dealt with formatted I/O. The internal representation of a value may differ from the external form, which is always a character string contained in an input or output record. The use of formatted I/O involves an overhead for the conversion between the two forms, and often a roundoff error too. There is also the disadvantage that the external representation usually occupies more space on a storage medium than the internal representation. These three actual or potential drawbacks are all absent when unformatted I/O is used. In this form, the internal representation of a value is written exactly as it stands to the storage medium, and can be read back directly with neither roundoff nor conversion overhead. Here, a value of derived type is treated as a whole and is not equivalent to a list of its ultimate components. This is another reason for the rule (Section 9.3) that it must not have a pointer component at any level of component selection.

This type of I/O should be used in all cases where the records are generated by a program on one computer, to be read back on the same computer or another computer using the same internal number representations. Only when this is not the case, or when the data have to be visualized in one form or another, should formatted I/O be used. The records of a file must all be formatted or all be unformatted (apart from the endfile record).

Unformatted I/O has the incidental advantage of being simpler to program since no complicated format specifications are required. The forms of the read and write statements are the same as for formatted I/O, but without any fmt= specifier:

```
read(unit=4) q
write(unit=nout, iostat=ios) a
```

Non-advancing I/O is not available (in fact, an advance= specifier is not allowed).

Each read or write statement transfers exactly one record. The file must be an external file. The number of values specified by the input list of a read statement must not exceed the number of values available in the current record.

On output to a file connected for sequential access, a record of sufficient length is created. On input, the type and type parameters of each entity in the list must agree with those of the value in the record, except that two reals may correspond to one complex when all three have the same kind parameter.

9.13   Direct-access files

The only type of file organization that we have so far dealt with is the sequential file, which has a beginning and an end, and which contains a sequence of records, one after the other. F permits another type of file organization known as *direct access* (or sometimes as random access or indexed). All the records have the same length, each record is identified by an index number, and it is possible to write, read, or re-write any specified record without regard to position. (In a sequential file, only the last record may be rewritten without losing other records; in general, records in sequential files cannot be replaced.) The records are either all formatted or all unformatted.

By default, any file used by a F program is a sequential file, unless declared to be direct access. This declaration has to be made using the access="direct" and recl=*rl* specifiers of the open statement, which is described in the next chapter, (*rl* is the length of a record in the file). Once this declaration has been made, reading and writing, whether formatted or unformatted, proceeds as described for sequential files, except for the addition of a rec=*i* specifier to the read and write statements, where *i* is a scalar integer expression whose value is the index number of the record concerned. Usually, a data transfer statement for a direct-access file accesses a single record, but during formatted I/O any slash edit descriptor increases the record number by one and causes processing to continue at the beginning of this record. A sequence of statements to write, read, and replace a given record is given in Figure 9.5.

Figure 9.5

```
      integer, parameter :: nunit=2, length=100
      real, dimension(length)        :: a
      real, dimension(length+1:2*length) :: b
      integer                        :: i, rec_length
      :
      inquire (iolength=rec_length) a       ! See Section 10.5
      open (unit=nunit, access="direct", recl=rec_length, &
                  status="scratch", action="readwrite")
                                      ! See Section 10.3
      :
  !   Write array b to direct-access file in record 14
      write (unit=nunit, rec=14) b
      :
  !
  !   Read the array back into array a
      read (unit=nunit, rec=14) a
      :
      do i = 1, length/2
         a(i) = i
      end do
  !
  !   Replace modified record
      write (unit=nunit, rec=14) a
```

The file must be an external file and list-directed formatting and non-advancing I/O are unavailable.

Direct-access files are particularly useful for applications which involve lots of hopping around inside a file, or where records need to be replaced, for instance in data base applications. A weakness is that the length of all the records must be the same, though on formatted output, the record is padded with blanks if necessary. For unformatted output, if the record is not filled, the remainder is undefined.

This simple and powerful facility allows much clearer control logic to be written than is the case for a sequential file which is repeatedly read, backspaced, or rewound. Only when direct-access files become large may problems of long access times become evident on some computer systems, and this point should always be investigated before heavy investments are made in programming large direct-access file applications.

Some computer systems allow the same file to be regarded as sequential or direct access according to the specification in the open statement or its default. The F language, therefore, regards this as a property of the connection rather than of the file. In this case, the order of records, even for sequential I/O, is that determined by the direct-access record numbering.

9.14   Execution of a data transfer statement

So far, we have used simple illustrations of data transfer statements without dependencies. However, some forms of dependency are permitted and can be very useful. For example, the statement

```
read (unit=*, fmt=*) n, a(1:n)                ! n is an integer
```

allows the length of an array section to be part of the data.

With dependencies in mind, the order in which operations are executed is important. It is as follows:

 i) identify the unit;

 ii) establish the format (if any);

 iii) position the file ready for the transfer (if required);

 iv) transfer data between the file and the I/O list;

 v) position the file following the transfer (if required);

 vi) cause the iostat and size variables (if present) to become defined.

The order of transfer is that of the I/O list. Each input item is processed in turn, and may affect later subobjects. All expressions within an I/O list item are determined at the beginning of processing of the item, and any zero-sized array is ignored.

When an input item is an array, no element of the array is permitted to affect the value of an expression within the item. For example, the cases shown in Figure 9.6 are not permitted. This prevents dependencies occurring within the item itself.

In the case of an internal file, an I/O item must not be in the file or associated with it. Nor may an input item contain or be associated with any portion of the established format.

Finally, a function reference must not appear in an expression anywhere in an I/O statement if it causes another I/O statement to be executed.

Figure 9.6

```
    integer, dimension(10) :: j
    :
    read *, j(j)                            ! Not permitted
    read *, j(j(1):j(10))                   ! Not permitted
```

9.15 Summary

This chapter has begun the description of F's extensive I/O facilities. It has covered the formatted I/O statements, and their associated format specifications, and then turned to unformatted I/O and direct-access files.

The syntax of the read and write statements has been introduced gradually. The full syntax is

   read (*control-list*) [*input-list*]

and

   write (*control-list*) [*output-list*]

where *control-list* contains one or more of the following:

   unit= *u*,
   fmt= *fmt*,
   rec= *i*,
   iostat=*ios*,
   advance= *advance*,
   size=*size*.

A *control-list* must include a unit specifier and must not include any specifier more than once. The iostat and size variables must not be associated with each other (for instance be identical), nor with any entity being transferred. If either of these variables is an array element, the subscript value must not be affected by the data transfer or by the evaluation of any other specifier in the statement.

There are a number of detailed changes with respect to Fortran 77, but the only features of F not in that language are non-advancing I/O and the es edit descriptor.

9.16 Exercises

1. Write suitable print or write statements to print the name and contents of each of the following arrays:

  a) real, dimension(10,10) :: grid, 10 elements to a line (assuming the values are between 1.0 and 100.0);

  b) integer, dimension(50) :: list, the odd elements only;

c) `character(len=10), dimension(20) :: titles,` two elements to a line;

d) `real, dimension(10) :: power,` five elements to a line in scientific notation;

e) `logical, dimension(10) :: flags,` on one line;

f) `complex, dimension(5) :: plane,` on one line.

2. Write statements to output the state of a game of tic-tac-toe (noughts-and-crosses) to a unit designated by the variable `unit_no`.

3. Write a program which reads an input record of up to 132 characters into an internal file and classifies it as an F comment line with no statement, an initial line, or a continuation line.

4. Write separate list-directed input statements to fill each of the arrays of Exercise 1. For each statement write a sample first input record.

5. Write the procedure `get_char`, to read single characters from a formatted, sequential file, taking account of the record structure.

10. Operations on external files

10.1 Introduction

So far we have discussed the topic of external files in a rather superficial way. In the examples of the various I/O statements in the previous chapter, an implicit assumption has always been made that the specified file was actually available, and that records could be written to it and read from it. For sequential files, the file control statements described in the next section further assume that it can be positioned. In fact, these assumptions are not necessarily valid. In order to define explicitly and to test the status of external files, three file status statements are provided: open, close, and inquire. Before beginning their description, however, two new definitions are required.

A computer system contains, among other components, a CPU and a storage system. Modern storage systems are usually based on some form of disc, which is used to store files for long or short periods of time. The execution of a computer program is, by comparison, a transient event. A file may exist for many years, whereas most programs run at most for a few hours. In F terminology, a file is said to *exist* not in the sense we have just used, but in the restricted sense that it exists as a file *to which the program might have access.* In other words, if the program is prohibited from using the file because of a password protection system, or because some necessary action has not been taken in the operating system which is controlling the execution of the program, the file 'does not exist'.

A file which exists for a running program may be empty and may or may not be *connected* to that program. The file is connected if it is associated with a unit number known to the program. Such connection is usually made by executing an open statement for the file, but many computer systems will *pre-connect* certain files which any program may be expected to use, such as terminal input and output. Thus we see that a file may exist but not be connected. It may also be connected but not exist. This can happen for a pre-connected new file. The file will only come into existence (be *created*) if some other action is taken on the file: executing an open, write, print, or endfile statement. A unit must not be connected to more than one file at once, and a file must not be connected to more than one unit at once.

There are a number of other points to note with respect to files:

- The set of allowed names for a file is processor dependent.

- Both sequential and direct access may be available for some files, but normally a file is limited to one or the other.

- A file never contains both formatted and unformatted records.

Finally, we note that no statement described in this chapter applies to internal files.

10.2   File positioning statements

When reading or writing an external file that is connected for sequential access, whether formatted or unformatted, it is sometimes necessary to perform other control functions on the file in addition to input and output. In particular, one may wish to alter the current position, which may be within a record, between records, ahead of the first record (at the *initial point*), or after the last record (at its *terminal point*). The following three statements are provided for these purposes.

10.2.1   The backspace statement

It can happen in a program that a series of records is being written and that, for some reason, the last record written should be replaced by a new one, that is, be overwritten. Similarly, when reading records, it may be necessary to reread the last record read, or to check-read a record which has just been written. For this purpose, F provides the backspace statement, which has the syntax

```
backspace (unit=u [,iostat=ios])
```

where *u* is a scalar integer expression whose value is the unit number, and the iostat specifier has the same meaning as for a read statement. The unit specifier need not come first.

The action of this statement is to position the file before the current record if it is positioned within a record, or before the preceding record if it is positioned between records. An attempt to backspace when already positioned at the beginning of a file results in no change in the file's position. If the file is positioned after an endfile record (Section 10.2.3), it becomes positioned before that record. It is not possible to backspace a file that does not exist, nor to backspace over a record written by a list-directed output statement (Section 9.9). A series of backspace statements will backspace over the corresponding number of records. This statement is often very costly in computer resources and should be used as little as possible.

10.2.2   The rewind statement

In an analogous fashion to rereading, rewriting, or check-reading a record, a similar operation may be carried out on a complete file. For this purpose the rewind statement,

```
rewind (unit=u [,iostat=ios])
```

may be used to reposition a file whose unit number is specified by the scalar integer expression u. Again, the unit specifier need not come first. If the file is already at its beginning, there is no change in its position. The statement is permitted for a file that does not exist, and has no effect.

10.2.3   The endfile statement

The end of a file connected for sequential access is normally marked by a special record which is identified as such by the computer hardware, and computer systems ensure that all files written by a program are correctly terminated by such an *endfile record*. In doubtful situations, or when a subsequent program step will reread the file, it is possible to write an endfile record explicitly using the endfile statement:

```
endfile (unit=u [,iostat=ios])
```

where u, once again, is a scalar integer expression specifying the unit number. Again, the unit specifier need not come first. The file is then positioned after the endfile record. This endfile record, if subsequently read by a program, must be handled using the iostat=*ios* specifier of the read statement, otherwise program execution will normally terminate. Prior to data transfer, a file must not be positioned after an endfile record, but it is possible to backspace or rewind across an endfile record, which allows further data transfer to occur. An endfile record is written automatically whenever either a backspace or rewind operation follows a write operation as the next operation on the unit, or the file is closed by execution of a close statement (Section 10.4), or by normal program termination.

If the file may also be connected for direct access, only the records ahead of the endfile record are considered to have been written and only these may be read during a subsequent direct-access connection.

Note that if a file is connected to a unit but does not exist for the program, it will be made to exist by executing an endfile statement on the unit.

10.2.4   Data transfer statements

Execution of a data transfer statement (read, write, or print) also affects the file position. If it is between records, it is moved to the start of the next record. Data transfer then takes place, which usually moves the position. No further movement occurs for non-advancing access. For advancing access, the position finally moves to follow the last record transferred.

10.3   The open statement

The open statement is used to connect an external file to a unit, create a file that is preconnected, or create a file and connect it to a unit. The syntax is

> open (unit=*u*, status=*st*, action=*act* [,*olist*])

where *olist* is a list of optional specifiers. The specifiers may appear in any order. A specifier must not appear more than once, and in the specifiers all entities are scalar. In character expressions, any trailing blanks are ignored and, except for file=, any upper-case letters are converted to lower case.

The non-optional specifiers are:

unit= *u* where *u* is a scalar integer expression specifying the external file unit number.

status= *st*, where *st* is a character expression that provides the value old, new, replace, or scratch. The file= specifier must be present if old, new, or replace is specified and must not be present if scratch is specified. If old is specified, the file must already exist. If new is specified, the action= specifier must not be read; the file must not already exist, but will be brought into existence by the action of the open statement and the status of the file then becomes old. If replace is specified and the file does not already exist, the file is created; if the file does exist, the file is deleted, and a new file is created with the same name. In each case the status is changed to old. If the value scratch is specified, the action= specifier must be readwrite; the file is created and becomes connected, but it cannot be kept after completion of the program or execution of a close statement (Section 10.4).

action= *act*, where *act* is a character expression that provides the value read, write, or readwrite. If read is specified, the write, print and endfile statements must not be used for this connection; if write is specified, the read statement must not be used (and backspace and position="append" may fail on some systems); if readwrite is specified, there is no restriction.

The optional specifiers are:

iostat= *ios*, where *ios* is a default integer variable which is set to zero if the statement is correctly executed, and to a positive value otherwise.

file= *fln*, where *fln* is a character expression that provides the name of the file. If this specifier is omitted and the unit is not connected to a file, the status= specifier must be specified with the value scratch and the file connected to the unit will then depend on the computer system. Whether the interpretation is case sensitive varies from system to system.

access= *acc*, where *acc* is a character expression that provides one of the values sequential or direct. For a file which already exists, this value must be an allowed value. If the file does not already exist, it will be brought into existence with the appropriate access method. If this specifier is omitted, the value sequential will be assumed.

form= *fm*, where *fm* is a character expression that provides the value formatted or unformatted, and determines whether the file is to be connected for formatted or unformatted I/O. For a file which already exists, the value must be an allowed value. If the file does not already exist, it will be brought into existence with an allowed set of forms that includes the specified form. If this specifier is omitted, the default is formatted for sequential access and unformatted for direct-access connection.

recl= *rl*, where *rl* is an integer expression whose value must be positive. For a direct-access file, it specifies the length of the records, and is obligatory. For a sequential file, it specifies the maximum length of a record, and is optional with a default value that is processor dependent. For formatted files, the length is the number of characters; for unformatted files it is system dependent but the inquire statement (Section 10.5) may be used to find the length of an I/O list. In either case, for a file which already exists, the value specified must be allowed for that file. If the file does not already exist, the file will be brought into existence with an allowed set of record lengths that includes the specified value.

position= *pos*, where *pos* is a character expression that provides the value rewind or append. It must be specified if the access method is sequential and must not be specified if the access method is direct. A new file is positioned at its initial point. If rewind is specified the file is positioned at its initial point; if append is specified and the file exists, it is positioned ahead of the endfile record if it has one (and otherwise at its terminal point).

An example of an open statement is

```
open (unit=2, iostat=ios, file="cities", status="new",      &
      access="direct", action="readwrite", recl=100)
```

which brings into existence a new, direct-access, unformatted file named cities, whose records have length 100. The file is connected to unit number 2 and will be both read and written. Failure to execute the statement correctly can be checked for by testing the value of ios.

The open statements in a program are best collected together in one place, so that any changes which might have to be made to them when transporting the program from one system to another can be carried out without having to search for them. Regardless of where they appear, the connection may be referenced in any program unit of the program.

A file already connected to one unit must not be specified for connection to another unit, nor can a fresh file be connected to a given unit without a close statement first being executed on it.

10.4 The close statement

The purpose of the close statement is to disconnect a file from a unit. Its form is

```
close (unit=u [,iostat=ios] [,status=st])
```

where *u* and *ios* have the same meanings as described above for the open statement. The specifiers may be in any order.

The function of the status= specifier is to determine what will happen to the file once it is disconnected. The value of *st*, which is a scalar character expression, may be either keep or delete, ignoring any trailing blanks and converting any upper-case letters to lower case. If the value is keep, a file that exists continues to exist after execution of the close statement, and may later be connected again to a unit. If the value is delete, the file no longer exists after execution of the statement. In either case, the unit is free to be connected again to a file. The close statement may appear anywhere in the program, and if executed for a non-existing or unconnected unit, acts as a 'do nothing' statement. The value keep must not be specified for a file with the status scratch.

If the status= specifier is omitted, its default value is keep unless the file has status scratch, in which case the default value is delete. On normal termination of execution, all connected units are closed, as if close statements with omitted status= specifiers were executed.

An example of a close statement is

```
close (unit=2, iostat=ios, status="delete")
```

In general, by repeated execution of the open and close statements on the same unit, it is possible to process in sequence an arbitrarily high number of files, whether they exist or not.

10.5   The inquire statement

The status of a file can be defined by the operating system prior to execution of the program, or by the program itself during execution, either by an open statement or by some action on a pre-connected file which brings it into existence. At any time during the execution of a program it is possible to inquire about the status and attributes of a file using the inquire statement. Using a variant of this statement, it is similarly possible to determine the status of a unit, for instance whether the unit number exists for that system (that is, whether it is an allowed unit number), whether the unit number has a file connected to it and, if so, which attributes that file has. Another variant permits an inquiry about the length of an output list when used to write an unformatted record.

Some of the attributes which may be determined by use of the inquire statement are dependent on others. For instance, if a file is not connected to a unit, it is not meaningful to inquire about the form being used for that file. If this is nevertheless attempted, the relevant specifier is undefined.

The three variants are known as inquire by file, inquire by unit, and inquire by output list. In the description of the inquire statement which follows, the first two variants will be described together. Their forms are

```
inquire (unit=u, ilist)
```

for inquire by unit, where *u* is a scalar integer expression specifying an external unit, and

inquire (file=*fln, ilist*)

for inquire by file, where *fln* is a scalar character expression whose value, ignoring any trailing blanks, provides the name of the file concerned. Whether the interpretation is case sensitive is system dependent. The unit or file need not be specified first, although this is usual. A specifier must not occur more than once in the list of optional specifiers, *ilist*. All assignments occur following the usual rules, and all values of type character, apart from that for the name= specifier, are in upper case. The specifiers, in which all variables are scalar and, for non-characters, are of default kind, are

iostat= *ios*, which has the meaning described in the open statement in Section 10.3. The iostat= variable is the only one which is defined if an error condition occurs during the execution of the statement.

exist= *ex*, where *ex* is a logical variable. The value true is assigned to *ex* if the file (or unit) exists, and false otherwise.

opened= *open*, where *open* is a logical variable. The value true is assigned to *open* if the file (or unit) is connected to a unit (or file), and false otherwise.

number= *num*, where *num* is an integer variable that is assigned the value of the unit number connected to the file, or -1 if no unit is connected to the file.

named= *nmd* and name= *nam*, where *nmd* is a logical variable that is assigned the value true if the file has a name, and false otherwise. If the file has a name, the character variable *nam* will be assigned the name. This value is not necessarily the same as that given in the file specifier, if used, but may be qualified in some way. However, in all cases it is a name which is valid for use in a subsequent open statement, and so the inquire can be used to determine the actual name of a file before connecting it. Whether the file name is case sensitive is system dependent.

access= *acc*, where *acc* is a character variable that is assigned one of the values SEQUENTIAL or DIRECT depending on the access method for a file that is connected, and UNDEFINED if there is no connection.

sequential= *seq* and direct= *dir*, where *seq* and *dir* are character variables that are assigned the value YES, NO, or UNKNOWN, depending on whether the file *may* be opened for sequential or direct access respectively, or whether this cannot be determined.

form= *frm*, where *frm* is a character variable that is assigned one of the values FORMATTED or UNFORMATTED, depending on the form for which the file is actually connected, and UNDEFINED if there is no connection.

formatted= *fmt* and unformatted= *unf*, where *fmt* and *unf* are character variables
that are assigned the value YES, NO, or UNKNOWN, depending on whether the
file *may* be opened for formatted or unformatted access, respectively, or
whether this cannot be determined.

recl= *rec*, where *rec* is an integer variable that is assigned the value of the record
length of a file connected for direct access, or the maximum record length
allowed for a file connected for sequential access. The length is the number
of characters for formatted records, and system dependent otherwise. If
there is no connection, *rec* becomes undefined.

nextrec= *nr*, where *nr* is an integer variable that is assigned the value of the
number of the last record read or written, plus one. If no record has been
yet read or written, it is assigned the value 1. If the file is not connected for
direct access or if the position is indeterminate because of a previous error,
nr becomes undefined.

position= *pos*, where *pos* is a character variable that is assigned the value REWIND
or APPEND, as specified in the corresponding open statement, if the file has
not been repositioned since it was opened. If there is no connection, or if the
file is connected for direct access, the value is UNDEFINED. If the file has been
repositioned since the connection was established, the value is processor
dependent (but must not be REWIND or APPEND unless that corresponds to
the true position).

action= *act*, where *act* is a character variable that is assigned the value READ,
WRITE, or READWRITE, according to the connection. If there is no connection,
the value assigned is UNDEFINED.

read= *rd*, where *rd* is a character variable that is assigned the value YES, NO or
UNKNOWN according to whether read is allowed, not allowed, or is undetermined for the file.

write= *wr*, where *wr* is a character variable that is assigned the value YES,
NO or UNKNOWN according to whether write is allowed, not allowed, or is
undetermined for the file.

readwrite= *rw*, where *rw* is a character variable that is assigned the value YES,
NO or UNKNOWN according to whether read/write is allowed, not allowed, or
is undetermined for the file.

A variable that is a specifier in an inquire statement or is associated with one
must not appear in another specifier in the same statement.

The third variant of the inquire statement, inquire by I/O list, has the form

inquire (iolength=*length*) *olist*

where *length* is a scalar integer variable of default kind and is used to determine
the length of an unformatted output list in processor-dependent units, and might

be used to establish whether, for instance, an output list is too long for the record length given in the `recl=` specifier of an `open` statement, or be used as the value of the length to be supplied to a `recl=` specifier, (see Figure 9.5 in Section 9.13).

An example of the `inquire` statement, for the file opened as an example of the `open` statement in Section 10.3, is

```
logical             :: ex, op
character (len=11) :: nam, acc, seq, frm
integer             :: irec, nr
inquire (unit=2, exist=ex, opened=op, name=nam, access=acc, &
     sequential=seq, form=frm, recl=irec, nextrec=nr)
```

After successful execution of this statement, the variables provided will have been assigned the following values:

ex	.true.
op	.true.
nam	cities*bbbbb*
acc	DIRECT*bbbbb*
seq	NO*bbbbbbbbb*
frm	UNFORMATTED
irec	100
nr	1

(assuming no intervening read or write operations).

The three I/O status statements just described are perhaps the most indigestible of all F statements. They provide, however, a powerful and portable facility for the dynamic allocation and deallocation of files, completely under program control, which is far in advance of that found in any other programming language suitable for scientific applications.

10.6 Summary

This chapter has completed the description of the input/output features begun in the previous chapter, and together they provide a complete reference to all the facilities available. The features not in Fortran 77 were `inquire` by I/O list and the additional specifiers for the `open` and `inquire` statements: `position`, `action`, `read`, `write`, and `readwrite`. There are also minor differences that accommodate other features of F not in Fortran 77.

10.7 Exercises

1. A direct-access file is to contain a list of names and initials, to each of which there corresponds a telephone number. Write a program which opens a sequential file and a direct-access file, and copies the list from the sequential file to the direct-access file, closing it for use in another program.

Write a second program which reads an input record containing either a name or a telephone number (from a terminal if possible), and prints out the corresponding entry (or entries) in the direct-access file if present, and an error message otherwise. Remember that names are as diverse as Wu, O'Hara and Trevington-Smythe, and that it is insulting for a computer program to corrupt or abbreviate people's names. The format of the telephone numbers should correspond to your local numbers, but the actual format used should be readily modifiable to another.

A. Intrinsic procedures

Name	Section	Description
abs (a)	8.3.1	Absolute value.
acos (x)	8.4	Arc cosine (inverse cosine) function.
adjustl (string)	8.5.2	Adjust left, removing leading blanks and inserting trailing blanks.
adjustr (string)	8.5.2	Adjust right, removing trailing blanks and inserting leading blanks.
aimag (z)	8.3.1	Imaginary part of complex number.
aint (a [,kind])	8.3.1	Truncate to a whole number.
all (mask [,dim])	8.10	True if all elements are true.
allocated (array)	8.11.1	True if the array is allocated.
anint (a [,kind])	8.3.1	Nearest whole number.
any (mask [,dim])	8.10	True if any element is true.
asin (x)	8.4	Arcsine (inverse sine) function.
associated (pointer [,target])	8.2	True if pointer is associated with target.
atan (x)	8.4	Arctangent (inverse tangent) function.
atan2 (y, x)	8.4	Argument of complex number (x, y).
bit_size (i)	8.8.1	Maximum number of bits that may be held in an integer.
btest (i, pos)	8.8.2	True if bit pos of integer i has value 1.
ceiling (a)	8.3.1	Least integer greater than or equal to its argument.

`char (i)`	8.5.1	Character in position i of the processor collating sequence.
`cmplx (x [,y] [,kind])`	8.3.1	Convert to complex type.
`conjg (z)`	8.3.2	Conjugate of a complex number.
`cos (x)`	8.4	Cosine function.
`cosh (x)`	8.4	Hyperbolic cosine function.
`count (mask [,dim])`	8.10	Number of true elements.
`cshift (array, shift` `[,dim])`	8.12.5	Perform circular shift.
`call date_and_time ([date]` `[,time] [,zone]` `[,values])`	8.14.1	Real-time clock reading date and time.
`digits (x)`	8.7.2	Number of significant digits in the model for x.
`dot_product (vector_a,` `vector_b)`	8.9	Dotproduct.
`eoshift (array, shift` `[,boundary] [,dim])`	8.12.5	Perform end-off shift.
`epsilon (x)`	8.7.2	Number that is almost negligible compared with one in the model for numbers like x.
`exp (x)`	8.4	Exponential function.
`exponent (x)`	8.7.3	Exponent part of the model for x.
`floor (a)`	8.3.1	Greatest integer less than or equal to its argument.
`fraction (x)`	8.7.3	Fractional part of the model for x.
`huge (x)`	8.7.2	Largest number in the model for numbers like x.
`iand (i, j)`	8.8.2	Logical and on the bits.
`ibclr (i, pos)`	8.8.2	Clear bit pos to zero.
`ibits (i, pos, len)`	8.8.2	Extract a sequence of bits.
`ibset (i, pos)`	8.8.2	Set bit pos to one.
`ichar (c)`	8.5.1	Position of character c in the processor collating sequence.
`ieor (i, j)`	8.8.2	Exclusive or on the bits.
`index (string, substring` `[,back])`	8.5.2	Starting position of substring within string.
`int (a [,kind])`	8.3.1	Convert to integer type. on a set of bits on the right.

ior (i, j)	8.8.2	Inclusive or on the bits.
ishft (i, shift)	8.8.2	Logical shift on the bits.
ishftc (i, shift [,size])	8.8.2	Logical circular shift on a set of bits on the right.
kind (x)	8.2	Kind type parameter value.
lbound (array [,dim])	8.11.2	Array lower bounds.
len (string)	8.6.1	Character length.
len_trim (string)	8.5.2	Length of string without trailing blanks.
log (x)	8.4	Natural (base *e*) logarithm function.
logical (1, [,kind])	8.5.3	Convert between kinds of logicals.
log10 (x)	8.4	Common (base 10) logarithm function.
matmul (matrix_a, matrix_b)	8.9	Matrix multiplication.
max (a1, a2 [,a3,...])	8.3.2	Maximum value.
maxexponent (x)	8.7.2	Maximum exponent in the model for numbers like x.
maxloc (array [,mask])	8.13	Location of maximum array element.
maxval (array [,dim] [,mask])	8.10	Value of maximum array element.
merge (tsource, fsource, mask)	8.12.1	tsource when mask is true and fsource otherwise.
min (a1, a2 [,a3,...])	8.3.2	Minimum value.
minexponent (x)	8.7.2	minimum exponent in the model for numbers like x.
minloc (array [,mask])	8.13	Location of minimum array element.
minval (array [,dim] [,mask])	8.10	Value of minimum array element.
modulo (a, p)	8.3.2	a modulo p.
call mvbits (from, frompos, len, to, topos)	8.8.3	Copy bits.
nearest (x, s)	8.7.3	Nearest different machine number in the direction given by the sign of s.

nint (a [,kind])	8.3.1	Nearest integer.
not (i)	8.8.2	Logical complement of the bits.
pack (array, mask [,vector])	8.12.2	Pack elements corresponding to true elements of mask into rank-one result.
precision (x)	8.7.2	Decimal precision in the model for x.
present (a)	8.2	True if optional argument is present.
product (array [,dim] [,mask])	8.10	Product of array elements.
radix (x)	8.7.2	Base of the model for numbers like x.
call random_number (harvest)	8.14.2	Random numbers in range $0 \le x < 1$.
call random_seed ([size] [,put] [,get])	8.14.2	Initialize or restart random number generator.
range (x)	8.7.2	Decimal exponent range in the model for x.
real (a [,kind])	8.3.1	Convert to real type.
repeat (string, ncopies)	8.6.2	Concatenates ncopies of string.
reshape (source, shape [,pad] [,order])	8.12.3	Reshape source to shape shape.
rrspacing (x)	8.7.3	Reciprocal of the relative spacing of model numbers near x.
scale (x, i)	8.7.3	$x \times b^i$, where b=radix(x).
scan (string, set [,back])	8.5.2	Index of left-most (right-most if back is true) character of string that belongs to set; zero if none belong.
selected_int_kind (r)	8.7.4	Kind of type parameter for specified exponent range.
selected_real_kind ([p] [,r])	8.7.4	Kind of type parameter for specified precision and exponent range.
set_exponent (x, i)	8.7.3	Model number whose sign and fractional part are those of x and whose exponent part is i.
shape (source)	8.11.2	Array (or scalar) shape.

`sign (a, b)`	8.3.2	Absolute value of a times sign of b.
`sin (x)`	8.4	Sine function.
`sinh (x)`	8.4	Hyperbolic sine function.
`size (array [,dim])`	8.11.2	Array size.
`spacing (x)`	8.7.3	Absolute spacing of model numbers near x.
`spread (source, dim, ncopies)`	8.12.4	`ncopies` copies of `source` forming an array of rank one greater.
`sqrt (x)`	8.4	Square root function.
`sum (array [,dim] [,mask])`	8.10	Sum of array elements.
`call system_clock ([count] [,count_rate] [,count_max])`	8.14.1	Integer data from real-time clock.
`tan (x)`	8.4	Tangent function.
`tanh (x)`	8.4	Hyperbolic tangent function.
`tiny (x)`	8.7.2	Smallest positive number in the model for numbers like x.
`transpose (matrix)`	8.12.6	Matrix transpose.
`trim (string)`	8.6.2	Remove trailing blanks from a single string.
`ubound (array [,dim])`	8.11.2	Array upper bounds.
`unpack (vector, mask, field)`	8.12.2	Unpack elements of `vector` corresponding to true elements of `mask`.
`verify (string, set [,back])`	8.5.2	Zero if all characters of `string` belong to `set` or index of leftmost (right-most if `back` true) that does not.

B. The statements of F

Note: Where no optional blank is indicated between two adjacent keywords, the blank is mandatory.

Statement	Section
NON-EXECUTABLE STATEMENTS	
Program Units and Subprograms	
program *program-name*	5.2
module *module-name*	5.5
end[ ]module *module-name*	5.5
use *module-name* [,*rename-list*]	7.7
use *module-name*, only: *only-list*	7.7
private [:: *access-id-list*]	7.4 & 7.5
public [:: *access-id-list*]	7.4
intrinsic *intrinsic-name-list*	8.1.3
[recursive] subroutine *subroutine-name*([*dummy-argument-list*])]	5.18
[recursive] function *function-name* ([*dummy-argument-list*])	
result(*result-name*)	5.18
contains	5.5
interface [*generic-spec*]	5.16
where *generic-spec* is *generic-name*, operator(*defined-operator*), or assignment(=)	
end[ ]interface	5.16
module procedure *procedure-name-list*	5.16
Data Specification	
type [,*attribute*]... :: *object-list*	7.9
where *type* is integer[(kind=*kind-value*)], real[(kind=*kind-value*)], logical[(kind=*kind-value*)], complex[(kind=*kind-value*)],	
character(len=*len-value*), or type(*type-name*)	7.10
and *attribute* is parameter, public, private, pointer, target,	

allocatable, dimension(*extent-list*), intent(*inout*), optional or   7.9
save

type, *access* :: *type-name*   7.8
where *access* is public or private   7.8
type [,*component-attr*] ... :: *component-name-list*   7.8
where *component-attr* is pointer, private or dimension(*extent-list*)
end[ ]type *type-name*   7.8

EXECUTABLE STATEMENTS
Assignment
variable = expr
where *variable* may be an array and may be a subobject   Chap. 3
pointer => target   3.12

Program Units and Subprograms
call *subroutine-name* ([*actual-argument-list*])   5.12
return   5.7
end[ ]*unit unit-name*   Chap. 5
where *unit* is program, subroutine, or function.

Dynamic Storage Allocation
allocate (*allocation-list* [, stat=*stat*])   6.5.2
deallocate (*allocate-object-list* [, stat=*stat*])   6.5.3
nullify (*pointer-object-list*)   6.5.4

Control Constructs
[*do-name*:] do [*do-variable = scalar-integer-expr,*   4.5
scalar-integer-expr [,*scalar-integer-expr*]
cycle [*do-name*]   4.5
exit [*do-name*]   4.5
end[ ]do [*do-name*]   4.5
if (*scalar-logical-expr*) then   4.2
else[ ]if (*scalar-logical-expr*) then   4.2
else   4.2
end[ ]if   4.2
select[ ]case (*scalar-expr*)   4.3
case (*case-value-list*)   4.3
case default   4.3

end[ ]select	4.3
stop	5.3
where (*logical-array-expr*)	6.8
elsewhere	6.8
end[ ]where	6.8

Input-Output

read (*control-list*) [*input-list*]	9.15
read *format* [, *input-list*]	9.7
write (*control-list*) [*output-list*]	9.15
print *format* [, *output-list*]	9.8
rewind (*position-list*)	10.2.2
end[ ]file (*position-list*)	10.2.3
backspace (*position-list*)	10.2.1
open (*connect-list*)	10.3
close (*close-list*)	10.4
inquire (*inquire-list*)	10.5
inquire (iolength = *length*) *olist*	10.5

B.1   Reserved words

The reserved words of F are listed in Figures B.1 and B.2. Regardless of case, no reserved word is permitted as a name.

Figure B.1

abs	allocate	atan2	close
achar	allocated	backspace	cmplx
acos	and	bit_size	complex
adjustl	anint	btest	conjg
adjustr	any	call	contains
aimag	asin	case	cos
aint	assignment	ceiling	cosh
all	associated	char	count
allocatable	atan	character	cpu_time

Figure B.2

cshift	go	min	return
cycle	goto	minexponent	rewind
date_and_time	gt	minloc	rrspacing
dble	huge	minval	save
deallocate	iachar	mod	scale
default	iand	module	scan
digits	ibclr	modulo	select
dim	ibits	mvbits	selectcase
dimension	ibset	ne	selected_int_kind
do	ichar	nearest	selected_real_kind
dot_product	ieor	neqv	set_exponent
dprod	if	nint	shape
elemental	in	not	sign
else	index	null	sin
elseif	inout	nullify	sinh
elsewhere	inquire	only	size
end	int	open	spacing
enddo	integer	operator	spread
endfile	intent	optional	sqrt
endforall	interface	or	stop
endfunction	intrinsic	out	subroutine
endif	ior	pack	sum
endinterface	ishft	parameter	system_clock
endmodule	ishftc	pointer	tan
endprogram	kind	precision	tanh
endselect	lbound	present	target
endsubroutine	le	print	then
endtype	len	private	tiny
endwhere	len_trim	procedure	to
eoshift	lge	product	transfer
epsilon	lgt	program	transpose
eq	lle	public	trim
eqv	llt	pure	true
exit	log	radix	type
exp	log10	random_number	ubound
exponent	logical	random_seed	unpack
false	lt	range	use
file	matmul	read	verify
floor	max	real	where
forall	maxexponent	recursive	write
fraction	maxloc	repeat	
function	maxval	reshape	
ge	merge	result	

C. Differences from Fortran 90

An F processor must use the ASCII character set. It does not interpret the first character of an output record as providing carriage control.

An F program is a Fortran 90 program and is interpreted according to the standard. In this appendix we list the restrictions that a Fortran 90 program must satisfy in order to be an F program. We group these by the chapters of this book.

C.1 Language evolution

- There is no use of an obsolescent feature of Fortran 90.

- There is no use of an obsolescent feature of Fortran 95, that is,

  i) Fixed source form.

  ii) Computed go to statement.

  iii) The character* form of character specification.

  iv) A data statement among the executable statements.[1]

  v) Statement functions.

  vi) Assumed character length of function results.

C.2 Language elements

- The free source form is in use.

- The include statement is not employed.

- There are no binary, octal, or hexadecimal constants.

- There are no labels.

- No token is continued from one line to another, even when an embedded blank is permitted, such as in end if.

- No continuation line begins with &.

---

[1] In F, no data statements are permitted.

- There are no ; statement separators.

- No name terminates with the character _.

- Each reference to the name of an entity uses the same case for each letter in the name.

- All the names listed in Section B.1 (Appendix B) are reserved words.

- All keywords are in lower case.

- Each kind value in a literal constant is a named constant.

- Each real literal constant has a decimal point preceded and followed by a digit string and does not have d as its exponent letter.

- The parts of a complex literal constant are real and have the same kind with the same named constant. If a kind type parameter value is explicitly specified for one part, it must be specified for both and with the same named constant.

- No character entity is specified with a kind parameter.

- Every character declaration has a specified character length.

- No apostrophe is used as a character string delimiter.

- No character constant is qualified by a substring.

C.3   Expressions and assignments

- The operators .eq., .ne., .lt., .le., .gt., .ge. are not used (replaced by ==, /=, etc.).

C.4   Control constructs

- No do statement has a comma after do.

- No do statement has a while clause.

- No do statement has a label.

- There is no go to statement.

- Each if statement is the leading statement of an if construct.

- There is no continue statement.

- No do index is a dummy argument, a pointer, a function result, or accessed by use or host association.

- No if or select case construct is named.

- No case statements have case values or expressions of type logical.

- Each case default selector is the final case selector of its construct.

C.5 Program units and procedures

- No stop statement has a stop-code.

- Each end statement takes its fullest form: end program *name*, end function *name*, etc.

- The type of a function result is not declared on the function statement.

- Each function statement has a result clause.

- No function changes the value of a dummy argument, modifies a value in a module, or relies on saved local data.

- No function performs input-output operations other than with a print statement or with a formatted read or formatted write statement for an internal file or for the unit designated with an asterisk.

- Functions may invoke subroutines only as defined assignments.

- Any subroutine called from a function, either by a defined assignment or indirectly, must obey all the rules for functions except that the first argument may have intent out or inout.

- There are no block data program units.

- There are no statement function statements.

- There is no entry statement.

- The main program has a program statement.

- There are no internal subprograms.

- External subprograms are written in another language (which might be Fortran 90) and have an interface in a module before the contains statement.

- In each dummy argument list, the non-optional arguments precede the optional arguments.

- The intent of each dummy argument is specified unless it is a pointer or a procedure.

- Each dummy argument of a function is of intent in unless it is a pointer or a procedure.

- Each procedure dummy argument of a function is a function.

- Each procedure actual argument is a module procedure.

- All procedures have explicit interfaces.

- No `call` or `subroutine` statement is without parentheses.

- The statements of a program unit or subprogram are ordered as shown in Figures 5.22, 5.23, 5.24, 7.1, and 7.2.

- Character dummy arguments are of assumed length.

- No two use statements in a scoping unit give access to the same module, even indirectly where a used module uses a previously used module.

- Generic identifiers are specified only for module procedures.

- No interface block has an empty body.

- No interface body includes a declaration of a variable or procedure that is not a dummy argument or function result.

- No generic name for a module procedure is identical to that of the procedure.

- In a module that extends an intrinsic procedure, an `intrinsic` statement declares the intrinsic name.

- Overloading does not lead to an ambiguous call with an intrinsic name.

C.6　Array features

- No array constructor index is a dummy argument, a pointer, a function result, or accessed by use or host association.

- No index variable of an array constructor is used outside an array constructor, initialized, or saved.

- There are no assumed-size arrays.

- Array dummy arguments are assumed-shape or pointers.

- Each `where` statement is the leading statement of a `where` construct.

C.7   Specification statements

- Each module with a use statement has a default accessibility statement.

- Each module with no use statements has no default accessibility statement.

- The body of a module with public default accessibility consists only of use statements followed by the public statement.

- All generic specifiers and procedures defined in a module must appear in an accessiblity statement there.

- No use statement renames an intrinsic procedure.

- No use statement has an empty only list.

- Kind selectors have the form (kind=*scalar-int-constant-name*).

- Length selectors have the form (len=*specification-expr*) or (len=*).

- No accessible name refers to more than one entity, even if not referenced.

- No accessible entity has more than one name.

- No main program variable has an initial value.

- No entity is given its type by implicit typing.

- All the attributes of an entity with a type are given on the type declaration statement.

- There is no intrinsic attribute (all intrinsic procedures are generic).

- No dimension or character length attributes are given after the :: token.

- The token :: is present wherever it is optional in Fortran 90.

- There are none of the following statements: allocatable, common, data, dimension, double precision, equivalence, external, intent, implicit, namelist, optional, parameter, pointer, save, sequence, target.

- Each object with an initial value has the save or parameter attribute.

- Derived-type definitions appear only in modules and include a specification of accessibility.

- No private type has a private statement.

C.8   Intrinsic procedures

- No reference is made to the intrinsics achar, dble, dim, dprod, iachar, lge, lgt, lle, llt, mod, transfer.

- Each kind value in an intrinsic procedure reference is a named constant.

C.9   Data transfer

- There is no format statement.

- There are no blank=, delim=, end=, err=, nml=, or pad= specifiers.

- In the the parenthetical list of an I/O statement, the forms unit= and fmt= are always used to specify a unit or format.

- No I/O statement has an implied-do.

- No comma is omitted in a format list.

- Blanks do not appear in formats except: either side of a comma, either side of a parenthesis, after a repeat count, before a field width, or before a tab count.

- There is no namelist I/O.

- No format contains a character string edit descriptor.

- No format contains a b, o, z, d, e, en, g, p, x, bn or bz edit descriptor (but E, d, D are acceptable alternatives for e in I/O data)

C.10   Operations on external files

- No backspace, endfile, or rewind statement is without a list.

- Each open statement has a status= specifier and its value is not unknown.

- Each open statement has a action= specifier.

- Each open statement for sequential access has a position= specifier and its value is not asis.

- Each open statement with a status= specifier value of scratch has an action= specifier with value readwrite.

- No open statement with a status= specifier value of new has an action= specifier with value read.

- No open statement is for a unit that is connected.

D. Pointer example

A recurring problem in computing is the need to manipulate a linked data structure. This might be a simple linked list like the one encountered in Section 2.13, but often a more general tree structure is required.

The example in this Appendix consists of a module that establishes and navigates one or more such trees, organized as a 'forest', and a short test program for it. Here, each node is identified by a name and has any number of children, any number of siblings, and (optionally) some associated real data. Each root node is regarded as having a common parent, the 'forest root' node, whose name is 'forest_root'. Thus, every node has a parent. The module provides facilities for adding a named node to a specified parent, for enquiring about all the nodes that are offspring of a specified node, for removing a tree or subtree, and for performing I/O operations on a tree or subtree.

The user-callable interfaces are:

start: must be called to initialize a forest.

add_node: stores the data provided at the node whose parent is specified and sets up pointers to the parent and siblings (if any).

remove_node: deallocates all the storage occupied by a complete tree or subtree.

retrieve: retrieves the data stored at a specified node and the names of the parent and children.

dump_tree: writes a complete tree or subtree.

restore_tree: reads a complete tree or subtree.

finish: deallocates all the storage occupied by all the trees of the forest.

The source code can be obtained by anonymous ftp to *jkr.cc.rl.ac.uk* (130.246.8.23). When prompted for a userid, reply with

```
anonymous
```

and give your name as password. The directory is */pub/MandR* and the file name is *appxd.f90*.

```
module directory
!
! Strong typing imposed
!
! Only subroutine interfaces, the length of the character
! component, and the I/O unit number are public
  public  :: start, add_node, remove_node, retrieve,              &
             dump_tree, restore_tree, finish
  private :: tree_out, find, look, remove
!
! Module constants
  character(len=*), private, parameter:: eot = "End-of-Tree....."
  integer, parameter, public :: unit = 4,   & ! I/O unit number
                          max_char = 16 ! length of character
                                        ! component
!
! Define the basic tree type
  type, private :: node
     character(len=max_char)    :: name    ! name of node
     real, pointer, dimension(:) :: y    ! stored real data
     type(node), pointer       :: parent ! parent node
     type(node), pointer       :: sibling ! next sibling node
     type(node), pointer       :: child   ! first child node
  end type node
!
! Module variables
  type(node), pointer, private  :: current    ! current node
  type(node), pointer, private  :: forest_root ! the root of the forest
  integer,private               :: max_data   ! max size of data array
  character(len=max_char), private, allocatable, target, dimension(:) &
                                            :: names
                          ! for returning list of names
! The module procedures

contains

  subroutine start ()
! Initialize the tree.
     allocate (forest_root)
     current => forest_root
     forest_root%name = "forest_root"
     nullify(forest_root%parent, forest_root%sibling, forest_root%child)
     allocate(forest_root%y(0))
     max_data = 0
     allocate (names(0))
  end subroutine start

  subroutine find(name)
     character(len=*), intent(in) :: name
```

```
! Make the module variable current point to the node with given name,
! or be null if the name is not there.
      type(node), pointer    :: root
! For efficiency, we search the tree rooted at current, and if this
! fails try its parent and so on until the forest root is reached.
      if (associated(current)) then
          root => current
          nullify (current)
      else
          root => forest_root
      end if
      do
          call look(root ,name)
          if (associated(current)) then
              return
          end if
          root => root%parent
          if (.not.associated(root)) then
              exit
          end if
      end do
end subroutine find

      recursive subroutine look(root, name)
          type(node), intent(in), target :: root
          character(len=*), intent(in)    :: name
! Look for name in the tree rooted at root. If found, make the
! module variable current point to the node
          type(node), pointer    :: child
!
          if (root%name == name) then
              current => root
          else
              child => root%child
              do
                  if (.not.associated(child)) then
                      exit
                  end if
                  call look(child, name)
                  if (associated(current)) then
                      return
                  end if
                  child => child%sibling
              end do
          end if
      end subroutine look

   subroutine add_node(name, name_of_parent, data)
       character(len=*), intent(in)                :: name, name_of_parent
```

```
! For a root, name = ""
      real, intent(in), optional, dimension(:) :: data
! Allocate a new tree node of type node, store the given name and
! data there, set pointers to the parent and to its next sibling
! (if any). If the parent is not found, the new node is treated as
! a root. It is assumed that the node is not already present in the
! forest.
      type(node), pointer :: new_node
!
      allocate (new_node)
      new_node%name = name
      if (present(data)) then
         allocate(new_node%y(size(data)))
         new_node%y = data
         max_data = max(max_data, size(data))
      else
         allocate(new_node%y(0))
      end if
!
! If name of parent is not null, search for it.
! If not found, print message.
      if (name_of_parent == "") then
         current => forest_root
      else
         call find (name_of_parent)
         if (.not.associated(current)) then
            print *, "no parent ", name_of_parent, " found for ", name
            current => forest_root
         end if
      end if
      new_node%parent => current
      new_node%sibling => current%child
      current%child => new_node
      nullify(new_node%child)
   end subroutine add_node

   subroutine remove_node(name)
      character(len=*), intent(in) :: name
! Remove node and the subtree rooted on it (if any),
! deallocating associated pointer targets.
      type(node), pointer :: parent, child, sibling
!
      call find (name)
      if (associated(current)) then
         parent =>  current%parent
         child => parent%child
         if (.not.associated(child, current)) then
! Make it the first child, looping through the siblings to find it
! and resetting the links
```

```
              parent%child => current
              sibling => child
              do
                 if (associated (sibling%sibling, current)) then
                   exit
                 end if
                 sibling => sibling%sibling
              end do
              sibling%sibling => current%sibling
              current%sibling => child
            end if
            call remove(current)
         end if
      end subroutine remove_node

      recursive subroutine remove (old_node)
    ! Remove a first child node and the subtree rooted on it (if any),
    ! deallocating associated pointer targets.
         type(node), pointer :: old_node
         type(node), pointer :: child, sibling
    !
         child => old_node%child
         do
            if (.not.associated(child)) then
              exit
            end if
            sibling => child%sibling
            call remove(child)
            child => sibling
         end do
    ! remove leaf node
         if (associated(old_node%parent)) then
            old_node%parent%child => old_node%sibling
         end if
         deallocate (old_node%y)
         deallocate (old_node)
      end subroutine remove

      subroutine retrieve(name, data, parent, children)
         character(len=*), intent(in)                :: name
         real, pointer, dimension(:)                  :: data
         character(len=*), intent(out)                :: parent
         character(len=*), pointer, dimension(:) :: children
    ! Returns a pointer to the data at the node, the name of the
    ! parent, and a pointer to the names of the children.
         integer :: counter, i
         type(node), pointer :: child
    !
         call find (name)
```

```
        if (associated(current)) then
            data => current%y
            parent = current%parent%name
! Count the number of children
            counter = 0
            child => current%child
            do
                if (.not.associated(child)) then
                    exit
                end if
                counter = counter + 1
                child => child%sibling
            end do
            deallocate (names)
            allocate (names(counter))
! and store their names
            children => names
            child => current%child
            do i = 1, counter
                children(i) = child%name
                child => child%sibling
            end do
        else
            nullify(data)
            parent = ""
            nullify(children)
        end if
    end subroutine retrieve

    subroutine dump_tree(root)
        character(len=*), intent(in) :: root
! Write out a complete tree followed by an end-of-tree record
! unformatted on the file unit.
        call find (root)
        if (associated(current)) then
            call tree_out(current)
        end if
        write(unit = unit) eot, 0, eot
    end subroutine dump_tree


        recursive subroutine tree_out (root)
! Traverse a complete tree or subtree, writing out its contents
        type(node), intent(in) :: root      ! root node of tree
! Local variable
        type(node), pointer    :: child
!
        write(unit = unit) root%name, size(root%y), root%y, &
                            root%parent%name
        child => root%child
```

```
        do
            if (.not.associated(child)) then
              exit
            end if
            call tree_out (child)
            child => child%sibling
        end do
      end subroutine tree_out

  subroutine restore_tree ()
! Reads a subtree unformatted from the file unit.
      character(len=max_char)         :: name
      integer :: length_y
      real, allocatable, dimension(:) :: y
      character(len=max_char)         :: name_of_parent
!
      allocate(y(max_data))
      do
          read (unit= unit) name, length_y, y(:length_y), name_of_parent
          if (name == eot) then
            exit
          end if
          call add_node( name, name_of_parent, y(:length_y) )
      end do
      deallocate(y)
  end subroutine restore_tree

  subroutine finish ()
! Deallocate all allocated targets.
      call remove (forest_root)
      deallocate(names)
  end subroutine finish

end module directory

module tree_print

  use  directory
  private
  public :: print_tree

  contains

  recursive subroutine print_tree(name)
! To print the data contained in a subtree
      character(len=*), intent(in)                      :: name
      integer                                           :: i
      real, pointer, dimension(:)                       :: data
      character(len=max_char)                           :: parent, self
```

```
          character(len=max_char), pointer, dimension(:)      :: children
          character(len=max_char), allocatable, dimension(:) :: siblings
!
          call retrieve(name, data, parent, children)
          if (.not.associated(data)) then
            return
          end if
          self = name
          write(unit=*,fmt=*) self, data
          write(unit=*,fmt=*) "   parent:   ", parent
          if (size(children) > 0 ) then
              write(unit=*,fmt=*)  "   children: ", children
          end if
          allocate(siblings(size(children)))
          siblings = children
          do i = 1, size(children)
              call print_tree(siblings(i))
          end do
      end subroutine print_tree
end module tree_print

program test
    use directory
    use tree_print
!
! Initialize a tree
    call start ()
! Fill it with some data
    call add_node("ernest","",(/1.0,2.0/))
    call add_node("helen","ernest",(/3.0,4.0,5.0/))
    call add_node("douglas","ernest",(/6.0,7.0/))
    call add_node("john","helen",(/8.0/))
    call add_node("betty","helen",(/9.0,10.0/))
    call add_node("nigel","betty",(/11.0/))
    call add_node("peter","betty",(/12.0/))
    call add_node("ruth","betty")
! Manipulate subtrees
    open(unit=unit, form="unformatted", status="scratch",    &
         action="readwrite")
    call dump_tree("betty")
    call remove_node("betty")
    write(unit=*,fmt=*)
    call print_tree("ernest")
    rewind (unit=unit)
    call restore_tree ()
    rewind (unit=unit)
    write(unit=*,fmt=*)
    call print_tree("ernest")
    call dump_tree("john")
```

```
   call remove_node("john")
   write(unit=*,fmt=*)
   call print_tree("ernest")
   rewind (unit=unit)
   call restore_tree ()
   write(unit=*,fmt=*)
   call print_tree("ernest")
! Return storage
   call finish ()

end program test
```

E. The terms of F

The following is a list of the principal technical terms used in this book and their definitions. To facilitate reference to the Fortran 90 standard, we have kept closely to the meanings used there. Where the definition uses a term that is itself defined in this glossary, the first occurrence of the term is printed in italics.

Actual argument An *expression*, a *variable*, or a *procedure* that is specified in a procedure *reference*.

Allocatable array A *named array* having the `allocatable` *attribute*. Only when it has space allocated for it does it have a *shape* and may it be *referenced* or *defined*.

Argument An *actual argument* or a *dummy argument*.

Argument association The relationship between an *actual argument* and a *dummy argument* during the execution of a *procedure reference*.

Argument keyword A *dummy argument name*. It may used in a *procedure reference* ahead of the equals symbol.

Array A set of *scalar data*, all of the same *type* and *type parameters*, whose individual elements are arranged in a rectangular pattern. It may be a *named* array, an *array section*, a *structure component*, a *function* value, or an *expression*. Its *rank* is at least one.

Array element One of the *scalar data* that make up an *array* that is either *named* or is a *structure component*.

Array pointer A *pointer* that is an *array*.

Array section A *subobject* whose *designator* contains a *subscript triplet*, a *vector subscript*, or an *array component selector* that is followed by one or more further component selectors.

Array-valued Having the property of being an *array*.

Assignment statement A *statement* of the form '*variable = expression*'.

Assignment token The *lexical token* = used in an *assignment statement*.

Association *Name association* or *pointer association*.

Attribute A property of a *data object* that may be specified in a *type declaration statement*.

Belong If an `exit` or a `cycle` *statement* contains a *construct name*, the statement **belongs** to the do construct using that name. Otherwise, it **belongs** to the innermost do construct in which it appears.

Block A sequence of *executable constructs* embedded in another executable construct, bounded by *statements* that are particular to the construct, and treated as an integral unit.

Bounds For a *named array*, the limits within which the values of the *subscripts* of its *array elements* must lie.

Character A letter, digit, or other symbol.

Character string A sequence of *characters* that is numbered from left to right 1, 2, 3, ...

Characteristics

  i) Of a *procedure*, its classification as a *function* or *subroutine*, the characteristics of its *dummy arguments*, and the characteristics of its *function result* if it is a function.

  ii) Of a *dummy argument*, whether it is a *data object*, is a *procedure*, or has the `optional` *attribute*.

  iii) Of a *data object*, its *type, type parameters, shape*, the exact dependence of an array bound or the character length on other entities, *intent*, whether it is optional, whether it is a *pointer* or a *target*, and whether the *shape*, or *character length* is assumed.

  iv) Of a *dummy procedure*, its characteristics as a procedure and whether it is optional.

  v) Of a *function result*, its type, type parameters, whether it is a pointer, rank if it is a pointer, shape if it is not a pointer, and the exact dependence of an array bound or the character length on other entities.

Collating sequence The ordering of all the different *characters*.

Component A constituent of a *derived type*.

Conformable Two *arrays* are said to be **conformable** if they have the same *shape*. A *scalar* is **conformable** with any array.

Connected

  i) For an *external unit*, the property of referring to an *external file*.

ii) For an *external file*, the property of having an *external unit* that refers to it.

Constant A *data object* whose value must not change during execution of an *executable program*. It may be a *named constant* or a *literal constant*.

Constant expression An *expression* satisfying rules that ensure that its value does not vary during program execution.

Construct A sequence of *statements* starting with a select case, do, if, or where statement and ending with the corresponding terminal statement.

Data Plural of *datum*.

Data entity An *entity* that has or may have a data value. It may be a *constant*, a *variable*, an *expression*, or a *function result*.

Data object A *datum* of *intrinsic* or *derived type* or an *array* of such *data*. It may be a *literal constant*, a *named* data object, a *target* of a *pointer*, or it may be a *subobject*.

Data type A *named* category of *data* that is characterized by a set of values, together with a way to denote these values and a collection of *operations* that interpret and manipulate the values. For an *intrinsic* data type, the set of data values depends on the values of the *type parameters*.

Datum A single quantity that may have any of the set of values specified for its *data type*.

Definable A *variable* is **definable** if its value may be changed by the appearance of its *name* or *designator* on the left of an *assignment statement*. A *allocatable array* that has not been allocated is an example of a *data object* that is not definable. An example of a *subobject* that is not definable is c(i) when c is an *array* that is a *constant* and i is an integer variable.

Defined For a *data object*, the property of having or being given a valid value.

Defined assignment statement An *assignment statement* that is not an *intrinsic* assignment statement and is defined by a *subroutine subprogram* and an *interface block*.

Defined operation An *operation* that is not an *intrinsic* operation and is defined by a *function subprogram* and an *interface block*.

Derived type A *type* whose *data* have *components* each of which is either of *intrinsic* type or of another derived type.

Designator See *subobject designator*.

Disassociated A *pointer* is **disassociated** following execution of a deallocate or nullify *statement*.

Dummy argument An *entity* whose *name* appears in the parenthesized list following the *procedure* name in a function *statement*, or a subroutine statement.

Dummy array A *dummy argument* that is an *array*.

Dummy pointer A *dummy argument* that is a *pointer*.

Dummy procedure A *dummy argument* that is a *procedure*.

Elemental An adjective applied to an *intrinsic operation, procedure*, or *assignment statement* that is applied independently to the elements of an *array* or corresponding elements of a set of *conformable* arrays and *scalars*.

Entity The term used for any of the following: a *program unit*, a *procedure*, an *operator*, an *interface block*, an *external unit*, a *type*, a *data entity*, or a *construct*.

Executable construct A case, do, if, or where *construct*.

Executable program A set of *program units* that includes exactly one *main program*.

Executable statement An instruction to perform or control one or more computational actions.

Explicit-shape array A *named array* that is declared with *explicit bounds*.

Expression A sequence of *operands, operators*, and parentheses. It may be a *variable*, a *constant*, a *function reference*, or may represent a computation.

Extent The size of one dimension of an *array*.

External file A sequence of *records* that exists in a medium external to the *executable program*.

External procedure A *procedure* that is defined by an *external subprogram* or by a means other than F.

External unit A mechanism that is used to refer to an *external file*. It is identified by a nonnegative integer.

File An *internal file* or an *external file*.

Function A *procedure* that is invoked in an *expression*.

Function result The *data object* that returns the value of a *function*.

Function subprogram A sequence of *statements* beginning with a function statement that is not in an *interface block* and ending with the corresponding end function statement.

Generic identifier A *name*, *operator*, or *assignment token* that is specified in an `interface` *statement* to provide an alternative means of invoking any of the *procedures* in the *interface block*.

Global entity An *entity* identified by a *lexical token* whose *scope* is an *executable program*. It may be a *program unit*, or an *external procedure*.

Host A *module* that contains a *module subprogram* or *derived type* definition is called the **host** of the module subprogram or derived type definition.

Host association The process by which a *module subprogram*, or a *derived type* definition accesses *entities* of its *host*.

Inquiry function An *intrinsic function* whose result depends on properties of the principal *argument* other than the value of the argument.

Instance of a subprogram The copy of a *subprogram* that is created when a *procedure* defined by the subprogram is *invoked*.

Intent Of a *dummy argument* that is a neither a *procedure* nor a *pointer*, whether it is intended to transfer data into the procedure, out of the procedure, or both.

Interface block A sequence of *statements* beginning with an `interface` statement and ending with the corresponding `end interface` statement.

Interface body A sequence of *statements* in an *interface block* beginning with a `function` or `subroutine` statement and ending with the corresponding `end` statement.

Interface of a procedure See *procedure interface*.

Internal file A character *variable* that is used to transfer and convert *data* from internal storage to internal storage.

Intrinsic An adjective applied to *types*, *operations*, *assignment statements*, and *procedures* may be used in any *scoping unit* without definition or specification.

Invoke

    i) To call a *subroutine* by a `call` *statement* or by a *defined assignment statement*.

    ii) To call a *function* by a *reference* to it by *name* or *operator* during the evaluation of an *expression*.

Keyword *Statement keyword* or *argument keyword*.

Kind type parameter A parameter whose values label the available kinds of an *intrinsic type* other than `character`.

Length of a character string The number of *characters* in the *character string*.

Lexical token A sequence of one or more characters with an indivisible interpretation.

Line A source-form *record* containing from 0 to 132 *characters*.

Literal constant A *constant* without a *name*.

Local entity An *entity* identified by a *lexical token* whose *scope* is a *scoping unit*.

Main program A *program unit* that is not a *module*.

Many-one array section An *array section* with a *vector subscript* having two or more elements with the same value.

Module A *program unit* that contains or accesses definitions to be accessed by other program units.

Module procedure A *procedure* that is defined by a *module subprogram*.

Module subprogram A *subprogram* that is contained in a *module*.

Name A *lexical token* consisting of a letter followed by up to 30 alphanumeric characters (letters, digits, and underscores).

Name association *Argument association*, *use association*, or *host association*.

Named Having a *name*.

Named constant A *constant* that has a *name*.

Numeric type Integer, real, or complex *type*.

Object *Data object*.

Operand An *expression* that precedes or succeeds an *operator*.

Operation A computation involving one or two *operands*.

Operator A *lexical token* that specifies an *operation*.

Pointer A *data object* that has the `pointer` *attribute*. It may not be *referenced* or *defined* unless it is *pointer associated* with a *target*. If it is an *array*, it does not have a *shape* unless it is pointer associated.

Pointer assignment The *pointer association* of a *pointer* with a *target* by the execution of a *pointer assignment statement* or the execution of an *assignment statement* for a *data object* of *derived type* having the pointer as a *subobject*.

Pointer assignment statement A *statement* of the form '*pointer => target*'.

Pointer associated The relationship between a *pointer* and a *target* following a *pointer assignment* or a valid execution of an `allocate` *statement*.

Pointer association The process by which a *pointer* becomes *pointer associated* with a *target*.

Present A *dummy argument* is **present** in an *instance* of a *subprogram* if it is *associated* with an *actual argument* and the actual argument is a dummy argument that is present in the invoking *procedure* or is not a dummy argument of the invoking procedure.

Procedure A computation that may be *invoked* during program execution. It may be a *function* or a *subroutine*. It may be an *intrinsic procedure*, an *external procedure*, a *module procedure*, or a *dummy procedure*.

Procedure interface The *characteristics* of a *procedure*, the *name* of the procedure, the name of each *dummy argument*, and the *generic identifiers* (if any) by which it may be *referenced*.

Processor The combination of a computing system and the mechanism by which *executable programs* are transformed for use on that computing system.

Program See *executable program* and *main program*.

Program unit The fundamental component of an *executable program*. A sequence of *statements* and comment lines. It may be a *main program* or a *module*.

Rank The number of dimensions of an *array*. Zero for a *scalar*.

Record A sequence of values that is treated as a whole within a *file* .

Reference The appearance of a *data object name* or *subobject designator* in a context requiring the value at that point during execution, or the appearance of a *procedure* name, its *operator* symbol, or a *defined assignment statement* in a context requiring execution of the procedure at that point. Note that neither the act of defining a *variable* nor the appearance of the name of a procedure as an *actual argument* is regarded as a reference.

Scalar

    i) A single *datum* that is not an *array*.

    ii) Not having the property of being an *array*.

Scope That part of an *executable program* within which a *lexical token* has a single interpretation. It may be an *executable program*, a *scoping unit*, a single *statement*, or a part of a statement.

Scoping unit One of the following:

i) A *main program*,

ii) A *derived-type* definition,

iii) An *interface body*, excluding any interface bodies contained within it,

iv) An *subprogram*, excluding any interface bodies contained within it, or

v) A *module*, excluding derived-type definitions, interface bodies, and subprograms contained within it.

Section subscript A *subscript*, *subscript triplet*, or *vector subscript* in an *array section selector*.

Selector A syntactic mechanism for designating

i) Part of a *data object*. It may designate a *substring*, an *array element*, an *array section*, or a *structure component*.

ii) The set of values for which a case *block* is executed.

Shape For an *array*, the *rank* and *extents*. The shape may be represented by the rank-one array whose elements are the extents in each dimension.

Size For an *array*, the total number of elements.

Standard module A *module* standardized as a separate collateral standard.

Statement A sequence of *lexical tokens*. It usually consists of a single line, but the ampersand symbol may be used to continue a statement from one line to another.

Statement entity An *entity* identified by a *lexical token* whose *scope* is a single *statement* or part of a statement.

Statement keyword A word that is part of the syntax of a *statement* and that may be used to identify the statement.

Stride The increment specified in a *subscript triplet*.

Structure A *scalar data object* of *derived type*.

Structure component The part of an *object* of *derived-type* corresponding to a *component* of its type.

Subobject Of a *named data object* or *target* of a *pointer*, a portion that may be *referenced* or *defined* independently of other portions. It may be an *array element*, an *array section*, a *structure component*, or a *substring*.

Subobject designator A *name*, followed by one or more *component selectors*, *array section* selectors, *array element* selectors, and *substring* selectors.

Subprogram A *function subprogram* or a *subroutine subprogram*.

Subroutine A *procedure* that is *invoked* by a `call` *statement* or by a *defined assignment statement*.

Subroutine subprogram A sequence of *statements* from a `subroutine` statement that is not in an *interface block* to the corresponding end `subroutine` statement.

Subscript One of the list of *scalar* integer *expressions* in an *array element selector*.

Subscript triplet An item in the list of an *array section selector* that contains a colon and specifies a regular sequence of integer values.

Substring A contiguous portion of a *scalar character string*. Note that an *array section* can include a *substring selector*; the result is called an array section and not a substring.

Target A *named data object* specified in a *type declaration statement* containing the `target` *attribute*, a data object created by an `allocate` statement for a *pointer*, or a *subobject* of such an object.

Transformational function An *intrinsic function* that is neither an *elemental function* nor an *inquiry function*. It usually has *array arguments* and an array result whose elements have values that depend on the values of many of the elements of the arguments.

Type *Data type.*

Type declaration statement An `integer`, `real`, `complex`, `character`, `logical`, or `type`(*type-name*) *statement*.

Type parameter A parameter of an *intrinsic data type*.

Type parameter values The values of the *type parameters* of a *data entity* of an *intrinsic data type*.

Undefined For a *data object*, the property of not having a determinate value.

Use association The relationship specified by a `use` *statement* between two *names* in different *scoping units*.

Variable A *data object* whose value can be *defined* and redefined during the execution of an *executable program*. It may be a *named* data object, an *array element*, an *array section*, a *structure component*, or a *substring*.

Vector subscript A *section subscript* that is an integer *expression* of *rank* one.

F. Solutions to exercises

Note: A few exercises have been left to the reader.

Chapter 2

1.

B is less than M	true
8 is less than 2	false
blank is greater than A	false
blank is less than 6	true

2.

`x = y`	correct
`a = b+c !  add`	correct, with commentary
`word = "string"`	correct
`song = "Life is just"&`	correct, initial line
`  //" a bowl of cherries"`	correct, continuation
`chide = "Waste not, &`	incorrect, " missing
` want not!"`	incorrect, //" missing
`c(3:4) = "up"`	correct

3.

`-43`	integer	`"WORD"`	character
`4.39`	real	`1.9-4`	not legal
`0.0001e+20`	real	`"stuff & nonsense"`	character
`.1`	not legal	`4.`	not legal
`4 9`	not legal	`(0.0,1.0)`	complex
`(1.0e3,2.0)`	complex	`"I CAN'T"`	character
`"(4.3e9, 6.2)"`	character	`.true._bit`	legal logical
`e5`	not legal	`'shouldn' 't'`	not legal
`1_short`	legal	`"O.K."`	character

4.

name	legal	name32	legal
quotient	legal	123	not legal
a182c3	legal	no-go	not legal
stop!	not legal	burn_	not legal
size	not legal	long__name	legal

5.

```
real, dimension(11)      :: a    a(1), a(10), a(11), a(11)
real, dimension(0:11)    :: b    b(0), b(9), b(10), b(11)
real, dimension(-11:0)   :: c    c(-11), c(-2), c(-1), c(0)
real, dimension(10,10)   :: d    d(1,1), d(10,1), d(1,2), d(10,10)
real, dimension(5,9)     :: e    e(1,1), e(5,2), e(1,3), e(5,9)
real, dimension(5,0:1,4) :: f    f(1,0,1), f(5,1,1), f(1,0,2), f(5,1,4)
```

Array constructor: (/ (i, i = 1,11) /)

6.

c(2,3)	legal	c(4:3)(2,1)	not legal
c(6,2)	not legal	c(5,3)(9:9)	legal
c(0,3)	legal	c(2,1)(4:8)	legal
c(4,3)(:)	legal	c(3,2)(0:9)	not legal
c(5)(2:3)	not legal	c(5:6)	not legal
c(5,3)(9)	not legal	c(,)	not legal

7.

a)
```
type, public :: vehicle_registration
    character(len=3) :: letters
    integer          :: digits
end type vehicle_registration
```

b)
```
type, public :: circle
    real                 :: radius
    real, dimension(2) :: centre
end type circle
```

c)
```
type, public :: book
    character(len=20)                :: title
    character(len=20), dimension(2) :: author
    integer                          :: no_of_pages
end type book
```

Derived type constants:

```
vehicle_registration("PQR", 123)
circle(15.1, (/ 0.0, 0.0 /))
book("Pilgrim's Progress", (/ "John  ", "Bunyan" /), 250 )
```

8.

t	array	t(4)%vertex(1)	scalar
t(10)	scalar	t(5:6)	array
t(1)%vertex	array	t(5:5)	array (size 1)

9.

a) `integer, parameter ::  twenty = selected_int_kind(20)`
    `integer (kind = twenty) counter`
b) `integer, parameter :: high = selected_real_kind(12,100)`
    `real(kind = high) big`

Chapter 3

1.

a+b	valid	-c	valid
a+-c	invalid	d+(-f)	valid
(a+c)**(p+q)	valid	(a+c)(p+q)	invalid
-(x+y)**i	valid	4.((a-d)-(a+4.0*x)+1)	invalid

2.

```
c+(4.0*f)
((4.0*g)-a)+(d/2.0)
a**(e**(c**d))
((a*e)-((c**d)/a))+e
(i .and. j) .or. k
((.not. 1) .or.  ((.not. i) .and. m)) .neqv. n
((b(3).and.b(1)).or.b(6)).or.(.not.b(2))
```

3.

3+4/2	= 5	6/4/2	= 0
3.0*4**2	= 48.0	3.0**3/2	= 13.5
-1.0**2	= -1.0	(-1.0)**3	= -1.0

4.

```
ABCDEFGH
ABCD0123
ABCDEFGu    u = unchanged
ABCDbbuu    b = blank
```

5.

.not.b(1).and.b(2)	valid	.or.b(1)	invalid
b(1).or..not.b(4)	valid	b(2)(.and.b(3).or.b(4))	invalid

6.

d <= c	valid	p < t > 0	invalid
x-1 /= y	valid	x+y < 3 .or. > 4.	invalid
d<c.and.3.0	invalid	q==r .and. s>t	valid

7.

a) 4*1
b) b*h/2.0
c) 4.0/3.0*pi*r**3

8.

```
integer :: n, one, five, ten, twenty_five
twenty_five = (100-n)/25
ten         = (100-n-25*twenty_five)/10
five        = (100-n-25*twenty_five-10*ten)/5
one         = 100-n-25*twenty_five-10*ten-5*five
```

9.

a = b + c	valid
c = b + 1.0	valid
d = b + 1	invalid
r = b + c	valid
a = r + 2	valid

10.

a = b	valid	c = a(:,2) + b(5,:)	valid
a = c+1.0	invalid	c = a(2,:) + b(:,5)	invalid
a(:,3) = c	valid	b(2:,3) = c + b(:5,3)	invalid

Chapter 4

1.

```
program reverse_order
   integer                :: i, j, k, temp
   integer, dimension(100) :: reverse
   do i = 1,100
      reverse(i) = i
   end do
   read *, i, j
   do k= i, i+(j-i-1)/2
      temp = reverse(k)
      reverse(k) = reverse(j-k+i)
      reverse(j-k+i) = temp
   end do
end program reverse_order
```

Note: A simpler method for performing this operation will become apparent in Section 6.10.

2.

```
program fibonacci
   integer :: limit, f1, f2, f3
   read *, limit
   f1 = 1
   if (limit>=1) then
      print *, f1
   end if
   f2 = 1
   if (limit>=2) then
      print *, f2
   end if
   do i = 3, limit
      f3 = f1+f2
      print *, f3
      f1 = f2
      f2 = f3
   end do
end program fibonacci
```

6.

```
program divide
   real :: x
   do
      read *, x
      if (x==-1.0) then
         print *, "input value -1.0 invalid"
      else
         print *, x/(1.0 + x)
         exit
      end if
   end do
end program divide
```

7.

```
type(entry), pointer :: first, current, previous
current => first
if (current%index == 10) then
   first => first%next
else
   do
      previous => current
      current => current%next
      if (current%index == 10) exit
   end do
   previous%next => current%next
end if
```

Chapter 5

1.

```
subroutine calculate(x, n, mean, variance, ok)
   real, dimension(:), intent(in) :: x
   integer, intent(in)            :: n
   real, intent(out)              :: mean, variance
   logical, intent(out)           :: ok
   integer :: i
   mean = 0.0
   variance = 0.0
   ok = n > 1
   if (ok) then
      do i = 1, n
         mean = mean + x(i)
      end do
      mean = mean/n
      do i = 1, n
         variance = variance + (x(i) - mean)**2
      end do
      variance = variance/(n-1)
   end if
end subroutine calculate
```

Note: A simpler method will become apparent in Chapter 8.

2.

```
subroutine matrix_mult(a, b, c, i, j, k)
   real, dimension(:,:), intent(in)  :: a
   real, dimension(:,:), intent(in)  :: b
   real, dimension(:,:), intent(out) :: c
   integer, intent(in)               :: i, j, k
   integer :: l, m, n
   c(1:i, 1:k) = 0.0
   do n = 1, k
      do l = 1, j
         do m = 1, i
            c(m, n) = c(m, n) + a(m,l)*b(l, n)
         end do
      end do
   end do
end subroutine matrix_mult
```

3.

```
subroutine shuffle(cards)
   integer, dimension(:), intent(out):: cards
   integer :: left, choice, i, temp
   real    :: r
   cards = (/ (i, i=1,size(cards)) /)    ! Initialize deck.
   do left = size(cards),1,-1   ! Loop over number of cards left.
      call random_number(r)     ! Draw a card
      choice = r*left + 1       !    from remaining possibilities
      temp = cards(left)        !    and swap with last
      cards(left) = cards(choice)!   one left.
      cards(choice) = temp
   end do
end subroutine shuffle
```

4.

```
function earliest(string) result(e)
   character (len=*), intent(in) :: string
   character(len=1) :: e
   integer          :: j, length
   length = len(string)
   if (length <= 0) then
      e = ""
   else
      e = string(1:1)
      do j = 2, length
         if (string(j:j) < e) then
            e = string(j:j)
         end if
      end do
   end if
end function earliest
```

5.

```
module calc
   public :: volume
contains
   function volume(radius, length) result(v)
      real, intent(in) :: radius, length
      real :: v
      v = acos(-1.0)*radius**2*length
   end function volume
end module calc
program sample
   use calc
   real :: r, l, v
   :
   r = 3.0
```

```
    l = 4.0
    v = volume(r, l)
    :
end program sample
```

7.

```
module string_type
   public :: assignment(=), operator(//), c_to_s_assign,   &
            s_to_c_assign, string_len,  string_concat
   intrinsic len
   type, public :: string
      integer              :: length
      character(len=80)    :: string_data
   end type string
   interface assignment(=)
      module procedure c_to_s_assign, s_to_c_assign
   end interface
   interface len
      module procedure string_len
   end interface
   interface operator(//)
      module procedure string_concat
   end interface
contains
   subroutine c_to_s_assign(s, c)
      type (string), intent(out)   :: s
      character(len=*), intent(in) :: c
      s%string_data = c
      s%length = len(c)
      if (s%length > 80) then
         s%length = 80
      end if
   end subroutine c_to_s_assign
   subroutine s_to_c_assign(c, s)
      character(len=*), intent(out) :: c
      type (string), intent(in)     :: s
      c = s%string_data(1:s%length)
   end subroutine s_to_c_assign
   function string_len(s) result(sl)
      type(string), intent(in) :: s
      integer                  :: sl
      sl = s%length
   end function string_len
   function string_concat(s1, s2) result(sc)
      type (string), intent(in) :: s1, s2
      type (string)             :: sc
      sc%string_data = s1%string_data(1:s1%length) // &
                       s2%string_data(1:s2%length)
      sc%length = s1%length + s2%length
```

```
            if (sc%length > 80) then
                sc%length = 80
            end if
        end function string_concat
    end module string_type
```

Note: The intrinsic len function, used in subroutine c_to_s_assign, is first described in Section 8.6.1.

Chapter 6

1.

   i) a(1, :)

   ii) a(:, 20)

   iii) a(2:50:2, 2:20:2)

   iv) a(50:2:-2, 20:2:-2)

   v) a(1:0, 1)

2.

```
    where (z > 0.0)
        z = 2*z
    end where
```

3.

```
    integer, dimension(16) :: j
```

4.

```
    a, b    assumed-shape
    d       pointer
    w       explicit-shaped
```

5.

```
    real, pointer, dimension(:, :, :) :: x
    x => tar(2:10:2, 2:20:2, 2:30:2)%du(3)
```

6.

```
    ll = ll + ll
    ll = mm + nn + n(j:k+1, j:k+1)
```

7.

```
    program main
        integer                  :: i, j, k
        integer, dimension(100) :: reverse
        reverse = (/ (k, k=1, 100) /)
        read *, i, j
        reverse(i:j) = reverse(j:i:-1)
    end program main
```

Chapter 7

1.

```
  i) integer, dimension(100) ::  bin

 ii) integer, parameter ::  kind64 = selected_real_kind(6, 4)
     real(kind=kind64), dimension(0:20, 0:20) ::  iron_temperature

iii) logical, dimension(20) ::  switches

 iv) character(len=70), dimension(44) ::  page
```

2.
Value of i is 3.1, but may be changed,
value of i is 3.1, but may not be changed.

3.

```
  i) integer, dimension(100) ::  i=0

 ii) integer, dimension(100) ::  i=(/ (0, 1, k=1, 50) /)

iii) real, dimension(10, 10) ::  x=1

 iv) character(len=10) ::  string = "0123456789"
```

4.

```
  i) type(person) boss = person("Smith", 48.7, 22)
```

  ii) This is impossible because a pointer component cannot be a constant.

5.
The following are not:
iv) because of the real exponent, and
viii) because of the pointer component.

Chapter 8

1.

```
    program qroots        ! Solution of quadratic equation.
!
    real :: a, b, c, d, x1, x2
!
    read(unit=*, fmt=*) a, b, c
    write(unit=*, fmt=*) " a = ", a, "b = ", b, "c = ", c
    if (a == 0.0) then
       if (b /= 0.0) then
          write(unit=*, fmt=*) " Linear: x = ", -c/b
       else
          write(unit=*, fmt=*) " No roots!"
       endif
    else
       d = b**2 - 4.0*a*c
       if (d < 0.0) then
          write (unit=*, fmt=*) " Complex", -b/(2.0*a),    &
```

```
        "+-", sqrt(-d)/(2.0*a)
      else
        x1 = -(b + sign(sqrt(d), b))/(2.0*a)
        x2 = c/(x1*a)
        write(unit=*, fmt=*) " Real roots", x1, x2
      endif
   endif
end program qroots
```

Historical note: A similar problem was set in one of the first books on Fortran programming — *A FORTRAN Primer* by E. Organick (Addison-Wesley, 1963). It is interesting to compare Organick's solution, written in FORTRAN II, on p. 122 of that book, with the one above. (It is reproduced in the *Encyclopedia of Physical Science & Technology* (Academic Press, 1987), vol. 5, p. 538.)

2.

```
subroutine calculate(x, n, mean, variance, ok)
   real, dimension(:), intent(in)  :: x
   integer, intent(in)             :: n
   real, intent(out)               :: mean, variance
   logical, intent(out)            :: ok
   ok = n > 1
   if (ok) then
      mean = sum(x)/n
      variance = sum((x-mean)**2)/(n-1)
   end if
end subroutine calculate
```

3.

```
F     p1 and p2 are associated with the same array elements,
      but in reverse order
T     p1 and p2(4:1:-1) are associated with exactly the
      same array elements, a(3), a(5), a(7), a(9)
```

4.

```
5   1     a has bounds 5:10 and a(:) has bounds 1:6
5   1     p1 has bounds 5:10 and p2 has bounds 1:6
1   1     x and y both have bounds 1:6
```

Chapter 9

1.

```
a) print "(a, /, (t1, 10f6.1))", " grid", grid
b) print "(a, tr1, 25i5)",        " list", (/ (list(i), i = 1, 49, 2)/)
or                                                list(1:49:2)
c) print "(a, /, (t1, 2a12))",    " titles", titles
d) print "(a, /, (t1, 5es15.6))"," power", power
```

```
e) print "(a, 1012)",                " flags", flags
f) write(unit=*,fmt="(a)",advance="no") "plane"
   do i = 1, 5
       write(unit=*,fmt="(a,2f6.1,a)",advance="no") "  (", plane(i), ")"
   end do
```

2.

```
     character(len=1), dimension(3,3) :: tic_tac_toe
     integer :: unit_no
     :
     write(unit=unit_no, fmt="(t1, 3a2)" ) tic_tac_toe
```

4.

```
(a) read(unit=*, fmt=*) grid
1.0 2.0 3.0 4.0 5.0 6.0 7.0 8.0 9.0 10.0

(b) read(unit=*, fmt=*) list(1:49:2)
25*1

(c) read(unit=*, fmt=*) titles
data transfer

(d) read(unit=*, fmt=*) power
1.0 1.0e-03

(e) read(unit=*, fmt=*) flags
t f t f t f f t f t

(f) read(unit=*, fmt=*) plane
(0.0, 1.0),(2.3, 4.0)
```

5.

```
subroutine get_char(unit_no, gc, ios)
    integer, intent(in)          :: unit_no
    character(len=*), intent(out) :: gc
    integer, intent(out)          :: ios
    integer :: i
    ! Allow one extra attempt to read to handle possible end-of-record,
    ! otherwise exit with error code.
    do i = 1, 2
        read(unit=unit_no, fmt="(a1)", advance="no", iostat=ios) gc
        if (ios == 0 ) then
            exit
        end if
    end do
end subroutine get_char
```

Index

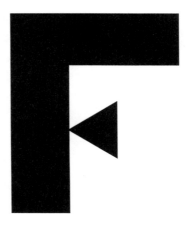